SINGLES GUIDE

to the

SAN FRANCISCO

BAY AREA

Where & How to Meet
a Romantic Partner
and New Friends

5th Edition

RICHARD GOSSE

Dedicated to Jeff Mulanax & Dorothy Schad

Published by
Marin Publications
4 Highland Avenue
San Rafael, CA 94901
(415) 459-3817

ISBN 0-934377-11-1

CONTENTS

Part One:

BEING SINGLE

IN THE BAY AREA

CHAPTER 1: THE BAY AREA SINGLES SCENE

Congratulations for choosing to live in the San Francisco Bay Area! You've chosen the best region in the country to be single. That's because the Bay Area has the highest per capita singles population in the United States. A majority of the adults are single. That's not true of other areas of the country where singles are often a minority looked upon with scorn or pity. Isn't it great to be part of the majority?

Over a million single adults in the Bay Area just like you are hoping to meet the right person for a lasting relationship. And we all have one thing in common. We all need love.

The tragedy is that most of us are too embarrassed to admit it. And we're too scared of rejection to reach out to each other. So we stay home and feel lonely. And complain about how hard it is to meet people. Single women are particularly pessimistic. Many complain that "all the men in San Francisco are either married, gay, or dead." That's simply not true. Noreen Goldman & Charles F. Westoff did a study of eligible men in the top 38 metropolitan areas of America (Money Magazine, December, 1984). They only counted eligible bachelors (men who were not gay and were open to marriage) and still concluded that San Francisco is the third best major city in the country to meet a husband!

I teach classes for singles at 55 colleges. Wherever I go I hear amazing statistics from women about the shortage of men. Some single women actually believe that there are 8 women for every man in their county!

The fact of the matter is that there is a tiny surplus of women in most counties and there actually is a surplus of men in Solano County! Listed below are the estimated populations of San Francisco and ten nearby counties, as of January 1, 1985, together with the male-female ratio:

Alameda County - Population 1,174,800; 51.4% women; 48.6% men
Contra Costa County - 703,400; 51.2% women; 48.8% men
Marin County - 223,200; 50.9% women; 49.1% men
Monterey County - 48.8% women; 51.2% men
Napa County - 102,200; 50.9% women; 49.1% men
San Francisco - 719,200; 50.2% women; 49.8% men
San Mateo County - 606,200; 51.3% women; 48.7% men
Santa Clara County - 1,376,900; 50.5% women; 49.5% men
Santa Cruz County - 51.1% women; 48.9% men
Solano County - 269,100; 49.3% women; 50.7% men
Sonoma County - 330,000; 51.6% women; 48.4% men

(Source: California Almanac, 1986-87, James S. Fay, et. al., which may be obtained from Presidio Press, 31 Pamaron Way, Novato, CA 94947).

Clearly there are literally hundreds of thousands of living, breathing, single men in the Bay Area who want to meet a special woman for a loving relationship.

Sometimes, of course, statistics can lie. These figures are misleading because they aren't broken down by age bracket. While there is a surplus of single women in most age brackets, there's actually a shortage of single women in San Francisco in the 20-29 age bracket. According to Goldman & Westoff, there are 136 eligible bachelors for every 100 single women in the 20-24 age bracket and 104 single men for every 100 single women in the 25-29 age bracket. This is despite the fact that an estimated 24% of men in San Francisco are gay.

Here are the statistics for the number of single men in their 20s and 30s per 100 single women. Salinas-Monterey-166; San Francisco-Oakland-115; San Jose-122; Santa Rosa-Petaluma-110; Vallejo-Fairfield-Napa-141. (For an 18" x 24" Singles Map of the best cities in America to meet single men send $9.95 to Map Makers, Box 97, Kenmore, NY 14217 or call (800) 388-6277).

Where does this surplus come from? Partly it's because of the fact that there are more boys born each year than girls (a surplus of 1% more male babies). Since men tend to marry women 2 - 3 years younger than they, there is a shortage of eligible women in their twenties.

Eventually, however, another factor moves in to reverse the imbalance: men tend to die seven years younger than women. At age 35, for example, enough men have died that there is an equal number of men and women in the United States. By age 60 there are 3 and 1/2 single women for every single man in the U.S. The odds are even worse than this statistic suggest because men 50 years old and over marry women an average of eight years younger than they. If you're a middle-aged woman, however, don't panic. The surplus of single women of your age isn't an insurmountable problem because most of these women aren't really much competition. The overwhelming majority of them either stay home almost all the time or don't have a clue as to where to meet single men. That's where you have the advantage. By following the simple suggestions in this book you can beat the odds and find the right man for a happy, loving relationship.

As for men, the odds get better each year. In San Francisco there are 91 eligible bachelors for every 100 single women in the 30-34 age bracket; 73 men, 100 women, ages 35-39; 58 men, 100 women, ages 40-44; 47 men, 100 women, ages 45-49; 41 men, 100 women, ages 50-54; 36 men, 100 women, ages 55-59.

Here are the figures for San Jose: 142 eligible bachelors for every 100 single women, ages 20-24; 100 men, 100 women, ages 25-29; 81 men, 100 women, ages 30-34; 63 men, 100 women, ages 35-39; 51 men, 100 women, ages 40-44; 42 men, 100 women, ages 45-49; 36 men, 100 women, ages 50-54; 31 men, 100 women, ages 55-59.

But enough of statistics. Regardless of how many single men or women there are to meet, Mr. or Ms. Right isn't going to knock on your door. You've got to go out of your way to find them. This Guide has all the information you'll need. But there's one missing ingredient. And that's you. You've got to be committed to implementing the suggestions in this Guide. That means hard work. And a lot of frustration. But in the end it will all be worth it. Because the pay-off will be a loving relationship that brings great joy to your life.

CHAPTER 2: HOW TO BE HAPPILY SINGLE

Most singles approach the single state as a cross to bear. They see bachelorhood as a way station between marriages. It's inconceivable to them that they could ever be happy as a single. Society reinforces this belief. It teaches us that happiness lies in the nuclear family. Singles are often dismissed as "old maids" or suspected of being gay. No wonder it's tough to be single in America!

The fact of the matter, however, is that single people are often far happier than couples. You can be happily single also. The first step is to get rid of the "grass is greener on the other side syndrome". You have to realize that being married isn't all it's cracked up to be. There are 3 ways to accomplish this.

1. **Make a List of All the Unhappy Couples You Know.** We all know couples that are continually fighting or ignoring each other. If you know a reasonable number of married people you should be able to write up a long list of unhappily married couples. That should help dispel the "grass is greener on the other side syndrome."
2. **Double Your List.** We all know that many people are phony. That holds true for a surprising number of supposedly happy couples. Secretly they hate each others guts, but publicly they put on a show of matrimonial bliss. We have all seen married couples who appear to be perfectly suited to one another. They make "a lovely couple" and are always kissing and hugging in public. A week later you read in the Society page that they're getting a divorce. You can safely assume that for every obviously unhappy couple you know there is another that is secretly unhappy.
3. **Count Your Blessings.** Make a list of all the advantages of being single. Think of all the things you are free to do that would be forbidden if you were coupled. Think of all the rotten habits you don't have to tolerate. Be imaginative. You should be able to come up with a long list of blessings that are associated with your single lifestyle.

Once you get over the "grass is greener on the other side syndrome' you're ready to make the most of being single. There are three keys to being happily single.

KEY #1: ACCEPTING YOURSELF

Several years ago I had the good fortune of spending a weekend at the Esalen Institute in Big Sur, California. I was with a group of about 20 people in an encounter group. There was one middle-aged gentleman who impressed me deeply. He appeared to be very happy and seemed to have a genuinely high opinion of himself. Believing that self-esteem was the most important key to happiness, I asked him for his secret.

His answer astounded me. He said, "I don't have high self-esteem. I know my limitations and I accept them. That's the key to my happiness."

Unfortunately society teaches that you should "live up to expectations—your own and those of others. That's great if you can live up to all of them. But what happens if you have contradictory expectations? Or what if you fail to meet some of them? Often the result is low self-esteem and misery for the rest of your life.

Think back to your childhood. Your parents always insisted that you be a good little boy or girl. You were taught that if you didn't meet those standards you were a rotten person. You were rejected and/or punished by your parents for being yourself and not being the person they wanted you to be.

When you went to school the same process continued. Your teachers rewarded you with compliments, smiles, gold stars, and good grades when you were "good". But if you were a lousy speller, couldn't memorize your times tables, or were noisy you were rejected and labeled as a "slow learner" or "discipline problem".

Likewise your peer group damaged your self concept. If you couldn't hit the ball as far as your friends or didn't have as pretty a dress you were shunned. You learned that you were an unattractive or bad person.

The process continues throughout life. Bosses, co-workers, employees, customers, clients, friends, lovers, spouses, children. All of them are in a position to do damage to your self-concept by insisting that you be something you aren't.

You can spend your entire life striving to meet those expectations. But that's not the road to happiness. The key to happiness is to dump all the expectations and give yourself permission to be yourself.

KEY #2: CHANGING YOURSELF

Most people will agree that accepting yourself is a key to happiness. But shouldn't you also strive to be the best person you can possibly be? Certainly there's nothing wrong with trying to change yourself for the better. Be careful to consider two points, however, before deciding to change yourself.

1. Will changing yourself make YOU happy or simply meet someone else's expectations? If it isn't going to make you happy, then why change just to appease someone else? You are under no obligation to meet their expectations. If you find yourself in a relationship with someone who won't be satisfied with you unless you change, wouldn't you be better off finding someone who likes you as you are?

2. Are you willing to pay the price to change? Change requires effort and often involves a great deal of pain. As a human being you are a creature of habit. The vast percentage of your actions and qualities are habitual. And habits are extremely difficult to change. If you don't believe this, ask smokers why they keep smoking despite the fact that they are slowly killing themselves.

Unless you are motivated to pay the price you're kidding yourself if you expect to change. As an example let's look at obesity. In our society women in particular are trained to be ashamed of their bodies because they're too fat. Hundreds of thousands of teenage girls are anorexic or bulemic (they starve themselves or throw up continuously) because of this neurotic American obsession with slimness. If you don't have the figure of a model you probably chastise yourself continuously.

Most American women (and many men) go from one crash diet to the next. This is despite the fact that 98% of the time they either don't lose a significant amount of weight or regain it all within two years.

Why is it so hard to lose weight and keep it off, despite the intense pressure placed on you to do so? Because being slim, for most people, involves paying a very high price—pain every day of your life. You can't be "good" every other day or every other week. You have to diet 7 days a week, 52 weeks a year—forever. Not many people are willing to pay this price.

So what do you do? You go on crash diets, lose weight, and then eventually get tired of the price and go back to being fat. Then you beat yourself up psychologically and the cycle resumes with another crash diet. The result: you wind up being as fat or fatter than before and your self-concept goes down the drain.

What's the solution? Ask yourself, "Am I willing to suffer every day for the rest of my life in order to be thin? Or will I be happier being fat?" If you aren't willing to pay the price for slimness the only rational alternative is to give yourself permission to be fat and abandon all dieting. Eat to your heart's content and become a happy fat person.

The same holds true for any other negative quality or habit. Be honest with yourself and ask whether you are willing to pay the price to rid yourself of your habits. If you aren't, then try to make the most of your life in spite of these qualities.

On the other hand, suppose you have a positive goal. For example, you may have a desire to become wealthy. If you're like most people you'll never achieve wealth—because you aren't willing to pay the price. You'll fantasize about great wealth. Or you'll wait for a miracle to happen—e.g. winning the Irish sweepstakes or marrying a millionaire. In the meantime you remain impoverished.

If you want to make a great deal of money you have to do it "the old-fashioned way", as the commercial goes. "You have to earn it". That means long, hard, tedious hours. It involves working when you'd rather play. It means taking chances. You'll have to live a frugal lifestyle so you can save the nest egg you need for starting a business or investing in real estate.

If you're not willing to pay the price to achieve wealth, give up the fantasy. Be realistic and face the fact that you have chosen to live comfortably now rather than sacrifice for the future. There's nothing wrong with a modest standard of living—as long as you have rationally decided that it's preferable to working to achieve great wealth.

KEY #3: CONTROLLING NEGATIVE EMOTIONS

One of the cardinal tenets of pop psychology is to "let it all hang out". You're supposed to unleash all of your anger, frustration, bitterness, and repression. That's supposed to be the key to emotional health.

There's an element of truth to this. If you keep your negative emotions locked up there is the danger that one day you'll explode. Ulcers and other negative symptoms may also result from keeping a lid on your emotions.

But there is a better way to deal with your negative feelings. You can take charge and control them, rather than sit back passively and allow them to control your life.

Your negative emotions don't just happen. They are the results of statements you make to yourself. Let's take jealousy as an example. Your sweetheart is flirting at a party. You react by saying to yourself: "My lover has no right to flirt with someone else. My lover should only flirt with me. This is unfair and cruel. I don't have to take this." Needless to say, if you make these statements you will feel jealous and miserable. You may wind up making a nasty scene, leaving in a huff, and refusing to have sex with your partner for a week as punishment for lack of fidelity. You suffer, your partner suffers, and the relationship deteriorates.

Sound familiar? The tragedy of this scene is that it didn't have to happen. You could have said to yourself, "My lover has a right to live his/her life as s/he wishes. That includes flirting." If you say this to yourself (and believe it) you won't feel upset at innocent flirting at a party.

Another negative emotion you can control is guilt. Beating yourself up psychologically over a past indiscretion serves no useful purpose. You can make yourself feel miserable for the rest of your life over past mistakes if you aren't careful. The solution is to control your guilt by changing the statements you make to yourself.

Let's take an extreme example. Suppose you murder someone. You go to prison and, like most murderers, you eventually are released. It would be easy to say to yourself, "I'm a rotten, disgusting human being. I don't deserve to live. What I did was horrible. I hate myself."

The only problem with these statements and the resulting guilt is that they serve no useful purpose. The person you murdered is dead. No amount of guilt will ever make up for your dastardly deed. The important thing now is to make sure that you never repeat your mistake and to try to make your life the best life possible.

Maybe you can help the family of your victim. Perhaps you will choose to devote some of your time to charitable endeavors. Whatever you do, don't wallow in guilt. Try to make the most of the rest of your life by saying, "I did something terribly wrong and will do everything I can to avoid repeating my mistake. In the meantime I will do my best to bring happiness into my life and the lives of others."

Worry is another negative emotion that must not be indulged. As an

How to Be Happily Single

example, supposed you fear your lover will dump you. Every time your lover comes home late, ignores you, or says something angry you conclude that the relationship is about to end. You spend a considerable amount of time each day worrying about being dumped. You probably drive your lover up the wall by neurotically demanding attention and reassurance. Meantime your constant worrying serves no purpose other than to make your life miserable. No amount of worrying will increase the chances of survival of your relationship.

The wise course would be to change your statements to yourself. Don't say, "My lover is going to leave me and my life will be ruined. I'm going to be miserable for the rest of my life." Instead say, "Maybe my relationship will end and I'll be miserable for a while. But millions of others have been dumped and have gone on to happy relationships. I can also. Besides, I don't know for sure this will end. Maybe if I sit down with my lover and share my feelings we can work things out."

What do you do if you find that you can't stop making statements that cause negative emotions? You may wish to use a thought-stopping technique, such as yelling "Stop!" at the top of your lungs. For example, every time you worry about losing your job, shout "Stop!". Obviously you won't feel comfortable doing this publicly. There are other techniques you can employ. For example, wear a rubber band around your wrist. Whenever you make negative statements to yourself that make you miserable, snap the rubber band. These techniques are so simple they may appear silly. They aren't. They are effective ways of avoiding a lifetime of misery.

Changing or stopping the statements you make to yourself aren't the only methods for controlling your negative emotions. There are many others. Relaxation techniques are an effective way of overcoming negative emotions such as anger or anxiety. When you feel under stress the first thing to is to concentrate on your breathing. You will find that you are breathing faster and less deeply than normal. Hopefully the simple process of monitoring your breathing will slow it down and cause it to become deeper. Negative emotions are usually associated with a tense body. If you can relax your body you will often find that your negative emotions dissipate.

CONCLUSION

If you're like most people, you bought this book because you wanted to meet someone special for a lasting, loving relationship. The information and techniques in this book will help you achieve that goal. But it's hard work. So before you get your hopes up, ask yourself if you're willing to pay the price for finding love.

In the meantime, don't put your life on hold. Make the most out of being single. Strive to be the happiest person you can possibly be. That way if someday you do choose to commit to someone, it won't be out of desperation. It will be because you have met someone wonderful and have succeeded in creating a beautiful relationship. Good luck!

CHAPTER 3: TEN RULES FOR DATING

If you're like most singles you work 40 or more hours a week at a job you don't particularly enjoy. The reason is that you value money very highly.

How many hours a week do you spend looking for love? Probably zero. And that's the problem. Here in America our value system is twisted. We're taught to value money a lot more highly than we do love. The result is millions of single people in America who have money but not happiness.

This Guide is based on a different value system. One that holds love to be the most precious thing in life. One that says that good friends are worth their weight in gold.

You can sit back and patiently wait for romantic partners and intimate friends to come your way. Or you can take the initiative and make things happen!

This Guide does the easy part. It tells you where to go to meet people. The hard part, however, is up to you. You've got to implement the suggestions in this Guide. And that takes hard work.

So before we talk about the hundreds of places to meet people in your area let's get to the unpleasant part. There are 10 rules for meeting someone special for a lasting, loving relationship. They aren't pleasant rules. And they aren't easy. But they work. If you're willing to follow these rules, you'll leave the ranks of those who are waiting for love and join those who have found love.

RULE #1: HAVE REALISTIC EXPECTATIONS

Have you ever noticed that 95% of us seem to be chasing after the same 5%. I call them the "lucky 5%". They have no trouble meeting someone for a romantic relationship. They are blessed with physical beauty or money or status or all three. Relationships come to them rather than the other way around. Looking at things logically, if 95% of us are chasing after the same 5%, each of them has to date 19 of us simultaneously in order to keep all of us happy. And that's not going to happen.

How realistic are your expectations? Take a good, long, honest look at yourself. "I've got a great personality and a heart of gold", you say. That's great, except that you live in a world in which people judge you initially by superficial things like facial beauty, the slimness of your body, the clothes you wear, the car you drive, and the job you hold.

So if people find your exterior to be unattractive, you've got a tough road ahead of you. For example, if you're a 3 on a scale of 10 in terms of initial attractiveness to the opposite sex, don't expect to attract a 9 or 10. If you're a woman, forget about Tom Selleck or a millionaire. If you're a man, forget about meeting a Playboy bunny. Settle for someone nice who finds you attractive.

"Does that mean I have to lower my standards?"

Sadly the answer is yes. I know it's hard to give up fantasies of Prince Charming or the beauty queen. Just remember that it's even harder to go through life without romantic love.

Newsweek Magazine's cover story for June 2, 1986 demoralized single women throughout the nation. The article claimed that if you are 30 years old, college-educated, and never been married, that you only have a 20% chance of ever finding a husband. If you reach age 35 without a spouse, your chances drop to 5%. And if you have the misfortune of being single at 40, according to Newsweek you have a greater chance of "being killed by terrorists" than finding a husband.

The Newsweek article was based on a study by two professors at Harvard and Yale Universities. Fortunately the figures have been discredited by the U.S. Census Bureau. For one thing, the Harvard-Yale Study was based on a relatively small sample. More importantly, it was based on a critical assumption: that single women in the United States would continue to follow three patterns in selecting a mate as they have in the past:

1. Marrying a man who is older than she. The average woman in America chooses a man two to four years older than she. Since men live seven years less than the average woman, this means that the older a woman becomes the fewer men are still left that are older than she. At birth there are more boy babies than girls (a 1% surplus of boys). This continues until age 35 where there is an equal ratio of single men to single women. From that point on the men start dying off so that at age 60 there are three and one half single women for every single man in the United States. This statistic becomes even more grim when you consider that many of these scarce 60 year single men are dating women in their forties and fifties! Obviously if single women continue to prefer older men their chances of finding a husband will diminish.

2. Marrying a man who is taller than she. Women who are tall (over 5'6") and like to wear high heels have a problem in meeting suitable men. I have spoken to many women who insist that a man be over 6 feet tall. That eliminates 90% of the single men in this country!

3. Marrying a man who earns more money than she. Even though women in this country still only earn 62 cents on the dollar in comparison to men, this doesn't apply to successful professional women, who have literally priced themselves out of the market! They have a very tough time finding a man who is older, taller, and wealthier than they.

The main flaw in the Harvard-Yale Study is that there's no reason why you can't adjust to these realities. Why not choose a man who is younger, shorter, or less prosperous? For years women have been complaining about how superficial men are. They chastise men for overlooking inner beauty, intimacy, and communication. Perhaps single women need to look at their own superficial prejudices regarding age, height, and money.

Single men have their own set of unrealistic expectations. They tend to prefer young, slim, pretty women. These women are at a tremendous premium. They have men standing in line for them. Unless you're rich and handsome, what are the chances that you'll attract one of these beauties?

The reality is that few women in this country have the slim figure of a model. Women begin with one third more fat than men. That is nature's way of preparing them for pregnancy. Otherwise our species might not be around today. The old adage that "beauty is only skin deep" may sound corny, but it's true. So don't worry if she is a few pounds overweight. Find yourself a loving woman with whom you can share a happy life.

RULE #2: TAKE ADVANTAGE OF YOUR FRIENDS

"Oh no, don't tell me I have to go on blind dates. You only get to meet losers."

The number one method for meeting people in this country is through mutual friends. Spread the word to your friends that you'd like to meet more people. Be sure to share with them exactly the qualities you are looking for. Ask them to include you on their guest list for dinners and parties. Have them introduce you to their friends, relatives, and co-workers as well.

Don't be afraid of blind dates. They are still a very common way of meeting people. Just don't expect too much. The likelihood is that on any particular blind date either you or the other person won't find the other to be attractive. So be patient.

RULE #3: EXPLOIT YOUR JOB

"Hey, wait a second. I'm not going to choose a job on the basis of whether it's a good place to meet people. I've got to put food on my table."

Most people choose a job on the basis of such things as money, status, enjoyment, and proximity to their homes. There's nothing wrong with that, but think about adding one more criterion: likelihood of meeting new friends. 10% of all romantic relationships begin between people who meet each other on the job, according to a study of 3000 singles. (Simenauer, J. and Carroll, D., Singles: The New Americans, N.Y., Simon & Schuster: 1982). Furthermore, according to a survey of 1,800 professional women between the ages of 21-45, "a romance between coworkers is four times more likely to last than one between a couple who met elsewhere.... About 20% of on-the-job romances lead to marriage." (Marin Independent-Journal, March, 25, 1986.)

What about the risks involved? Will you have to find another job if your office romance doesn't work out? According to the survey of professional women cited above, "only 5.3% of the women said ... their relationship had hurt their career. Only 1 in 400 reported losing her job."

If possible choose a job where you are dealing with the public on a daily basis. Unfortunately these are often low-paying jobs (e.g., waiters and waitresses, bank tellers and cashiers.) The pay-off is that you meet lots of new people. Another option is to choose an office where there are plenty of attractive single people of the opposite sex.

What if you don't work and don't need the money? Consider a volunteer job. There are all kinds of interesting opportunities to help others and make your community a better place to live. Call up your local volunteer bureau to find out how. Along with "contributing to society" you'll also increase your visibility in the community and meet new friends. See the chapter on Volunteer Work.

RULE #4: GET OUT OF THE HOUSE

Staying home is natural. It's comfortable. It's safe. It's inexpensive. There's only one problem. You'll never meet anybody by staying at home. Most singles spend almost all of their free time at home. Then they wonder why they never meet anybody!

How often should you get out of the house to meet people? That depends on how soon you want to meet someone special. If you're willing to wait 20 years, then don't sweat about it. Once a month is fine. On the other hand, if you want to meet someone soon, remember that every night you go out looking hastens the day when you succeed.

RULE #5: HANG AROUND STRANGERS ALONE

When we're kids our parents warn us to stay away from strangers. That's good advice at the time. Strangers are dangerous. What's also true, however, is that the love of your life is probably a stranger to you right now. So if you want to meet that person you're going to have to forget what your parents taught you about strangers. A good example of the problem is the following conversation:

Julie: "Are you going to the party Saturday night?
Sally: "No, I don't think so."
Julie: "Why not?"
Sally: "I won't know anyone there."

Sally's attitude is typical. She's afraid to go to a party full of strangers. But that's exactly the party she should go to. She'll have the greatest chance of meeting someone special if she knows few of the guests. In fact, the ideal party would be one where you knew absolutely no one, not even the host. In other words, a party you crashed.

The hardest part of Rule #5 is the word "alone". If you're like most single people, when you go to social functions you usually drag along your friends. I call them bodyguards. Their purpose is to insure that you won't meet anyone new. As long as you have your friends to engage in conversation, you won't have the motivation to meet new people.

Hanging around your friends is a particularly serious problem if you are a single woman, because your bodyguards make you unapproachable. Most men are scared to approach you if you're alone, due to fear of rejection. Think of how much more intimidating it is for a single man to approach you if you are part of a group! A man will wait patiently for the magic moment that never comes—the time when the women stop talking so he can introduce himself.

RULE #6: HANG AROUND THE OPPOSITE SEX

"Don't insult my intelligence. Of course I know that I've got to hang around people of the opposite sex in order to find a romantic partner."

It sounds a little ridiculous to make something so obvious into a rule. Unfortunately what is obvious isn't always followed. Most people feel most comfortable hanging around their own sex. Don't believe what you read about women's liberation or men's liberation. The fact of the matter is that men and women are very different. Men usually prefer to do "masculine" things and women like to do "feminine" things. As a result, more times than not the sexes don't mingle.

If you want to meet a man, ask yourself this question: "What do women hate to do that men love to do?" If you're a man ask yourself, "What do men hate to do that women love to do?" Whatever it is, do it. You'll find that there will be very little competition. You'll have all those attractive men or women to yourself. For example, if you're a woman, the best place to meet men is at a basketball gym.

"Are you crazy? I'm only 5 foot 2 and I have long nails. How am I going to play basketball?"

Who said anything about playing basketball? What's to prevent you from going down to the gym to watch?

"But what if a guy comes up to me and asks what I'm doing there?"

You have two options: you can tell the truth or you can lie. If you have the courage, by all means tell the truth: "I'm here to meet men." If you haven't the guts to be honest, then lie: "I thought the NBA game was on tonight and was dying to see some good basketball." All's fair in love and war. If you have to tell a lie that hurts no one in order to find someone for a loving relationship, isn't it worth it?

So rush down to the gym. If nothing else you'll get to see a bunch of good looking hunks all night running around in their underwear!

In general just about any sport is a good place to meet single men. Some sports, of course, have a greater surplus of men than others. The rule of thumb is "the bloodier, more violent, more dangerous, more demanding the sport, the greater the surplus of men". Boxing, martial arts, wrestling, and hockey have a greater surplus of men than tennis or bowling, which are quite popular among women. See the chapter on **Sports** for specific places to watch or participate in individual sports.

"Enough of this advice for women. What about us guys? Where are all the women hanging out?"

Try an aerobics class. The ratio is usually 10 women for every man! Or try folk dancing. Here the ratio is usually three to one. In fact you'll usually find more women than men in any kind of event that features dancing (other than singles bars). Women are also more likely to attend classes, seminars, pot luck dinners, and singles clubs in general.

RULE #7: INITIATE CONTACT

"Oh, oh. I knew there was a catch. I'm willing to lower my expectations, get out of the house, and hang around strangers of the opposite sex. But don't ask me to put my ego on the line and initiate contact. I might get rejected!"

When you get right down to it, it's the fear of rejection that causes millions of singles to remain single. We're all just plain chicken.

"All right, I'll admit it. I'm chicken. So what's the solution? How do I overcome the fear of rejection?"

There's only one way: go out and get rejected. Each time you get rejected you build up scar tissue. You'll find it a little easier to approach someone the next time. Pretty soon you'll be desensitized to the pain of rejection to the point where your fear is manageable.

But don't expect to ever get rid of the pain of rejection. That will always remain. I've been rejected many, many times, but it still hurts. It's just that the pain has subsided to the point where I don't have a nervous breakdown each time I get turned down. So go out there and make contact!

"Hold it a second. Men don't like women who initiate contact."

This is pure b.s. I've asked hundreds of men in my classes this question and over 90% of them answer that they love women to take the initiative. If you're a woman, put yourself in the shoes of single men. All your life the pressure has been on you to initiate contact. You've been rejected countless times. Wouldn't you love to reverse the tables?

Where does this myth come from that men don't like forward women? I think it has to do with the **Law of Rejection:** Unless you're one of the lucky 5%, most single people will not find you attractive. In other words, most men are going to reject you. It has nothing to do with them not liking women who take the initiative. They just don't like you.

"O.k., you've talked me into it. But how should I initiate contact?"

The first thing is to make eye contact with someone you find attractive and smile. If they return the smile, you're in! If they turn away or fail to smile, things get riskier. If you approach them you know there's a high probability they're going to reject you. On the other hand, they may just be shy. There's only one way to find out. Take the plunge.

Most singles procrastinate for an hour before making their move. They keep waiting for an opening where they can come over comfortably and initiate contact. Before that happens usually one of two things occurs: the person leaves before you meet them or someone else beats you to the punch. In either case you lose out because you waited for the perfect opportunity.

The secret to initiating contact is to do it right away before you have time to talk yourself out of it.

"But what do I say? Give me a sure-fire opening line."

Sorry, there's isn't one guaranteed to work with everyone. You've just got to come up with the best line you can and hope for the best. If you try a funny line you may impress someone with your sense of humor or you may just end up with egg on your face.

If you try the straightforward approach, "Hi, I'm Charlie", they may dismiss you as a nerd. So you can't win all the time. But that's not the point. Nobody's keeping score! You only have to win once. Then you're set for the rest of your life. So don't worry about the flops. "Damn the torpedoes; full speed ahead!"

RULE #8: HAVE SUPERFICIAL CONVERSATIONS

"Wait a second, did I read that right? Have superficial conversations? That's the whole problem with meeting people, you wind up talking about Reagan, the weather, or the latest sports scores. BORING!"

Do you expect people to spill their guts the first five minutes they meet you? If so, you're very unrealistic. People usually want to feel you out before they open up. They want to make sure it's safe.

Every intimate conversation with a stranger begins on a superficial level. You have to kiss a lot of frogs to find one prince. A dozen phony, boring conversations may be the price you pay for one sincere conversation with someone special.

RULE #9: PIN DOWN YOUR NEXT CONTACT

Does this situation sound familiar? You meet someone special. You get involved in a superficial conversation. Before you know it, both of you start opening up with private things and feelings. You start laughing. You almost feel like you've known each other all your lives. Could this be the big one? After all the searching, is this it?

But then the moment of truth arrives. If you meet at the beach, eventually the sun's gonna set. If it's at a bar, at 2 a.m. it's closing time. Sooner or later, wherever you met, the party's over. Before you leave, one of you has to end the conversation. So the two of you stand up and stare at each other, nervous and hesitant. Finally you break the silence. "I had a real nice time talking to you. Hope to see you again." Your new friend replies, "Yeah, catch you next time.

Disaster can strike so quickly at the moment of truth. Let's look at things logically. If you've seen this person once in forty years, what's the likelihood that you'll ever see each other again? Both of you have blown it. It's back to the drawing board.

This kind of tragedy happens all the time. Two people meet,

obviously are attracted to each other, but then fail to follow through. And so all is for nought.

"But wait. I'd never be so dumb as to say 'catch you next time'. I'd exchange phone numbers."

That's a little better, but not much. Think of all the times you've exchanged phone numbers in the past. How many times did you actually get to see the other person again. Probably less than 50%.

People always are puzzled about this. The women all ask, "How come I meet this guy, we have a great conversation, he asks for my number, I give it to him, and then he never calls? What's wrong with men?"

Many women are quite bitter about this. They feel betrayed. Often they rush home from work the next three nights expecting him to call. The silence is deafening. What's going on here? There are many reasons why a man doesn't call after asking for your phone number:

1. He lost it.
2. He forgot who you were. This is common in situations where a great deal of drinking has gone on.
3. He remembered who you were, but forgot what a great time he had with you.
4. He fantasized that you might reject him and therefore chickened out.
5. He called a few times, nobody answered, so he gave up.

"But wait a second, I have an answering machine. Why didn't the jerk leave a message?"

Many people hate or fear answering machines. Just count the number of times people call and fail to leave a message. In a stressful situation like calling someone for a date, is it that surprising that he might hang up?

Of course the guys have their version of the story. "How come I run into women all the time who give me their number and then come up with a song and dance about how busy they are each time I call to ask them out?"

There are many reasons why a woman might not respond positively to your telephone call:

1. She forgot who you were.
2. She lost interest once she sobered up.
3. She is genuinely very busy.
4. She's afraid of dating.
5. She never intended to go out with you in the first place.

The last reason is the hardest for men to deal with. "If she didn't want to go out with me then why did she give me her damn number?" The best way to answer that question is to pretend you're an attractive woman. All your life men have come on to you and asked you out or for your telephone number. It's hard to say to someone, "I find you unattractive" or "I don't want to go out with you" or "No, you can't have my telephone number". So what do you do? You give up your telephone number, hoping he'll never call. If he does call, you lie. You say that you're busy Saturday night or you have a boyfriend.

It would be great if we lived in a world where people were honest and didn't play these games. Unfortunately, such is not the case. The price you pay for flirting with women and asking them out on dates is that a certain percentage will lie and pretend to want to go out with you. If you were a woman you'd probably do the same thing.

One piece of advice that is critical for both men and women is to always confirm a date ahead of time. Occasionally you will find that the phone number that was given to you is a phony or that the person has no intention of meeting with you. You can avoid the pain, frustration, and anger of being stood up by taking this simple precaution.

RULE #10: DON'T FALL IN LOVE WITH THE WRONG PERSON

The great American fantasy is to fall in love and live happily ever after. Unfortunately your heart is a poor judge of character. Many single people fall in love with the wrong person and live miserably ever after. Following your feelings can be a recipe for disaster unless they are based on sound information about this person. How do you get the facts about a potential spouse? The answer is you ask.

Unfortunately most singles are afraid to getting personal for fear of scaring off a potential loving partner. So they "play it cool" at the beginning of a relationship. They especially avoid "heavy" subjects like sex.

That's fine as long as your feelings towards each other are casual. But what happens when you fall in love? All of a sudden you panic and realize that you know very little about this special person. So now you start with the personal questions. Then disaster strikes. You discover a fatal flaw. For example, you want to have children and they don't. You want marriage and they don't. They want to move to Denver and you love the Bay Area.

Now you're on the horns of a terrible dilemma. You can drop the person and go through the agony of a broken relationship. Or you can do what most people do: marry them and hope to change them. Fat chance! You'll probably end up being married to someone inappropriate and resent them for not changing. The way to avoid disastrous relationships is to get personal early in a relationship.

"Hold it a minute. Get personal with a stranger? That's too risky. They're going to think I'm nosy if I ask intimate questions.

There's no doubt that it's risky to get personal. Some people can't handle intimacy. They are closed and feel uncomfortable being around someone who wants to share secrets and intimate feelings. But don't you want to find that out as soon as possible? Or would you rather date a guy for 6 months before discovering that he's an emotional cripple?

Of course there's nothing wrong with playing it cool for a while. At some point, however, you're going to have to bite the bullet. You're going to have to do two things: pry and reveal. When you pry you ask personal questions. When you reveal you let the other person learn personal things about you. That's all there is to it.

If you want to play it safe, pry and reveal simultaneously. For example, suppose you're talking to someone who mentions that they were recently living with someone but moved out. Here's your chance to get personal and raise your superficial conversation to an intimate level. You could ask, "Were you dumped or did you do the dumping?" That's getting personal, but there's a good chance you're going to offend the other person with such a heavy-handed question. An alternative is to say, "I was in a relationship until three months ago, but it broke up very painfully for me. How did yours end?"

"How soon should I get personal?"

That depends on how long you're willing to wait before falling in love. If you want to chitchat for six months before getting serious about someone, that's o.k. Just remember that you are not allowed to fall in love unless you have the answers to your critical questions. I call them **killer questions**. If any of them are answered incorrectly the relationship is dead. You drop the person immediately.

1. Are you single? Pretty obvious, isn't it? You'd be surprised how many people assume that someone by themselves at a party or a dance is single. Always ask. In addition, it makes particular sense for women to ask a man for his home telephone number. If he hands you a business card ask him to write his home number down as well. And be sure to call that number to make sure he isn't married or living with a woman. Be careful with people who answer that they are separated. "Have you moved out?" and "Have you filed for divorce?" are indispensable killer questions. If they are still living with their spouses or haven't yet filed for divorce, it's best you pass and move on to greener pastures.
2. Are you involved with someone romantically? Here's where you avoid someone who already loves someone else.
3. Why didn't your other romantic relationships last? Find out as much as you can about their marriage(s) or past relationships. Hopefully you'll find out their negative qualities. Then you can decide whether you can live with that flaw or should move on to someone different. You can also find out if they are incompatible with a certain kind of person. For example, maybe they can't stand being with someone who is possessive and is always checking up on them. If you are that kind of person, you can move on to someone compatible with your flaws.
4. How do you deal with conflict and problems in relationships? If their preference is to sweep problems under the rug or to fall into a rage, they are not good relationship material.
5. Do you have children? How many? Do you want children? How many? How **soon** do you want to have children? I have dated two

questions first; fall in love later.
6. What are your long term goals? Do you want to get married? Do you want to change careers? Do you plan to go back to school? Are you happy in this area or would you prefer moving elsewhere?
7. What do you like to do sexually? What are your sexual fantasies? Most singles are squeamish when it comes to asking these questions. The result is marriages that are unfulfilling sexually for one or both partners. Another potential result is your partner fulfilling their fantasies with others rather than you. Sexual questions are particularly important if you don't believe in pre-marital sex. In that case there's only one way to find out their sexual preferences—ask.
8. Do you have any contagious diseases? Have you engaged in high risk behavior (intravenous drugs or sex with bisexual or homosexual males)? These are literally killer questions. Falling in love with the wrong person can kill you.
9. How much do you drink? Which drugs do you do, and how often?

Here's a homework assignment. Develop your own list of killer questions. The way to do it is to analyze your previous love relationships. What character trait or behavior pattern of a romantic partner destroyed the relationship? Formulate a question to find out whether a prospect has this trait.

"How do I know that my prospective romantic partner is answering my killer questions honestly?"

Unfortunately you can't always trust people. They're going to be tempted to tell you what you want to hear rather than the truth. One way of getting around this is to quiz their parents, relatives, and friends. The ideal person to ask, of course, is their ex-spouse. Find out the "dirt" about a prospective romantic partner before you fall in love. This advice is decidedly unromantic, but it sure beats finding out disastrous information after you fall in love.

"If my partner finds out I've been snooping around their private life, there's going to be hell to pay!

That's true, so you have to be very subtle.

CHAPTER 4: DATING ETIQUETTE

There was a time when dating was simple. Men were expected to be gentlemen and women were expected to be ladies. Their roles were clear-cut. Today single people are often mixed up about proper dating etiquette. This is particularly true if you are re-entering the singles scene after years of being half of a married couple. It can be quite traumatic to play the "dating game" without knowing the rules.

Singles often feel in a "damned if I do, damned if I don't" situation. For example, if you're a man and automatically pick up the check at a restaurant, you may gain points with one woman but antagonize another. If you're a woman and prefer to pay your own way you'll find that some men love it and others hate it. So what are the rules for dating in America in the Eighties?

There are none. What works with some singles, doesn't work with others. It may be helpful therefore, to do 2 things:

1. Communicate with your dating partners. Let them know your preferences in terms of male/female roles, and find out theirs. For example, if you are a man who enjoys opening the door for a woman, ask her if she's comfortable with that or prefers to open her own door. If you're a woman who likes to pay her own way, check that out with your partner before the date.
2. Be tolerant of your date's desires. Again using the example above, if she says she doesn't want you to open her door, then don't. Don't get upset or try to persuade your date to give in your expectations.

There are 3 issues that come up most often during dates.

Issue #1: Who Initiates the Date?

Despite what you hear about women's liberation, the man usually initiates dates in America. But it also is socially acceptable for a woman to initiate a date. So do what feels comfortable.

Issue #2: Who Controls the Date?

Some men enjoy the "masculine" role of deciding where to go on a date. Many women feel quite comfortable with this. In that case, there's nothing wrong with an "old-fashioned date" with the man making the decisions. Many men and women, however, want a more equal relationship where both share in the decisions. It's important, therefore, to communicate your preferences and try to come to an accommodation with your partner.

Issue #3: Who Pays?

Here again you can't believe all you read and hear about women's liberation. The fact of the matter is that most women in California expect the man to pick up the check at restaurants, bars, etc. If you're a man, therefore, expect to pay most of the time.

Some men feel uncomfortable with picking up the bill. They prefer a "Dutch treat" where the bill is split. That's fine, as long as you have discussed this earlier with your date and she has agreed to it. Otherwise, it's quite rude to ask a woman out to a movie, for example, and announce to her at the ticket window that she has to pay for her own ticket.

Dating Etiquette 25

Men who would prefer that the woman "pay her fair share" often feel uncomfortable about discussing these matters. They are afraid that the woman will consider him to be cheap. This is indeed a possibility. Many women expect to be treated generously by a man. Some want to be taken to expensive restaurants, night clubs, etc. They may expect the man to bring flowers, a bottle of wine, or candy on a date when he comes to pick her up.

What do you do if you're a man and feel uncomfortable with all this? Don't date that kind of woman. There are plenty of women who are willing to pay their own way. They are the minority, but still a sizable one.

Some men feel quite bitter about society's expectation that they pick up the tab on dates. They can't understand why women are so "unfair". The most obvious reason is tradition. Throughout history men have been the "providers" and women have been the "homemakers". Today, with a significant percentage of the American work force composed of women, this is no longer always the case. But old traditions die slowly.

Another explanation is the fact that women only earn 72% of what men do in our society. For this reason many women feel that it is quite fair that the man pay for activities on dates.

One way the issue of equity is often settled is by the man paying for out-of-pocket expenses and the woman repaying him by having him over for dinner. This is a very fair way of handling the issue since most single men don't eat very good meals and really appreciate a home-cooked meal.

If you are a woman, you may have a problem adjusting to the expectations of different men on this issue. One man may be offended if you offer to pay your half. The next may be delighted. Again communication and tolerance are the keys. Normally it's assumed that the man will pay, but if you prefer to pay your own way you should discuss this ahead of time, preferably on the phone before your first date. Come to an agreement on who is to pay.

What do you do if the man insists on paying? You can call him a male chauvinist pig and refuse to go out with him again. Or you can accede to his wishes and let him pay. This has obvious financial advantages. There often is a disadvantage, however. Some men believe that if they spend money on a woman this entitles them to sexual favors. Don't allow yourself to fall into this trap. If you're going to feel pressured to give in sexually to a man who spends a lot of money on you in an evening then insist on paying your own way. If he won't agree to this, then cancel the date.

In other words, stick up for your rights. Try to be accommodating to the needs of your date, but not at the cost of sacrificing your own values or comfort.

The most difficult issues of all often pertain to sex. They are discussed in the next chapter.

CHAPTER 5: SEX AND THE SINGLE PERSON

One of the myths in our society is that the difference between men and women is that men want sex more. The fact of the matter is that women want sex and enjoy sex just as much as men. So what's the difference between the sexes?

The difference is that men want sex today. And that's where the conflict arises. As a general rule women want emotional intimacy before physical intimacy. They don't feel comfortable sleeping with a man they hardly know. Men tend to be the opposite. They've been conditioned by our society to seek sex immediately and with as many different partners as possible, regardless of how emotionally close or distant they may be.

Of course these are generalizations. Many men feel uncomfortable with casual sex, just as there are many women who love it. But as a general rule men want sex earlier in a relationship than women do.

The result is what I call the natural incompatibility of the sexes. Men and women are in a constant struggle whereby the men try to seduce every woman they find attractive while the women fight to maintain their "virtue". The result is a great deal of frustration and bitterness. And the death of many a promising relationship.

Both men and women often find themselves in uncomfortable positions regarding sex. The man often wants to sleep with a woman but is afraid of making a move for fear that she will be insulted or angered. The woman wants to postpone sexual intimacy until after emotional closeness, but she's afraid to say no for fear that the man will lose interest and move on to another woman who says yes.

And so both walk a tightrope between asserting their needs and acceding to those of their partners. Often neither feels very good about it all.

In order to get along with the opposite sex it is important to understand them. Below is information about the opposite sex together with suggestions on how to get along.

WHAT MEN NEED TO KNOW ABOUT WOMEN

Are you often puzzled by women's sexual behavior? For example, you meet a woman at a party. While slow dancing she rubs your hand and appears to be very comfortable in your tight embrace. Later in the evening she invites you into her home for some coffee. She responds positively to touching and hugging and kissing. But just as you try to escalate physical intimacy, all of a sudden she pulls back and says "not tonight". What's going on here? Why do women appear to be ready for sex and suddenly "chicken out"? There are many reasons:

1. She sees sex as inextricably entwined with love. Since she doesn't love you, she doesn't feel comfortable having sex with you.

2. She is afraid that if she has sex with you early in a relationship that you'll think she's "cheap" and promiscuous and therefore drop her.
3. She's afraid of pregnancy or disease.
4. She is having her menstrual period.
5. She finds that when she engages in casual sex she usually feels empty or ashamed the next morning. In other words, she enjoys the casual sex as it happens but regrets it the next morning.

Whatever the reason, the fact is that most women don't want to engage in casual sex. They want to get to know you first. How do you deal with this? One way is to be patient and wait for when she's ready for more physical intimacy. Another option is to try to persuade her to become more intimate with you sexually, but respect her right to say no.

What if you get tired of waiting? At some point you might frankly tell her, in a non-demanding tone of voice that you aren't getting your needs met in the relationship. At that point she has the choice of compromising with you or sticking to her guns. If she isn't willing to compromise then you have a choice. You can continue the relationship or move on to greener pastures.

WHAT WOMEN NEED TO KNOW ABOUT MEN

How could a man want to sleep with a complete stranger? Wouldn't he feel uncomfortable? Wouldn't he feel empty? Why doesn't he go slow, get to know a woman, and then move on to sexual contact? These are questions that boggle most women's minds.

The answer is that men have been conditioned to sleep with every attractive woman they meet. They are taught that they are more masculine and have greater value if they sleep with many women. The old "notch in the belt" analogy that women hate so much is sadly appropriate in many cases. Some men do indeed count their "conquests". They achieve self-esteem by seducing women.

The other thing you need to know about men is that often they find it very difficult to achieve emotional intimacy. Men are taught to hide their feelings. It's difficult for them to open up and share their inner selves. Most men seek intimacy but are frightened by emotions. Therefore they attempt to gain the intimacy they need in what to them is a safer means--through sex.

Whatever the reason, the fact is that often a man will try to seduce you. He will use all kinds of tricks to try to accomplish this objective:
1. He will play caveman and attempt to physically overwhelm your defenses.
2. He will try to get you drunk. He knows that this greatly increases his chances of seducing you.
3. He will lie to you and tell you that he loves you. Some women are dumb enough to fall for that kind of line.
4. He will accuse you of hating sex or being frigid.
5. He will threaten to drop you if you don't have sex with him.

How do you handle all this? There are several options. One is to hate men and dismiss them as insensitive, selfish brutes. Many women choose this course. They become quite bitter about men and often refuse to date. This is obviously a foolish choice.

A second option is give in. This is also a foolish strategy if you're going to regret it the next morning.

A third option is to insist that he respect your needs. If he is unwilling to do so, he's probably not the man for you. Find one who is.

The important thing is to accept the facts of life. Many men like to seduce women. You don't have to like it. Just accept it and learn to deal with it.

How do you avoid having casual sex?

1. Don't drink. The more alcohol you consume the less resistance you will have to his sexual advances.
2. Don't invite him into your home after a date. Most men will interpret your invitation to come in for a cup of coffee or a drink as a invitation to have sex as well.
3. Let him know that you don't want to have sex with him tonight.
4. Don't hug and kiss all night long and then think you can cut him off anytime you please without suffering certain negative consequences. Some men will either attempt to physically overpower you or get angry that you are a "tease".

SEXUAL MORALITY

All your life people have been telling you how you should behave sexually. Parents, siblings, teachers, clergymen, friends, and potential romantic partners all have advice on what is best for you. I don't choose to join these unsolicited counselors. Instead my suggestion is that you think things through yourself and develop a moral system that works for you.

How do you go about doing this? The first step is to throw out all the conditioning from the past. That's not easy to do, but the key is to realize that the advice you have been getting from others is hopelessly contradictory. One person advises you to avoid all sexual contact outside marriage. The next person suggests that you "loosen up" and enjoy yourself. You can't follow everyone's advice, so why not chuck it all and start from scratch?

What sexual code will make you happy? That's the place to start. Consider your physical and emotional needs. Develop a moral code that you can live with. Otherwise you're going to violate it anyway and wind up feeling guilty. Better to be realistic and develope a code of conduct that works for you.

What about your moral responsibility to others? It would be great if what made you happy also made others happy. Unfortunately that's not always true. Occasionally you're faced with sexual dilemmas. Do you make yourself or someone else happy? That's for you to decide.

A.I.D.S.

Once upon a time sexual promiscuity was the "in thing to do" in the American singles scene. That's no longer true. First there was herpes. Now there's Acquired Immune Deficiency Syndrome (AIDS). Estimates are that most if not all people who carry the virus will eventually die from it.

Before you panic, however, it's important to realize some important facts. First, AIDS is extremely difficult to catch. You have to go out of your way to get it. You cannot be infected through normal, everyday contact. Second, the vast majority of cases have been limited to a few high-risk groups: homosexual and bisexual men; intravenous drug users; hemophiliacs. Finally, AIDS is easily prevented. Here's how to do it:

1. Avoid sexual contact with the high risk groups listed above.
2. Don't be promiscuous. The more people you sleep with the greater the likelihood that you will catch AIDS. One of the reasons that so many members of the gay community became infected is because they tended to be far more promiscuous than heterosexuals.
3. Avoid sexual contact with promiscuous people (for the reasons given above).
4. Avoid anal intercourse.
5. Use a condom with new sexual partners or partners who may be promiscuous.

Of course the surest way to avoid AIDS is to refrain from sex altogether. After all, you can never be 100% certain that even a spouse isn't secretly consorting with someone who has AIDS. Obviously this is carrying things to an extreme. There's a difference between being reasonably cautious and being paranoid. Only a tiny percentage of the heterosexual population of the United States is carrying the AIDS virus. If you follow the suggestions above the chances of catching AIDS are minuscule.

Even if you fail to follow the recommended precautions, a study at the University of California at San Francisco concluded that there is only one chance in five million that you will catch AIDS if you have sexual intercourse with someone who does not belong to a high risk group. This "is about the same as the risk of being killed in a traffic accident while driving 10 miles to that encounter." (San Francisco Chronicle, April 22, 1988, p. A2.)

Remember that life involves a certain amount of risk. Every time you get on the highway you are risking being crippled or killed. That doesn't mean you stay off the freeway. It just means that you have to be careful. So too with AIDS. Don't let fear dominate your life to the point that you don't get your needs met for physical intimacy.

HERPES

Before the AIDS epidemic herpes was the main cause of paranoia in the singles community. Today many singles are still scared to death of herpes. Which is quite foolish. The facts about herpes are as follows:

1. Many people with herpes never have a recurrence. In other words, it was an unpleasant one-time illness. They won't ever infect anyone.
2. Those who do have recurrences usually have them infrequently (a few times a year at most). The chances of infecting someone are small.
3. The vast majority of herpes attacks are mild (ranging from itching to flu symptoms.

In view of these three facts, isn't it amazing how frightened people are of herpes? People don't dread catching the flu. So why are they so afraid of herpes? The main reason is that it is a sexually transmitted illness. In our society anything dealing with sex becomes magnified. That's because here in America we have an unhealthy attitude about sex. If we regarded it as other physical functions like eating and sleeping, there wouldn't be any emotional charge associated with sexually transmitted illnesses.

What should you do if you are infected with herpes at one time or another?

1. Don't be ashamed. You don't feel guilty when you catch the flu. Why should you feel any differently about herpes?
2. Accept the moral responsibility to avoid infecting others. That involves examining yourself frequently and avoiding sex when it appears that you are experiencing a flare-up.

Of course the big moral dilemma is "Should I tell a new romantic partner that I have had herpes?" That's a tough one. There's no right or wrong answer. Some people will be very grateful that you told them. Their esteem for you will increase because you were honest. Others may reject you, however, if they find out you have had herpes. In the worst case, they may share your secret with other people.

In weighing this decision it might be wise to try to calculate the chances that you might inadvertently transmit herpes to someone new. If the chances of transmitting the illness are slim, you may decide to keep your past experience to yourself and just be very careful.

On the other hand, if you have frequent recurrences there is a much larger chance that you will infect someone. If you do, they will be extremely angry and bitter. This will put a tremendous strain on your relationship with them.

So think carefully about this dilemma. Consider the happiness of others. But also don't lose sight of your responsibility to do what makes YOU happy.

For some people, herpes is far worse than the flu. Some people have severe attacks. Others chronically experience recurrences. So avoiding herpes is certainly a prudent policy. Many of the steps for preventing herpes are the same as those for AIDS:

1. Don't be promiscuous. The more people you sleep with the greater the likelihood that you will catch herpes.
2. Avoid sexual contact with promiscuous people, since they are more likely to be infected.
3. Use a condom with new sexual partners or partners who may be promiscuous.

CHAPTER 6: MARRIAGE

85% of singles in this country want to happily married. The problem is that close to half of all marriages in this country end in divorce. Why? The primary cause is that most singles get married for the wrong reasons. For example:

1. A high percentage of brides are pregnant on their wedding day. Many of them get married to avoid having an illegitimate child.
2. Many singles are lonely and unhappy. They get married out of desperation.
3. Many people get married because they are madly in love.
4. Some singles get married because "it's the thing to do". Their parents, friends, or society in general expect it of them.
5. Women over 30 worry about the biological clock. They see time running out and the day approaching when they will be too old to have children.

With reasons like this it's no wonder that a third of all marriages in America end tragically. How can you avoid divorce?

1. Don't get pregnant.   With Planned Parenthood and other organizations to assist you, there's no excuse for unwanted pregnancy.
2. Don't turn to marriage as a lifeboat that will rescue you from your unhappiness. Unhappy singles usually become unhappy couples. Become a happy single and then become married.
3. Don't get married because you're madly in love. The word "madly" should tip you off. You want to make an intelligent, rational decision to get married. Erich Fromm, in The Art of Loving, differentiates between "falling" in love and "standing" in love. When you fall in love you are not in contact with reality. You are idealizing your partner and blind to their shortcomings. After you get through the honeymoon stage you'll discover all of their negative qualities. Then it will be too late to decide intelligently about whether or not to get married.
4. Don't succumb to pressure from outside. The people who are advising you to get married aren't going to have to live with your spouse. You are. Being single is more socially acceptable today than ever before. So don't worry about what others think. Do what's right for you.
5. Don't get married because you want to have a child. You'll wind up raising your child in an unhappy marriage or broken home.
6. Don't expect to change your partner. People are remarkably resistant to change. If you can barely tolerate your partner during the engagement period you'll hate them later.

But enough of the "don't"s. What positive things can you do to increase your chances for a happy marriage?

1. Be patient. Don't marry the first decent person that comes along. Wait for someone right for you.
2. Play the numbers game. The more singles you meet the more choices you'll have.
3. Get to know someone well and make sure they know you well. Let them see your "worst foot" instead of always putting your best foot forward. Insist that they do the same. If you've never had a fight, if all is sweetness and light, don't get married! Sooner or later you're going to discover areas of incompatibility. It's wise to do so before the marital vows.
4. Make sure that there's more than just sexual attraction binding you together. It is very difficult to sustain a passionate relationship over the years. What usually holds marriages together is friendship and intimacy. If you don't truly like each other and enjoy each others company your marriage will not be a happy one.

The best way to insure a happy marriage is to be happily single first! How do you do that? The most important thing is to realize how lucky you are to be single. Instead of being in a rotten marriage like so many people in America, you have the freedom to remain single or marry someone special. That's quite a luxury.

Of course the grass always looks greener on the other side. You see married couples all the time who appear to be experiencing unlimited bliss. What you don't see are all the arguments and unmet needs. People have an uncanny knack for putting a good face on an unhappy marriage. So don't take the marriages around you at face value. Unless they're newly-weds, they all have their secret problems.

On the other hand, avoid becoming so bitter and disillusioned with your past relationships that you decide to remain single for the rest of your life. The fact of the matter is that there are millions of happy marriages in America. Yours can be one of them.

Part Two:

SINGLES

ORGANIZATIONS

OVERVIEW OF SINGLES CLUBS

There are hundreds of clubs in the Bay Area created specifically to meet the need of singles. Most people who attend these clubs are hoping to meet someone special for a romantic relationship. A smaller number aren't ready for romance (they're bouncing back from an unpleasant experience with the opposite sex), but they're still looking for new friends.

What is the typical age of people who attend singles clubs? That varies from club to club. Most singles who attend are 40+. Usually there is a shortage of men at these clubs, since there is a surplus of women in America in the 40+ age bracket. There are some clubs, however, that cater specifically to singles in their 20s or 30s. The **Singles Club Directory** that follows specifies which clubs attract younger singles.

Many people refuse to go to singles clubs. You may be one of them. You probably have one or more reasons for this:

1. **"Only losers go to singles clubs".** The fact of the matter is that you get a cross-section of people at singles clubs. Some are winners and some are losers, as in any other social situation. You are just as likely to run into losers at work, at church, on the beach, or at private dinner parties. If you want to avoid meeting losers, stay home. Otherwise, take your chances at singles clubs.
2. **"I went to a singles club once and didn't meet anybody."** That's usually the case. You can't expect to fall in love the first time you attend a singles club. Keep on going anyway. If you visit singles clubs often enough eventually you'll meet the kind of man you want.
3. **"I don't want to broadcast to the world that I'm single and looking."** Here's pride rearing its ugly head. Are you going to let it get in the way of meeting new friends or a romantic partner?

TYPES OF SINGLES CLUBS

1. CHRISTIAN CLUBS

Most singles clubs meet at churches. One reason is that churches usually provide meeting sites at little or no cost. Another reason is that many churches believe they are obligated to have a Singles Ministry committed towards reaching out to single people in the area to help them meet their spiritual, social, and emotional needs.

Many singles shy away from clubs that meet at churches because they don't belong to the particular denomination. That's a mistake. All church clubs are open to singles of all faiths (and even to singles with no faith at all).

Church-sponsored singles clubs fall into two categories: religiously oriented and secular. A religiously oriented club often features Sunday school classes, worship services and/or Bible study specifically for singles. Obviously, if you are non-religious, you might feel uncomfortable attending. Most church-sponsored singles clubs, however, are more secular in their orientation. Typically they sponsor lectures, discussions, potlucks, picnics, parties, dances, trips, and sports. You will rarely hear any mention of religion at their activities.

Many women in particular prefer going to singles clubs that meet at churches, because they provide a very safe environment for meeting people. Because of this, however, there usually is a shortage of men.

Catholic Singles Clubs

There was a time when churches were negative towards divorced people, particularly the Catholic Church. This is no longer true. Separated & Divorced Catholic Support Groups meet at churches throughout America. Typically they have a free weekly support group. In addition they often sponsor parties, potlucks, and dances. The Catholic Church also sponsors **Beginning Experience**, which is a weekend retreat for newly separated, divorced, and widowed. Catholic Alumni Clubs, for college graduates eligible to marry within the Catholic Church, are located in most major cities in the U.S.

Protestant Singles Clubs

Most Protestant denominations sponsor singles activities, particularly Presbyterians, Methodists, Lutherans, Baptists, Assembly of God, and Mormons. Often their groups are called FOCAS (Fellowship of Christian Adult Singles) or FOCUS (Fellowship of Christian United Singles).

Many Protestant churches sponsor COLLEGE/CAREER groups for singles in their 20s and early 30s who have postponed marriage in order to pursue their education or careers.

Unitarian Singles Clubs

What do you do if you're uncomfortable going to Catholic, Protestant, or Jewish places of worship? Go to the Unitarian Church. Unitarians don't have any dogmas, so theoretically we're all Unitarians. Most Unitarian churches have singles clubs.

2. JEWISH CLUBS

Jewish Community Centers (JCCs) almost always have singles clubs. Jewish synagogues and temples also frequently sponsor activities for singles. In addition, the JCC is similar to a YMCA or YWCA in terms of a host of activities such as lectures, discussions, dancing, swimming, and volleyball. These are great ways to meet people. JCCs in large cities also operate JASSline, a 24 hour recording of Jewish singles activities.

As with the clubs that meet at Christian churches, you need not be Jewish to attend a Jewish singles club, although many Jews, however, have a strong preference to marry within the Jewish faith. Most Jews are open to dating people of all faiths and a sizable minority actually prefer non-Jews.

3. SINGLE PARENTS CLUBS

Do you have kids? Sometimes they can cramp your social life when you can't find a babysitter. But for every cloud there's a silver lining. Parents Without Partners (PWP), has over 700 chapters throughout the U.S. In order to join you have to be the single parent of a living child. Your child could be 50 years old. You're still eligible to join PWP, and you don't even have to have custody of your 50 year old!

PWP sponsors dozens of activities for singles each month. Some are family-oriented and others are for adults only. To learn more about PWP call the local chapter listed in the white pages of your phone book. The first step is to attend an orientation meeting (free). If you aren't a single parent you are still invited to attend their monthly open dances. In addition to P.W.P., there are many other single parents clubs.

4. WIDOW/WIDOWERS CLUBS

For obvious reasons these clubs usually attract older members. There are a few young widow/widowers clubs, however.

5. EXCLUSIVE CLUBS

Some singles clubs claim to cater specifically to single professionals. They request that men wear a coat & tie. Usually they meet at country clubs, luxurious private homes, or elegant hotels. They also tend to be more expensive than other singles clubs.

Despite the aura of exclusivity, however, these groups seldom turn anyone away for reasons of income or occupation. In other words, the only thing you know about the men who attend is that they have a coat and tie and the price of admission that evening!

One group that limits its parties to invited guests is Who's Who International, with chapters in most major U.S. cities.

6. SPECIAL ACTIVITY CLUBS

Many singles clubs specialize in one or more activities. For example, there is a league of singles ski clubs in the Bay Area. They are listed under skiing in the Sports chapter. Singles Club Association of California includes many singles clubs in the Bay Area that specialize in ballroom dancing. They are listed in the Dancing chapter. Singles clubs specializing in other activities are also listed under different activity chapters or in the Singles Club Directory that follows. You will find that regardless of what you like to do in your spare time there probably is a club of singles that would like to do it with you!

Overview of Singles Clubs

STARTING YOUR OWN SINGLES CLUB

Are you unhappy with the choices for singles activities in your area? Why not start your own singles club! Here's the easy way to do it.

1. Enlist the help of your single friends. Call a meeting at your home for anyone who might be interested in helping to start a singles club. "Many hands make light work."
2. Choose a free or inexpensive meeting place or places for your group. Private homes are an obvious option. Your local church is another. Most churches are conscious of the need for a "singles ministry" and are receptive to singles clubs meeting at the church for little or no cost.
3. Publicize your group free through the news media. Most newspapers have an events calendar for non-profit organizations. Local radio and television stations may be willing to run a free public service announcement about your meetings.
4. Make newcomers feel welcome at your meetings. First-timers usually feel uncomfortable and need to be greeted warmly, introduced to other members, and then encouraged to participate in club activities.
5. Be sure to notify me about your singles club for a free listing in the next edition of this book. Send information to American Singles, 4 Highland Avenue, San Rafael, CA 94901, (415) 459-3817.

LOCATING SINGLES CLUBS

I have listed below as many singles organizations as I could locate. Unfortunately there are many more that are so obscure that I've never heard of them. Singles Clubs usually don't have an advertising budget, so it's difficult to find out about them other than through word of mouth.

If you know of any singles clubs that were omitted or if you are aware of any inaccuracies please contact me so I can include the information in the next edition of this book. The address once again is: American Singles, 4 Highland Ave., San Rafael 94901, (415) 459-3817.

Please don't be offended if some of the listings below are outdated. When your new telephone directory arrives on your doorstep each year, many of the listings are already obsolete. The same holds true with listings of singles clubs.

One method for locating other singles clubs in your area is to call your local churches. They usually sponsor a singles club or can tell you of a church nearby that does.

Another method is to check the listings in the calendar or events sections of your local newspapers. Many of the singles clubs receive free listings due to the fact that they are non-profit organizations.

A third method is to attend meetings of different singles clubs and ask people where other clubs meet.

A fourth method is to consult one of the singles club calendars below.

Singles Club Calendars

Enjoy Life Singles Magazine, Box 2593, Santa Rosa 95405, (707) 575-1006. Violet Young, Editor. North Bay singles calendar each month.

In the Know, 1042 Sanchez, San Francisco 94114, (415) 647-5567. Juliette Smith, Editor. Monthly. Singles parties and other activities.

Lifestyle, 421 W. MacArthur Blvd., Oakland 94609, (415) 420-1381. David Sawle, Publisher. Bi-monthly. Singles parties and other activities.

Party Fax Line, (415) 929-7500. Edited by Arden Van Upp. You need a computer and modem to access this publication of parties for singles.

Single Events of the Bay Area, (900) 844-3556. 95 cents per minute.

Trellis Singles Magazine, 1260 Persian Dr., Sunnyvale 94089, (415) 941-2900 or (408) 747-1455. Bi-monthly singles calendar. Singles events listings over the phone, (900) 844-4445. 89 cents per minute.

CHRISTIAN SINGLES CLUBS

ALAMEDA

H.O.T. Singles, Home of Truth Church, 1300 Grand Ave., Alameda 94501, (415) 522-3366.

St. Joseph's Parish Ctr Separated & Divorced Catholic Support Group, 1119 Lafayette, Alameda 94501, 865-0653. Potlucks, odd Thursdays, 7pm. Discussion & support group, even Fridays, 7:30pm.

ANTIOCH

1st Assembly of God Church Singles, 640 E. Tregallas, Antioch 94509, (415) 757-1837. Sundays, 9:30am. Tuesdays, 7pm.

Contra Costa Christian Singles, 2809 Minta Ave., Antioch 94509.

Delta Christian Singles, 2713 Garrow Dr., Antioch 94509

Separated & Divorced Catholic Support Group, Antioch, Bob Arieta, 197 Oakview, Pleasant Hill 94523, (415) 939-1356.

APTOS

Assembly of God Singles, 7200 Freedom Blvd., Aptos 95003, 688-3312.

Twin Lakes Baptist Church, 2701 Cabrillo College Dr., Aptos 95003, (408) 475-5284. 3 singles clubs: 1. New Life (mainly 45-65), (408) 475-5284. 2. Prime Time, ages 30-55. 3. In Step, ages 23-33. Sunday school classes for singles, Bible study, game nights, sports, socials.

BENICIA

Benicia Fellowship Church Divorce Recovery, 963 Jefferson, (707) 746-5673. Bill Price, Pastor. One evening per week for 8 weeks.

BERKELEY

Berkeley Singles Ward (Mormon), 2368 Le Conte, 848-1918. Sunday church services, camping, hiking, white water rafting, and socials.

1st Presbyterian 20-20 Singles, 2407 Dana, Berkeley 94704, 848-6242. Fellowship Sundays, 5:45pm. 22-35. Also Divorce Recovery Wksp.

Unitarian Singles, 1 Lawson, Kensington 94706, 891-9672 (Margaret). Discussions, Sundays, 7:30pm. Also socials. Mainly 35+.

BURLINGAME

1st Presbyterian Church, 1500 Easton, Burlingame 94010, 342-0875. 3 singles groups: 1. New Beginnings Transition Support Grp 2. Single Friends of Burlingame (30+). 3. YAMS (Young Adult Singles, 22-30), 347-7265. Wednesdays, 7:30pm.

CAMPBELL

Home Church Singles, 1711 S. Winchester, Campbell 95008, (408) 370-1500. 1st Fridays, 7pm. Non-sectarian. All ages. William Ray.

Spirit Group, 264 E. Everett St., Campbell 95008.

CASTRO VALLEY

Cathedral at the Crossroads 3 Crosses Singles, 20600 John Dr., C.V. 94546, 537-4690. M. Cash.

1st Baptist Church Singles, 18550 Redwood Rd, C.V. 94546, 582-0515.

1st Presbyterian Church Alive for Christ, 2490 Grove Way, C.V. 94546, 581-6203. Bible Study, Sunday nights. Also movies, potlucks. 26+.

Redwood Chapel Community Church (nonsectarian), 19300 Redwood Bl, C.V. 94546, 886-6300. Socials. 3 clubs: 1. Chai Alpha (18-early 20s), Sunday school, 11am. 2. 20-20 Singles (24-30), Sunday school, 8:10am, Little Chapel. 3. Single Career (working full-time, mainly 30s), Sunday school, 11am. Bible study, Wednesdays, 7pm.

CONCORD

Bethel Baptist Church Singles, 3578 Clayton, Concord 94521, 798-7470. Bible study, Sundays, 9 & 10am. Also potlucks & parties. All ages.

Calvary Baptist Church Singles, Hwy. 24 at Olivera Ct., Box 846, Concord 94522, (415) 685-1424. Craig Hadingor.

Concord Christian Ctr Singles, 4255 Clayton Rd, Concord 94521, 687-2020. Potlucks, singing at convalescent homes, socials. 25+.

Fairoaks Baptist Church Singles 1925 Risdon Rd., Concord, 687-4810. Sundays, 9am. Potlucks, barbecues, swimming.

1st Presbyterian Church Contra Costa Christian Singles, Colfax & Salvio, Concord 94520, 458-5470, 682-4241. 1st Fridays. Volleyball, potlucks, parties, fellowship. Nonsectarian.

Full Gospel Church Singles, 2120 Olivera Ct., Concord 94520.

Gateway Singles Ministries, 3018 Willow Pass #204, Concord 94519, (415) 686-5851. Mondays, 7:30-9, Fubar's Comedy Club, 1150-C Arnold Dr., Martinez. Lectures, discussions, concerts, sports.

Tabernacle Baptist Church Singles, 4380 Concord Bl, Concord 94521.

Trinity Baptist Church People's Group, 3525 Chestnut, Concord 94514, 686-1400 or 945-8147. mainly singles under 30, most of whom have never been married. Bible study and socializing Sundays, 6:30pm.

DALY CITY

Grace Presbyterian Singles, 515 Winchester, DC 94014, 586-5681.

DANVILLE

Community Presbyterian Church Christian Singles, 222 El Pintado, Danville 94526, 837-5525 or 947-1842. 30+. Religious service, speaker, social, Wednesdays, 7:30pm. Bible study, Fridays, 7pm.

Mormon Church Singles, 655 Old Orchard Dr., Danville 94568, (415) 743-1547. Dances for singles, 3rd Fridays.

DUBLIN
 Valley Christian Ctr Singles, 10800 Dublin Blvd., Dublin 94568, 828-4549. 2 grps: FOCAS (30+) and LOGOS (25-35). Bible study and socials.
EL CERRITO
 St. John the Baptist Church Separated & Divorced Catholic Support Group, 11150 San Pablo Ave., E.C. 94530, (415) 525-6577.
EL SOBRANTE
 Church of the Nazarene Singles, 4600 Appian Way, (415) 223-1576.
 El Sobrante Church Singles, 670 Appian Way, Richmond 94803.
FAIRFIELD
 Community United Methodist Singles Circuit, 1875 Fairfield, 428-3558 (Sherwood) or 422-3752 (Ruth Anne). Sundays, 7-9pm. Lectures, dancing, and parties.
 Mormon Singles Hotline, Fairfield, (707) 426-4950.
 Our Lady of Mt. Carmel Catholic Divorced And Widowed Neighbors (DAWN), 2700 Dover, Fairfield 94533, (707) 426-0920 (Phil) or 425-8623 (Mary). Support group, Wednesdays, 7pm.
FOSTER CITY
 Central Peninsula Church Singles Community Groups, 1005 Shell Blvd., F.C. 94404, 349-1132. Bible study and socials every other Wednesday, 7:30pm. Also socials. All ages, mainly 20s.
FREMONT
 Centerville Presbyterian Church Genesis (22-35), John Knox House, 4360 Central, Fremont 94536, 793-3575. Bible Study, Wednesdays, 7pm. Also brunches & socials. Garrett Starmer, Minister.
 1st Assembly of God Singles Alive, 4760 Thornton, Fremont 94536, 793-8687. Worship, Wednesdays, 7:30pm. Also picnics, barbecues, & potlucks. All ages & all faiths. Roger McCarthy, Singles Pastor.
 Fremont Community Church, 39700 Mission Bl, Fremont 94539, 657-0123. Bible study, socials. 2 nonsectarian groups: 1. College/Career Singles (never-married, 18-24), Sunday school, 9am. 2. 25+ group, Sunday school, 10:45am.
 St. Leonard's Catholic Church Reaching Out Support Group, 3600 St. Leonard's Way, Fremont 94538, 651-8009 (Jerry) or 489-1355 (Betty). Wednesdays, 7:30pm. Lectures, picnics, dining, movies, socials.
 Tri-City Church of Religious Science Serendipity Grp, 40155 Blacow, Fremont 94538, 656-9955. Dinners, beach parties, and discussions.
GILROY
 Gilroy Presbyterian Church Singles, 842-3000. Dinners & trips.
HAYWARD
 Black Catholics, 21062 Gary #113, Hayward 94546, 582-7632. Support Grp, wine tastings, potlucks, fundraisers, workshops.
 Elmhurst Baptist Church, 380 Elmhurst, Hayward 94544, 783-8062. Bible study & fellowship, Sundays, 9am. Nonsectarian. Divorce Recovery Workshop. Also parties, dances, sports. Mainly 25-50.
 Hayward Bible Chapel Singles, 22416 Meekland, Hayward 94541.
 Successful Christian Singles, 354 B St., Hayward 94541. Carl Serfass.

LAFAYETTE

Lafayette Orinda Presbyterian Church, 49 Knox, Lafayette 94549, 283-8722. Giant meetings, Sundays, 7:30pm, $3, featuring your choice of a Transition Support Grp, a Newcomers Grp, or any of 3 speakers. Socializing afterwards at WPLG's Cocktail Lounge in W.C. & other cocktail lounges. Discussions, parties, volleyball, and other activities throughout the week. 4 groups: 1. Castaways (born after 1955), 284-1425. 2. Shipmates (born after 1940). 3. Single Ship (40+). 4. Transition Support Group for singles less than 6 months out of a relationship. Members provide support and acceptance.

Our Savior Lutheran Church Singles, 1035 Carol, Lafayette 94549, 283-3722. Brunches, fellowship, retreats, dinners, lectures. 30+.

Touchstone, Box 494, Lafayette 94549, (415) 686-5851. Mondays, 7:30-9pm. Bible study, concerts, theatre, speakers, parties. Nonsectarian.

LIVERMORE

Tri-Valley Community Singles, Box 3015, Livermore 94551, 447-2573. Sundays, 7:15-9:30pm, Livermore Presbyterian Church, 5th & L, Rm. 10. Lectures, potlucks, dinners, plays, and hiking. 35+.

LOS ALTOS

1st Baptist Church College/Career Singles (20s), 625 Magdalena Ave., Los Altos 94022, (415) 948-5698. Rev. Roger Draves.

St. Nicholas Catholic Church New Dawn Support Group, Lincoln & Sherman, (415) 948-2158. 3rd Tuesdays. Monthly potlucks. (415) 961-6102 (Molly) or 948-5208 (Marion), or 961-3286 (Kay).

LOS GATOS

Los Gatos Christian Church Singles 16845 Hicks Rd., Los Gatos 95032, (408) 268-1411. Parties, games, socials. Nonsectarian.

St. Mary's Catholic Church New Vistas Support Group, N Ave. Socials. (408) 246-2153 (Loretta).

MENLO PARK

Menlo Park Presbyterian Church, 950 Santa Cruz, M.P. 94025. 4 grps: 1. Singles Together, 40+. Sundays, 11am, free. Parties, dances, dinners, rafting, performing arts, retreats. 2. Middle Singles (30s-early 40s), Dinner & lecture, every other Friday, 6:45-10pm. 3. Young Adult Fellowship (20s & 30s), 323-8631. Sundays, 6pm. Also rafting, dinners, parties. 4. Divorce Recovery Group.

New Life Church Singles, 71 Bay Rd., Menlo Park 94025, (415) 322-3696. Charismatic church. Mondays, 7:30pm.

MILL VALLEY

MAC Singles, Miller Avenue Church, 285 Miller Ave., M.V. 94941, 388-5993 (church) or 927-1895 (Nancy). Bowling, sports, parties, dinners, movies. Divorce Recovery Workshop, Wednesdays.

United Methodist Church Jugglers, 410 Sycamore, M.V. 94941, (415) 383-2368. Single parent support group. Potlucks, 1st Thursdays.

MILPITAS

Calvary Assembly of God College/Career Singles, (Pentecostal), 1115 Ayer, Milpitas 95035, 262-6551 (The Tolberts). Bible study & fellowship, Thursdays, 7pm, private home. Also socials. All faiths.

MONTEREY
Church of Religious Science Singles, 400 W. Franklin, Monterey 93940, (408) 372-7326.

Emmanuel Fellowship Singles, 761 Lighthouse, (408) 646-0121.

1st Presbyterian Church Singles, 501 E. Dorado, Monterey 93940, (408) 373-3031. 30s & 40s.

MORAGA
Lamorinda Connection, St. Monica's Catholic Church, Box 128, Moraga 94556, 376-6900. Also St. Perpetua's Church (Lafayette) & St. Maria's Church (Orinda). Trips, retreats, lectures, support group.

MORGAN HILL
1st Assembly of God Church Singles, Box 755, Morgan Hill 95037.

Hillside Nondenominational Church Singles, Morgan Hill.

Mormon Singles Hotline, (408) 779-0670

MOUNTAIN VIEW
Judean Society Catholic Support Group, 1075 Space Park Way #336, Mt. View 94043, (415) 964-8936 (Frances Miller).

South Bay Christian Ctr Singles 1134 Miramonte Ave., Mt. View 94040, (415) 961-5781. Tuesdays, 7pm.

NAPA
Catholic Social Services Support Group for Separated & Divorced, 2510 Old Sonoma, Napa 94558, 224-4403. Wednesdays, 7-9pm. All faiths & ages. Also therapy.

1st Christian Church Singles, 2659 1st St., Napa 94558, 253-7222. Bible study & fellowship, Mondays, 7pm. Also movies, bowling, camping. 20s & 30s. Open to all faiths.

Hillside Christian Ctr Singles (Assembly of God), 100 Anderson, Napa 94559, (707) 255-3036. Bible reading & fellowship, Tuesdays, 7pm. Also potlucks, water/snow skiing, trips to the city, game nights, and camping. 20-45. All faiths. Mark Hawkins.

Support Group for Separated, Divorced, or Widowed, Napa County Mental Health, 253-7715. Thursdays, 7-9pm, Adult Services Bldg, 2344 Old Sonoma Rd., Napa 94558. Free.

NOVATO
Church of the Open Door Singles, 897-5556 or 897-8206 (Phil & Vickie Holmes). Bible study, socials.

Our Lady of Loretto Church Separated & Div. Catholic Support Group, 1806 Novato Bl, Novato 94947, 897-9116. 2nd Fridays.

OAKLAND
Allen Temple Baptist Young Adult Singles, 8500 A St, Oakland 94621, 569-9418. 1st Saturdays. Workshops, potlucks, theater. Mainly singles, 23-38.

Beginning Experience, 185 Wildwood Ave., Piedmont 94610, 654-9588. Weekend workshops for newly single Catholics.

Greek Orthodox Church of the Ascension, 4700 Lincoln Ave., Oakland 94602, (415) 531-3400. Spiritual and social activities. Limited to Greek, Russian, and Antioch Orthodox. Attracts members from all over N. Calif. 2 clubs: Orthodox Singles (25-40) & 39ers (39+).

OAKLAND (continued)
Mormon Singles Hotline, (415) 531-6686.
Northern California Christian Singles, Shiloh Christian Fellowship,
3295 School, Oakland 94602, 261-2052 or 843-9117. Annual retreat,
with 30 churches attending. Nonsectarian. Sunday school, 9am.
Oakland Bible Church Singles, 2640 108th, Oakland 94605. B. Reese.
PACIFICA
Beginning Experience, Dorothy Stanek, Box 1074, Pacifica 94044, (415)
355-7236. Weekend workshops for newly single Catholics.
PACIFIC GROVE
1st United Methodist Church Singles, Box 60, P.G. 93950, 372-5875.
PALO ALTO
1st Methodist Church Singles, 625 Hamilton, P.A. 94301. Mary Kelly.
Grace Lutheran Church Singles, 3149 Waverly St., Palo Alto 94306.
Mormon Singles Hotline, Stanford, (408) 494-9136.
Palo Alto Singles Ward (Mormon), 3865 Middlefield, Palo Alto, (415)
494-8899. Sunday worship, camping, hiking, rafting, volleyball.
Peninsula Bible Church Singles, 3505 Middlefield Rd., P.A. 94306, 494-
3840. Worship service & small group discussion & socializing,
Sundays, 9-10:45, at Menu Tree, Showers Dr., Mt. View. Also
parties & dances. Mainly 20-49.
Unity Palo Alto Community Church Singles, 3391 Middlefield, P.A.
94303, (415) 969-1167. Even Thursdays, 7:30pm. Metaphysically
oriented. Discussions, lectures, parties, potlucks, weekend hikes.
UU South Bay Singles, Unitarian Church, 505 E. Charleston Rd., Palo
Alto 94306, (415) 494-0541, (415) 967-8764 (Sandy), or (408)554-6360
(Lisa). Socials co-sponsored by Unitarian Churches in Redwood
City, Palo Alto, San Jose, and Los Gatos.
PLEASANT HILL
Hope Ctr (Evangelical Church), 2275 Morello Ave., Pleasant Hill
94523, 685-4673. Carpenters (18-25), discussion group, Sundays,
6pm, free. Also parties, dinners, and skiing.
Christian Fellowship Church Contacts, 40 Cleveland, 676-1584.
Sundays, 8:30-10am, Oaks Restaurant in Walnut Creek. Also socials.
Hope Ctr (Evangelical Church) Lighthouse 2275 Morello, Pleasant Hill
94523, 685-4673. Discussion group, Thursdays, 7:30pm, free. Also
parties, dinners, skiing. 25+.
PLEASANT HILL (continued)
Separated & Divorced Catholic Support Group, Family Life Ctr, 2446
Estand Way, P.H. 94523, 671-9339 (Diocese of Oakland), 939-1356
(Bob Arieta) or 228-3389 (Kit Wilkinson). Tuesdays, 7:30pm,
discussion group for newly single. Thursdays, 7:30pm, discussion
on being happily single. 1st Wednesdays, 8pm, $1. Beginning
Experience, weekend workshops for newly single Catholics.
PLEASANTON
Single Women's Group, 4725 1st St. #205, Pleasanton 94566, 846-2085.
St. Augustine's Catholic Church Genesis Support Grp, 900 E. Angela,
846-3531. Serves the Tri-Valley area. Every other Monday, 7:30pm.

REDWOOD CITY

Beginning Experience, Redwood City, (415) 366-0323 (Christine Kenny). Weekend workshops for newly single Catholics.

Redeemer Lutheran Church Singles, 468 Grand St., Redwood City 94062. St. Pius Church Separated & Div. Catholic Support Group, 1110 Woodside, R.C. 94061, 322-7694 or 322-2220.

SALINAS

Cypress Community Church Singles, Monterey Hwy, 484-2141. Every other Fri. Bible study, potlucks, discussions, lectures, games. 2 clubs, 21-32 and all ages.

1st Baptist Church New Life Singles, 1130 San Vicente, Salinas 93901, (408) 663-2724. Volleyball, Thursdays, 7:30pm.

1st Presbyterian Church Single & Single Again (S.A.S.A.), 830 Padre Dr., Salinas 93901, (408) 422-7811. Socials, lectures, divorce recovery. Pete Cantu, Singles Minister.

Sacred Heart Catholic Church New Directions, 14 Stone, 424-1458 or 757-4568. Guest speaker & support group, Thursdays, 7:30pm.

Vineyard Christian Fellowship, The Gathering, 1000 S. Main St. #216B, Salinas 93901, (408) 422-5321.

Word of Life Christian Fellowship Singles (Evangelical), Box 4657, Salinas 93912, (408) 449-1030 or 675-3272.

SAN BRUNO

St. Robert's Church Separated & Divorced Catholic Support Group, 1380 Crystal Spgs, S.B. 94066, 873-7399 or 285-1219. 2nd Thurs.

SAN FRANCISCO

Beginning Experience, (415) 921-1367 (Barbara Elliott) or 469-9842 (Sue Brumer). Weekend workshops for newly single Catholics.

Bethel Temple Caring Christian Singles, 1325 Valencia, San Francisco 94110, 285-1433. Discussions, brunches, T.G.I.F., volleyball, concerts,

Calvary Presbyterian Church Singles Together 2515 Fillmore, S.F. 94115, 346-3832, 221-3821 (Ron) or 692-7439 (Frank). Parties, potlucks, movies, theatre outings, hiking, barbecues. 30s and 40s.

Catholic Young Adults, Chris Fitzsimmons, 755 Ashbury, San Francisco 94117, 665-4400. 21-35.

Divorced Catholics, Archdiocese of San Francisco, Sister Jane McKinlay, 445 Church, San Francisco 94114, 565-3624. Divorce adjustment program, support groups, socials.

SAN FRANCISCO (continued)

1st Baptist Church, Market & Octavia, 863-3382. Sunday school, 9am. Bible study, picnics, fairs, charitable, socials. 3 groups: 1. 40+. 2. 25-40. 3. College/Career (mainly college age).

1st Unitarian Church Singletarians, 1187 Franklin, San Francisco 94109, 776-4580. 40+. Potluck/Dance, last Saturdays.

Mormon Singles Hotline, (415) 345-0077 or 572-9273.

19th Ave. Baptist Church Singles 1370 19th Ave., 564-7721 (Bill Smith). Bible Study, Sundays, 10am. Socials. 24-40s.

San Francisco Singles Ward (Mormon), Pacific & Gough, 441-9897, (415) 441-4983.

SAN FRANCISCO (continued)

St. Peter Church Separated & Divorced Catholic Support Group, (Spanish speaking). 1st Tuesdays, St. Peter School, 1200 Florida, San Francisco 94110. 469-8765 or 826-4457.

St. Stephen's Catholic Church New Dimensions Support Group, 475 Eucalyptus, S.F. 94132, 586-4154 (Janet Arpin) Even Mondays.

St. Vincent de Paul Catholic Church New Tomorrow Support Grp, 2320 Green, San Francisco 94123. 346-7733. Odd Wednesdays.

Univ. of San Francisco New Wings Catholic Support Group, Turk & Parker, S.F. 94117, 661-4198 (Cliff Pfluger). Even Wednesdays.

Urban Life Ctr Christian Singles, 1101 O'Farrell, S.F. 94114, 333-6019. Bible study, Sundays, 6pm. Mid 20s-mid 40s. Socials.

Valley Baptist Church Singles 305 Raymond, San Francisco 94134, 467-6055. Jim Pittman, Minister. Potlucks and socials.

SAN JOSE

Agape Singles (Christian), Box 6531, S.J. 95150, 236-3396. Socials.

Almaden Neighborhood Church Singles, Box 20696, San Jose 95160.

Beginning Experience, 1879 Bethany, S.J. 95132, 926-3929 or Box 36003, S.J. 95158, 244-3684. For newly single Catholics.

Bethel Assembly of God Church (Pentecostal) Singles, 1201 S. Winchester, S.J. 95128, 246-6790. Outings, barbecues, parties, potlucks, lectures, films. All faiths. 3 groups: 1. Agape Singles (55+). Sunday classes, 9:30am. 2.Career Singles (20s & 30s), Sundays, 11a.m. 3. Single Spirit (30s-50s), Sunday classes. Also Santa Clara Valley Christian Singles sponsors large combined events with singles clubs at 6 churches. Open to all faiths.

Calvary Community Church Singles, 1175 Hillsdale Ave., S.J. 95118.

Cathedral of Faith Chapel Singles Helping Singles (Pentecostal), 2315 Canoas Garden, S.J. 95125, 267-4691. Worship & speaker, Sundays, 9:15 am, & Wednesdays, 7:30pm. Also dinners, beach parties, and retreats. 25+. Mike Garcia, Pastor.

Crossroads Bible Church, 1670 Moorpark. Seminars.

1st Baptist Church Singles, 800 Ironwood Dr., (408) 265-9000.

1st Church of Religious Science Phoenix Singles, (408) 294-1828.

1st Congregational Church Singles, 1980 Hamilton, San Jose 95125. 688-6611. 45+. Brunches, cards, theater, golf.

Gloria Dei Lutheran Church Singles, 121 S. White Rd., San Jose 95127.

Holy Family Catholic Church New Horizons Support Grp, 4848 Pearl, S.J. 95136, 267-2574 or 265-4040 (Fr. Pat Doherty). 1st & 3rd Sundays.

Immanuel Presbyterian Church Divorce Recovery, 3675 Payne, S.J. 95117, (408) 244-5298.

Jubilee Christian Ctr Singles, 110 Nortech Pkwy., S.J. 95134, 262-0900.

Mormon Singles Hotlines, Almaden, 268-7677; East San Jose, 259-5740; San Jose (408) 448-1113 or 298-5156 .

Queen of Apostles Church Separated/Divorced Catholics, 4911 Moorpark, S.J. 95129, 253-7560, 253-7560, 448-3268. Odd Tuesdays.

SAN JOSE (continued)

Solo Notes, 99 Almaden Blvd. #400, San Jose 95113, (408) 287-7383. Cocktail parties for singles at symphony performances.

St. Christopher's Catholic Church Four Seasons Support Group, 1576 Curtner, San Jose 95125, (408) 269-2226.

St. Frances Cabrini Church Separated & Divorced Catholic Support Group, 15333 Woodard, S.J. 95124, (408) 629-8160.

St. Martin of Tours Church Separated & Divorced Catholic Support Group, 200 O'Connor, S.J. 95128, (408) 294-8953. Even Sundays, 7-9pm, 20s & 30s.

St. Patrick's Catholic Church New Goal in Your Life Support Group, 389 E. Santa Clara, S.J. 95113, 294-8120 or 292-2782. Spanish speaking. 2nd Wednesdays.

St. Victor's Church, Separated & Divorced Catholic Support Group, 3108 Sierra, S.J. 95132, 259-0713, 262-6506 or 272-0295. 25-45. Crossroads sponsors a support group for newly divorced and separated odd Sundays. 252-7560, 251-7712, or 272-8421.

Trinity Presbyterian Church Singles, 3151 Union Ave., San Jose 95124.

Vineyard Christian Fellowship Singles, 3550 Stevens Creek Bl #345, S.J. 95117, (408) 243-7238.

SAN LEANDRO

Beginning Experience, 1392 Advent Ave., San Leandro 94579, (415) 357-2988. Weekend workshops for newly single Catholics.

Calvary Lutheran Church Singles, 17200 Via Magdalena, S.L. 94580.

Singletarians, 14316 Mendocino, S.L. 94579

St. Felicitas Church Separated & Divorced Catholic Support Group, 1604 Manor, S.L. 94579, 657-6956 (Chuck). Thursdays, 7pm.

SAN MATEO

Crystal Springs Bible Church College/Career Singles, 2645 Alameda de las Pulgas, S.M. 94403, (415) 341-5096.

1st Baptist Church Christian Singles Fellowship, 2801 Alameda de las Pulgas, S.M. 94403, 345-1965. Bible study, Thursdays, 7pm. Socials. 22-37.

SAN PABLO

St. Paul's Catholic Church Young Adult Fellowship, 1845 Church, S.P. 94806, 232-5931. 25-35. All faiths. Outings, sports, discussions, potlucks, picnics, and Bible sharings. Brother Rufino, Director,

SAN RAFAEL

Beginning Experience, Marin, Jack France, (415) 472-2477. Weekend workshops for newly single Catholics.

Christ Presbyterian Church Singles, 620 Del Ganado, S.R. 94903.

1st Presbyterian Ch. Sojourners, 1510 5th, S.R. 94901, 456-6760. 40+.

1st United Methodist Church Single Parent Coalition, 9 Ross Valley Dr, San Rafael 94901, 453-8716. Betty Pagett.

Marin Covenant Church, 195 N. Redwood Dr., S.R. 94903, 479-1360. All ages. No alcohol. 3 groups: 1. Career Singles (24-31). 2. Divorce Recovery Workshops. 3. Me & the Kids, 892-3319, potluck & discussion, odd Thursdays, 6pm. Child care. $2.

Christian Singles Clubs

SAN RAMON
Eagles Nest Single Fire, 833-8283. Bible study & dinner. Mainly 18-35.
Life Community Church Singles, 2525 San Ramon Valley Rd., San Ramon 94583, 867-4640.

SANTA CLARA
1st Baptist Church Singles, 3111 Benton St., S.C. 95051, (408) 241-7635.
1st Presbyterian Church Singles, 2499 Homestead, S.C. 95050, 984-0804.
Mormon Singles Hotline, (408) 446-4636
Progressive Christian Singles, 2408 Karen Dr. #D, Santa Clara 95050.
Resurrection Lutheran Church Singles, 2495 Cabrillo Ave., SC 95051, (408) 241-2728.
United Methodist Church Singles, 1700 Lincoln, S.C. 95050, (408) 296-7411.

SANTA CRUZ
1st Church of Religious Science Uno's, 429 Pennsylvania, Santa Cruz 95062, 423-9520 or 426-5999 (Gwen Lee).
Mormon Singles Hotline, (408) 423-8516.
Star of the Sea Catholic Church New Expectations, 515 Frederick, 438-3190 (Pat). Lectures, 2nd & 4th Wednesdays, 7pm. Also socials, dances, raps, potlucks, breakfasts, games.
Unity Temple Singles, 407 Broadway, Santa Cruz 95060, 423-8553 or 462-4152. Volleyball, potlucks, dances, parties.

SANTA ROSA
Christian Covenant Community Church Singles, 1315 Pacific, S.R. 95404.
Christian Singles, 1620 Sonoma Ave., Santa Rosa 95405.
Church of Religious Science Single Fellowship, 1033 4th St., Santa Rosa 95404, (707) 585-8378. Softball, dances.
Presbyterian Church of the Roses Simply Friends, 2500 Patio, Santa Rosa 95405, 542-4272. Potluck & program, 2nd Thursdays, 7:30pm. Dining out, card nights, Sunday brunches, weekend retreats. 40+.
Resurrection Life Ctr Singles Outreach, 50 Mark West Springs Rd., Santa Rosa 95403, (707) 526-7752.
St. Eugene's Catholic Church, 2325 Montgomery, S.R. 95405, 542-6984.
New Dawnings Support Group (non-sectarian), Box 9565, S.R. 95405, 538-3391 (Kathy). Wednesdays, 7:30pm, free. 30s-60s.

SARATOGA
Congregation Beth David Singles, 19700 Prospect, Saratoga 95070, (408) 257-3333 (Lynda Weiss) or 866-0365. Shabbat services/socials, 1st Fridays, 9pm.
Mormon Singles Hotline, (408) 867-5267

SCOTTS VALLEY
1st Baptist Church Singles, 5000 Granite Creek Rd., Scotts Valley 95066.

SEBASTOPOL
West Community Church Sebastopol Singles, Box 1046, Sebastopol 95473, 823-7299 or 769-8533.

SUNNYVALE

1st Baptist Church Singles, 445 S. Mary, Sunnyvale 94086, 736-3120.

Sunnyvale Presbyterian Church Singles in Touch, 728 W. Fremont, Sunnyvale 94087, 739-1892. Dinners, brunches, camping, lectures. 35+.

TIBURON

Tiburon Baptist Church Singles & Co, 445 Greenwood Beach, Tiburon 94920, 388-5403. Bible study, Sundays, 9am, Strawberry Joe's, Mill Valley. Also canoeing, trips, seminars, potlucks, parties, lectures, & discussions. Mainly 18-40. David Gragg, Singles Minister,

VACAVILLE

1st Baptist Church Singles, 1127 Davis, Vacaville 95688, 448-6209 or 447-0273. Fridays, 7pm. Aerobics, diet, nutrition, bowling. Bob Sorensen.

Valley Evangelical Free Church Singles, 5063 Maple Rd., Vacaville 95688.

VALLEJO

1st Assembly of God Singles on a Rock (SOAR), 21 Locust, Vallejo 94542, 644-4451. Bible study & fellowship, Tuesdays, 7pm. Also potlucks, parties, cruises, and rafting.

1st Baptist Church Bereavement Recovery Club, 2025 Sonoma Bl., 644-4064 or 642-7148 (Stanley Cornils).

Open Door Church Singles, 1004 Marin, Vallejo 94590, 648-8888. Brunches, socials.

Vallejo Revival Ctr Singles, 324 Mini, Vallejo 94589, (707) 642-2010. Singles lead church service 1st/2nd Fridays, 8pm. Socials. Mainly black singles, 25-35.

WALNUT CREEK

Community Presbyterian Church Christian Singles, 1450 Creekside Dr. #18, Walnut Creek 94596.

Evangelical Free Church, 2303 Ygnacio Valley, W.C. 94598, 934-1273. 4 grps: 1. Carpenter's Union (college-age). 2. Single Adult Fellowship (50s-60s). 3. Thirst Quenchers (20s). 4. New Joy (30s-40s)

Mormon Singles Hotline, (415) 935-0128 or 932-2903.

Single Adults, Dorothy Mitchell, 146 The Trees, Concord 94518, 689-9329, 932-5151. Coffee, fellowship, Bible study, Sundays, 9am, Mr. Steaks, 313 N. Civic Dr., Walnut Creek.

St. Paul's Episcopal Church Singles, 1924 Trinity, Walnut Creek 94596, (415) 934-2326.

Unity Center of Walnut Creek Singles, 1871 Geary, Walnut Creek 94596, 937-2191 or 938-2836 (Hank Visscher). Personal growth discussions followed by coffee and/or dancing, Sundays, 7-9pm.

Walnut Creek Presbyterian Church Singles, 1720 Oakland Bl, Walnut Creek 94596, 935-1574 or Katherine & Scott Anthony, 686-3251. Dinners, volleyball, special events, plays, picnics, beach parties, water skiing. 2 groups: 1. Kayaks (30+). 2. College/Career (20s).

WATSONVILLE
  Beginning Experience, Monterey Bay Chapter, 144 Holm Rd. #20,
Watsonville 95076, (408) 728-1177 or Tom Tanner at (408) 424-1458.
  Corralitos Methodist Church Singles, 26 Browns Valley, Watsonville
    95076, 722-4363.
MISCELLANEOUS
  Catholic Alumni Club, (415) 344-7952, 441-8470, 447-3312 or (408) 479-
    1846. For singles eligible for marriage within Catholic Church.

JEWISH SINGLES CLUBS

The Jewish Community Center (JCC) is a great place to meet Jewish
singles. The JCC is similar to a YMCA or YWCA in terms of a host of
activities such as lectures, discussions, dancing, swimming, and
volleyball. JCC almost always have singles clubs as well (see below).
Jewish synagogues and temples also frequently sponsor singles clubs.
A 24 hour hotline of weekly events for Jewish singles is provided by
BAYJASS (Bay Area Jewish Association of Singles Services), 3200
California, San Francisco 94118, (415) 931-JASS or (408) 356-0058.

BELMONT
  Mid-Peninsula Jewish Singles, 2440 Carlmont Dr., Belmont 94002,
    (415) 591-4438 or 334-0749 (Jack). Dances, house parties,
    lectures/discussions, camping. 35+. Co-sponsored by Peninsula
    JCC, Temple Sholom, & Temple Beth El. Parties, discussions.
BERKELEY
  East Bay Jewish Singles, Box 9792, Berkeley 94709, 540-5403. Cocktails,
    Wednesdays, 5:30-7:30pm, H's Lordships Rest. 35+.
  Temple Beth El Singles, Arch & Vine, Berkeley, 848-3988 or 464-5063.
  Temple Beth El Jewish Community Ctr Singles, 920 Bay, 423-3012.
    Parties, hikes, beach, picnics, theater.
LOS ALTOS HILLS
  Temple Beth Am, 26790 Arastradero, (415) 493-4661 or 965-3913.
    Weekly support group, hiking, wine tastings, picnics, dances, pool
    parties, discussions. 2 groups: 35+ Singles & Chai Society (21-35).
LOS GATOS
  Congregation Shir Hadash Singles, 16555 Shannon Rd., L.G. 95032,
    (408) 358-1751. 21-40.
LOS GATOS (continued)
  South Bay Jewish Community Ctr Singles, 14855 Oka Rd., Los Gatos
    95030, (408) 358-3636. Parties, dances, biking, sports, cultural,
    barbecues, discussions. Mindy Goodman. 3 groups: 1. 20-50. 2.
    Single Parents. 3. Young Energetic Single Seniors (YES), 60+.
OAKLAND
  Committee for Jewish Involvement Singles, Jewish Federation of the
    Greater East Bay, 401 Grand, Oakland 94610, 839-2900 (David
    Cohen). Social, educational, & cultural activities.

OAKLAND (continued)

Jewish Federation, 3245 Sheffield Ave., Oakland 94602, 533-7462.

Oakland/Piedmont Jewish Community Ctr Single Persuasion, 3245 Sheffield, Oakland 94602, 653-9790 (Lisa Wadsworth). Volleyball, films, tours, dinners, discussions, Shabbat dinners. 30-55.

PALO ALTO

Albert C. Schultz Jewish Community Ctr Singles, 655 Arastradero, P.A. 94306, (415) 493-9400. Volleyball, Tuesdays, 8-10pm, $1, (415) 424-9045. Also canoeing, sailing, tennis, hiking, potlucks, dining, wine tasting, workshops, games, bridge, discussions. 35-50.

Congregation Kol Emeth Singles, 4175 Manuela Ave, (415) 948-7498.

SAN FRANCISCO

Congregation Sherith Israel Modern Community of Adults, 2266 California, 346-1720 (Don Plansky). Monthly Shabbat services. Speakers, dances, cultural/socials.

Jewish Singles Over 40, Box 15055, San Francisco 94115, (415) 243-9202. Lectures, 1st Thursdays, 5:30-7:30pm, Hyatt-Union Square Hotel. Also parties, swing dances, dinners, art galleries.

L'Chaim Singles, Ed Epstein, 31 Meadowbrook, S.F. 94132, 731-9166. Sundays, 7:30-9pm. Games, speakers, dances, dinners. 50+.

San Francisco Jewish Community Ctr Singles, 3200 California, S.F. 94118, 346-6040. Sunday brunches, lectures, workshops. Going Places (ages 20-40) sponsors Wine & Cheese/Lectures, Tuesdays. Also skiing, river rafting, brunches, dinners, concerts, dances. Shabbat Dinner for singles, 1st Fridays.

Temple Emanu-El Singles, 2 Lake (at Arguello), Box 18247, S.F. 94118, 751-2535. Shabbat dinners/speakers. 2 grps: 1. Circle (20s & 30s); Singles Plus (40+).

Young Jewish Singles, Jewish Comm. Fed., Young Adult Division, 121 Steuart, San Francisco 94105, 777-0411. Blue Monday dances. Cultural, social, & fund-raising. 21-39.

SAN MATEO

Jewish Singles Over 40, Box 4156, San Mateo 94404, (415) 243-9202 (Ellen Sandler). Socials, speakers.

Temple Beth El Young Singles, 1700 Alameda de las Pulgas, S.M. 94403, 341-7701. Dances, dinners, shows, parties. 18-30.

SAN RAFAEL

Bay Area Jewish Singles Hiking Club, 30 N. San Pedro Rd., San Rafael 94903, (415) 479-2000 (Jeanette Carr). Hikes throughout the Bay Area. Activities include trips to Yosemite and skiing. 21+.

SAN RAFAEL (continued)

North Bay Jewish Adults, Marin JCC, 30 N. San Pedro, San Rafael 94903, 479-3441 or 499-1223 (Sharon). Discussions & socials. 25-50.

SUNNYVALE

Community Singles Shabbat Services (Jewish), 1537 Bedford, Sunnyvale 94087, (408) 968-0736 (Arnie Benowitz). Quarterly Shabbat services at various synagogues.

WALNUT CREEK
B'Nai Shalom Jewish Singles, 74 Eckley, 934-9446. 21-39.
Contra Costa Jewish Comm Ctr Singles, 2071 Tice Valley, Walnut Creek 94595, 938-7800. Lectures, Mondays, 7:45pm, $2. Also dinners, dances. 1. Jewish Singles, 40+. 2. Singles Chavarim, 21-40.

SONOMA COUNTY
Sonoma County Jewish Singles, 795-3553. 35-60 age group.

SINGLE PARENT CLUBS

ALBANY
Single Adoptive Parents, Sandy McQuillin, 1309-B Solano, Albany 94706, 236-4064. Workshops for singles who want to be parents.

ANTIOCH
Parents Without Partners, Box 1317, Antioch 94509, (415) 757-3591.

APTOS
Twin Lakes Baptist Church Single Parents Support Group, 2701 Cabrillo College Dr., Aptos 95003, (408) 475-5284. Potlucks, 4th Fridays, 6:30pm, at church. (Mainly 21-35).

BURLINGAME
Single Parents Drop-in Discussion Group, 696-5400. Tuesdays, 7-9pm, Peninsula Hospital, 3rd Floor Solarium, 1783 El Camino Real, Burlingame 94010. $2.

CONCORD
Parents Without Partners, Box 6347, Concord 94520, 689-1826. Dances, Sundays, 9pm, Sheraton Hotel, 45 John Glenn, Concord. $2.

FAIRFIELD
Parents Without Partners, Box 277, Fairfield 94533, (707) 429-1526.

FREMONT
Parents Without Partners, Box 1814, Fremont 94538, 796-4327. Dancing with DJ, Thursdays, 8:30pm, Fremont Inn, 46845 Warm Springs Bl, free. 40+.

GILROY
Parents Without Partners, Gilroy Chapter, Box 969, M.H. 95037.

HAYWARD
Parents Without Partners, Box 3341, Hayward 94540, 357-1768.

LIVERMORE
Parents Without Partners, Box 303, Livermore 94550, 443-0458 or 443-0802.

LOS ALTOS
1st Baptist Church Singles Single Parents Club, 625 Magdalena Ave., Los Altos 94022, (415) 948-5698 or (408) 948-5698.

LOS GATOS
South Bay Jewish Community Ctr Single Parents, 14855 Oka Rd., Los Gatos 95030, (408) 358-3636.

MILPITAS
Parents Without Partners, Box 360277, Milpitas 95035, (408) 251-7982.

MONTEREY COUNTY
    Parents Without Partners, Monterey County, Box 4382, Salinas 93912.
MORGAN HILL
    Parents Without Partners, Box 969, M.H. 95037, (408) 778-2128.
MT. VIEW
    Parents Without Partners, Mt. View, (415) 224-0118, 557-4308, 224-2512, 643-5470.
NOVATO
    Single Fathers, (415) 266-9213. 2nd Tuesdays, 7-8pm, Alvarado Inn, 250 Entrada Dr., Novato.
OAKLAND
    Parents Without Partners, Box 1497, Oakland 94604, (415) 893-5995.
PACIFICA
    Parents Without Partners, Box 745, Pacifica 94044, (415) 359-3779.
PALO ALTO
    Parents Without Partners, Box 60834, Palo Alto 94306, (415) 326-0426.
SALINAS
    Parents Without Partners, Box 4382, Salinas 93912, (408) 449-3511, 757-8532, 424-0562, 757-1640.
SAN JOSE
    Parents Without Partners, Box 5096, San Jose 95150, (408) 225-4415.
SAN MATEO
    Parents Without Partners, Box 1954, San Mateo 94401, 344-6406.
    Singles Adjustment Group, Mondays, 7:30pm, Belmont Community Center, 592-1576 or 369-8551.
SAN RAFAEL
    Apple Single Parent Support Group, 7 Skyview Terrace, S.R. 94903, 492-0720. Potluck/discussion, odd Mondays, 6-8pm, Corte Madera. $2 + potluck contribution. Child care. Also meets in Novato.
    Me & the Kids, Marin Covenant Church, 195 N. Redwood, S.R. 94903, 479-1360/892-3319. Potluck & discussion, odd Thursdays, 6pm.
    Single Parent Resource Ctr, 408 4th St., San Rafael 94901.
SANTA CLARA
    Parents Without Partners, Box 2265, Santa Clara 95054, (408) 984-1088.
SANTA ROSA
    Parents Without Partners, Box 6267, Santa Rosa 95406, (707) 664-1308.
SARATOGA
    Parents Without Partners, Box 442, Saratoga, (408) 866-0800.
SEBASTOPOL
    Just Me & the Kids, Box 1046, Sebastopol 95473, 769-8533. Even Sundays, West County Community Church.
SUNNYVALE
    Parents Without Partners, Box 60791, Sunnyvale 94088, (408) 245-3127.
VALLEJO
    Parents Without Partners, Box 144, Vallejo 94590, (707) 644-6407.
WALNUT CREEK
    Parents Without Partners, Box 5693, W.C. 94596, (415) 820-5160.

WIDOWS & WIDOWERS CLUBS

1st Baptist Church THEOS Widows Group, Richmond, (415) 234-4395 or 724-9124.

Lafayette Orinda Presbyterian Church Bereavement Outreach, 49 Knox Dr., Lafayette 94549, (415) 283-8722 or 938-3292. Support group & info for widowed, odd Thursdays.,

Mid-Peninsula Widows & Widowers, Box 4043, Mt. View 94040, (408) 395-0903 or (415) 941-9171. Tuesdays, 7:30pm and 3rd Thursdays, 7:30pm, at Los Altos Lutheran Church, Cuesta at El Monte, Los Altos.

St. Martin of Tours Church Catholic Widows or Widowers, 200 O'Connor, S.J. 95128, 294-8953 or 354-0371. Odd Sundays, Dinners, 3rd Saturdays.

Widow & Widowers Club, 725 Hemlock, South San Francisco 94083, (415) 583-0449.

Widowed Men & Women of N. Calif., 422-1153 (Nick). 3rd Mondays, 7:30pm, Chabot Community Ctr, 4637 Chabot. Parties, dancing, dinner, trips every weekend. Members from throughout East Bay.

Widowed Person's Association, Box 5014, Santa Rosa 95402, (707) 823-7011. Dining, socials. Mainly 40-65.

Widowed Persons of California, Marin Chapter, (415) 453-6562.

Widowed Person Support Group, John Muir Hospital, 1601 Ygnacio Valley Rd., Walnut Creek 94598, 939-3000 x 20372 or 938-5246. Counselors from JFK Univ.

Young Widows-Widowers, (415) 938-4483. Frances Freewater, MFCC.

MISCELLANEOUS SINGLES CLUBS

ALAMEDA
    40+ Singles, 119 Central Ave., Alameda 94501, (415) 522-8851
BELMONT
    Singles Adjustment Meetings, 592-1573. Free weekly discussions.
BERKELEY
    Berkeley Singles, Box 456, Berkeley 94710, (415) 236-8840. Ballroom dancing to live music, even Fridays, 8:30pm-12:30am, Cerrito City Club, Potrero & Kearney, El Cerrito. Mainly 40+.

    Cal Singles, Alumni Association of UC Berkeley, 642-1945. Dances, speakers, trips. Mainly 40+. You do not have to have attended Cal in order to join.

    Single Adults Counseling Group, 3048 Deakin St., Berkeley 94705, (415) 548-3434 (Joe Cristofalo, MFCC) or 653-5665 (Alice Large, LCSW).

    Single Gourmet, social dining, 25-60s. Karen Nordeen, Dakota Grill & Bar, Shattuck Hotel, Berkeley 94707, 841-2848.

BURLINGAME

Burlingame Recreation Department Singles Dances, 850 Burlingame Ave, Burlingame 94010, 344-6386. 250+ singles, live band. 35+.

Guys & Dolls, Box 5, Burlingame 94010, (415) 342-8471 (Laverne Parker). Ballroom dancing, live music, Fridays, Burlingame Women's Club, 241 Park Rd., Burlingame. Mainly 40+.

Men-Gals, Box 1145, Campbell 95009, 298-6391 (Kathleen). Ballroom dancing, odd Fridays, 9pm, American Legion Hall, 1344 Dell. 40+.

CASTRO VALLEY

Friends First, Box 20189 #200, C.V. 94546. Socials. Mainly 20s.

CONCORD

Yellow Rock Singles, 1844 Clayton, Concord 94520, 671-0730 (Mervin Burnworth). Square Dancing.

Merry Mixers, Box 993, Concord 94522. Odd Fridays, Sportsman Club, Evora Rd., Concord. Mainly 40+. For singles only.

Singles Drop-in Support Group, 1810C Willow Pass Rd., Concord, (415) 676-2399. Thursdays, 7:30-9pm. $10 per session. Led by Mae Bragen, M.F.C.C.

Singles Scene, Box 4242, Concord.

DALY CITY/COLMA

The Love of Your Life, 205 Village Lane, Colma 94015, 991-0288. Workshops, classes, and support groups on creating ideal relationships. Susan Scott, Dir., also does counseling for singles.

DUBLIN

Shannon Community Ctr Seniors Dance Club, Shannon & San Ramon Rd., Dublin, (415) 828-9394. Tuesdays, 1-4pm. Free.

EAST BAY

Dinners for Eight at popular East Bay Restaurants, (415) 339-2666.

FAIRFIELD

Bereavement Recovery Club, Fairfield Senior Ctr, 1200 Civic Ctr Dr., 642-7148 (Stanley Cornills). 2 Thursdays each month, 10:30am.

Creative Living Ctr Singles, (707) 429-6931 or 864-1334. Wed. & Thurs., 10am-2pm, at Moose Lodge, 623 Taylor St. Trips, crafts, arts, games. All ages. Sponsored by Solano County Health Dept. and Fairfield & Suisun City Adult School.

Singles Outdoor Activities & Recreation (SOAR), (707) 422-4694.

FOSTER CITY

Foster City Singles. Even Thursdays, Recreation Ctr, 650 Shell. Also dances with live music, 2nd Fridays. 35+.

FREMONT

New Horizons, 34469 Shenandoah, Fremont 94536, 794-8596. House parties, activities, volleyball, rafting. Mainly 35-45.

KENTFIELD

Single Cyclists, Box 684, Kentfield 94904, 258-8067. Bike trips. 25+.

Single Soles, Box 726, Kentfield 94904.

LAFAYETTE

Single Scene America, Mary Berkowitz, 3361 McGraw Lane, Lafayette 94549. Soup, sandwiches, & discussion of world-wide topics.

LOS GATOS
Selective Singles, Fridays, 7:30pm, Los Gatos Neighborhood Ctr. Discussions, lectures, game night, potlucks, and hiking.
Your Winning Edge, 15466 Los Gatos Blvd. #109-317, L.G. 95032, 354-7060. Offers Side by Side, a relationships seminar.

MARIN
Best Parties in Marin, (415) 381-5640.

MARTINEZ
Diablo Singles, 26 Lagunitas Ct., Martinez 94553, 228-3654 or 798-5797. Square dancing, Thursdays, 7:30pm, Fair Oaks Sch.

MENLO PARK
Singles Supper Club, (415) 321-0388 or 327-4645.

MOUNTAIN VIEW
Apres Singles Ski Club, Box 1027, M.V. 94042, 377-5966 or 259-5142. Even Thursdays, 8pm, Sunnyvale Elks Club, 375 N. Pastoria.
Bay Area Winners, 801 W. El Camino #189, Mountain View 94040. Discussions, seminars, socials.
Dinners for Singles, 224-6631 or 255-1327. Socials & dinners.
Napa Valley Singles, (707) 255-1327, 255-0268. Hiking, potlucks, overnights, brunches, dining out.
Sierra Singles, Loma Prieta Chapter, Box 391775, Mountain View 94039. 21+.
Singles Network, (707) 257-8525. Dancing, odd Thursdays, 8:30pm, Joe's Bar, Embassy Suites Hotel, Napa. Free. Mainly 40s & 50s.
Snow Drifters Singles Ski Club, Box 396, Mountain View 94042, 265-4206 (Bill Turner). Odd Wednesdays, 8pm, at The Bold Knight, 769 N. Mathilda Ave.
Support Group for Separated, Divorced, or Widowed, Napa County Mental Health, 253-7715. Thursdays, 7-9pm, Adult Services Bldg, 2344 Old Sonoma Rd., Napa 94558. Free.

NAPA
Napa Valley Singles, Box 10223, Napa 94581, 965-2290. Odd Thursdays, 8:30pm, Joe's, Embassy Suites, 1075 California. Free. 30s-50s.
Singles Outdoor Activities & Recreation (SOAR), (707) 255-8610.

OAKLAND
Alliance for Displaced Homemakers, 3800 Harrison, Oakland 94611.
Graduate Degrees, 421 W. MacArthur Blvd., Oakland 94609. (415) 420-1381. Socials in San Francisco and East Bay for singles with masters degrees or higher.
Happy-Go Lucky Singles, 3059 Georgia #3, Oakland 94602, 530-4483. Dining, dancing, barbecues, min. golf, bowling, picnics, parties.

OAKLAND
Lifestyle Dining Club, 419 W. MacArthur Blvd., Oakland 94609, (415) 420-1381. Meets at restaurants in San Francisco & Alameda County.
Powder Hounds Singles Ski Club, Box 12763, Oakland 94604, (415) 769-7669. Tuesdays, 8pm, Sheanigans, Jack London Square.
Sierra Singles, Bay Area Chapter, 6014 College, Oakland 94618, 548-0591, (Phil Gale). 21-40.

OAKLAND (continued)
Solo Sierrans, Sierra Club, 568 Fairmount Ave., Oakland 94624, 658-9977, or 654-4163 (Joe Dorst). 40+.
Treasure, 5461 Lawton, Oakland 94618, 655-9990. Lectures, parties, and dances in East Bay, San Francisco, Marin, San Mateo. Mainly 30s and 40s. Jim Spillane, Director.
PACIFIC GROVE
Monterey Outdoor Singles Society (M.O.S.S.) Box 51416, Pacific Grove 93950, (408) 445-1850. Mainly 30-60. Dancing, beach parties, hikes.
PALO ALTO
Inner Growth Seminars, Box 1107, Palo Alto 94302, (415) 328-8552. Gloria Wilcox leads "Breaking Through Barriers to Intimacy".
Singles Supper Club, (415) 321-0388. Barbara Millin, Director.
Stanford Bachelors, Box 2345, Stanford 94305. Large singles dances at hotels & country clubs from to San Jose. Coat & tie.
Stanford Singles, (415) 859-5341, 322-7280. Lectures, parties. 40+.
TGA Singles, YWCA, 4161 Alma St., Palo Alto, 494-0972 or 969-9772 (Antonio Fernandes). Ballroom Dancing, odd Saturdays & dance classes, Tuesdays, 7-8pm, followed by dancing.
PETALUMA
Petaluma Singles, 726-0749 (Charlene). Dances, happy hours, potlucks, hiking.
PINOLE
How to be Single & Happy Growth Group, (415) 787-1360. Thursdays, 7:30-9:30pm, at the Pinole YMCA.
PLEASANT HILL
Tons of Fun Social Club, 334 Strand, P.H. 94523, 676-3635, 841-7946, 676-4875. For overweight, all ages. Speakers, socials games.
PLEASANTON
Bota Baggers Singles Ski Club, Box 772, Pleasanton 94566, 443-4451 (tape) or 275-0317. Tuesdays, 8pm, Velvet Turtle, Sheraton Hotel.
Pleasanton Singles, (415) 484-3513 or 449-7015. Square dancing at Camp Parks, RFTA, Bldg. 790, Dublin.
Single Women's Group, 4725 1st St. #205, Pleasanton 94566, 846-2085.
RICHMOND
Singles Class, 3037 Groom Dr., Richmond 94806.
SAN ANSELMO
Marin Solos, Box 335, Novato 94948, 456-9890. Ballroom dancing, live music, 1st Saturdays, 8:30pm, $6, Isabel Cook Recreation Ctr, 1000 Sir Francis Drake Bl, San Anselmo. Dress code. Mainly 40+.
SAN FRANCISCO
Bachelors 'n' Bachelorettes, John Kelly, 55 Garcia 94127, 566-3563 or (415) 681-4843. Square dancing.
Commonwealth Club of California, 681 Market, San Francisco 94105, (415) 362-4903. Occasionally sponsors lectures for singles.
Creative Cooking for Singles, Carl Levinson, 1508 Taylor #4, San Francisco 94133, 441-0675. Weeknights, 6-8:30pm. Mainly 25-45.

Miscellaneous Singles Clubs

SAN FRANCISCO (continued)

Finance Meets Fashion sponsors a gigantic dance party and fashion show each year, co-produced by Camp Productions, 931-6591 and San Francisco Modeling Company, 626-1191.

Guardsmen, 115 Sansome #310, San Francisco 94104, 781-6785. Businessmen who sponsor parties to raise money for charity.

Have I Got a Friend for You, 15 Gerke #1, S.F. 94133, (415) 399-0695. Singles parties, 20s & 30s.

Molly Z Presents, 2269 Chestnut St. #298, San Francisco 94123, (415) 979-4488 (24 hr Party Line). Large theme parties. 25-45 age group.

Mothers Without Custody, Helga McCamley, 1040 Carolina, San Francisco 94107, 824-8052. Support group.

Musical Theater Lovers United, Box 4384, San Francisco 94101, 552-5045 or 552-2222. Bonnie Weiss. Sing-alongs and parties.

Pacific Heights Club, Ed Woods, 808 Post #709, S.F. 94109, 641-4909. Parties throughout Bay Area. Coat & tie. Mainly 30s & 40s.

Positive Connections, 1461 Broadway #205, S.F. 94109, 775-6517 (Georgina Ong). Progressive Dinners & social events.

Renaissance School of Dance, 285 Ellis, 474-0920. Buffet dinner & dance lesson & party for singles, Fridays.

San Francisco Club, Box 26347, SF 94126, (415) 673-9938. Parties. Proceeds go to charities.

San Francisco Singles Ski Club, Box 421765, San Francisco 94101, (415) 337-9333. Tuesdays, 7pm, Duffy's Tavern, 451 Pine St. at Kearny.

Singles Dining Out Club, 1978 23rd Ave., San Francisco 94116, 731-8026. Visits restaurants, wineries, & breweries. Mainly 30s & 40s.

Star Sport & Social Club, 870 Market #755, San Francisco 94102 (415) 956-1110 or (800) 242-3648

Tuesday Night Tennis, (415) 521-0440. Mixed doubles for single people, Tuesdays during summer, 6:30-8pm, at Golden Gate Park Tennis Courts. Dinner afterwards at a member's home. Another group meets at Golden Gate Park on Wednesdays.

SAN JOSE

Avatar Association, San Jose, (408) 249-3953.

Bachelors 'n' Bachelorettes, Bill Gates, 965 Katherine, San Jose 95126, 249-1609, or Mike, (408) 374-6148. Mainly 40+. Square dancing.

Exploring Singles Perspective (ESP), 737-8254. Discussions, dances.

Live Entertainment Going Singles (LEGS), C. Kelleher, 1048 Oaktree, San Jose 95129. 253-5353. Excursions to live entertainment.

Over 40 Singles, Box 9593, San Jose 95157. Ballroom dancing.

Professional Guild, Ron Hanner, 1211 Utopia Place, San Jose 95127, 272-3966. Parties for single professionals in elegant settings.

Singles Dinner Club, (408) 257-1450. Monthly dinners at gourmet restaurants, ski, trips.

Single Squares, 720 Laguna Seca Ct, San Jose 95123, 227-2162 (G. Carnes). Square dancing.

Solo Notes, 99 Almaden Blvd. #400, San Jose 95113, (408) 287-7383. Cocktail parties for singles at symphony performances.

Miscellaneous Singles Clubs

SAN LEANDRO

Soiree Socials, Box 2493, C.V. 94546, (415) 886-1625 (24 hr. hotline) or 568-5086. Volleyball, Mondays. Parties, dances, lectures, T.G.I.F.s. Mainly 40+.

SAN LORENZO

Eden Singles, 21455 Birch St., Hayward 94541. Ballroom dancing, 3rd Saturdays, San Lorenzo Community Ctr, 377 Paseo Grande, S.L.

San Lorenzo Singles, 16871 President, S.L. 94578, 278-6957 (Eldon) or 490-4096. Square & round dancing Tuesdays, 7:30-10pm, Ashland Community Ctr, 167th Ave., in San Leandro. Mainly 40+.

SAN MATEO

Bachelors 'n' Bachelorettes, Marvin G. Smith, 3633 Colegrove #12, San Mateo 94403, (415) 345-9853, or Ben, 278-3290. For singles only.

SAN MATEO

Inskiers Singles Ski Club, Box 5065, S.M. 94402, 494-8243 or 364-5490 (Sandy). Tuesdays, 8 pm, Sand Bar Cocktail Lounge, San Mateo Municipal Golf Course. Also potlucks, happy hours.

Peninsula Singles, Brookridge Institute, 349-9675. Potlucks, 3rd Saturdays, 7:30 -10:30pm, 1209 Palm Ave. Singles interested in consciousness, spirituality, parapsychology, and new connections with Greens, Elmwood Institute, USSR/US Initiatives, Beyond War.

SAN RAFAEL

American Singles, 4 Highland, S.R. 94901, (415) 456-5683. Lectures, classes, and parties throughout Bay Area. Nationwide organization.

Fall Line Singles Ski Club, Box 2367, S.R. 94912, 492-9293. Odd Tuesdays, Strawberry Joe's, Strawberry Shopping Ctr, Mill Valley.

Friendship Garden, Box 150446, SR 94915, 456-3341. Even Saturdays, discussion & potluck, N/S, N/D, vegetarian $8/dish. All ages.

In Interest Of, 714 C St. #201, S.R. 94901, (415) 456-7596 (De). Catered socials, private homes throughout Marin, 2nd Tuesdays, $15.

Single Parent Resource Ctr, 408 4th St., San Rafael 94901.

Team Singles, Box 13072, S.R. 94913, 461-2090, 456-3331 or 456-1748. Dances to live music, 4th Saturdays, 9pm, Masonic Lodge, 1122 Magnolia, Larkspur, $7. Also parties, lectures, trips, biking. 45+.

SANTA CLARA

Single Ballroom Dancers, (408) 268-6042 (Dick Wilson). Thursdays, 8-11pm, Senior Ctr, Fremont & Monroe, Santa Clara.

Single Clara, 1802 Amelia #2, S.C. 95050, 244-1668. Square dancing.

SANTA CRUZ

Attractions meet every Thursday, 7-9pm at the Barn, S. Park Way, in Santa Cruz. Activities include discussions and outings.

Green Earth Singles, Box 7933, Santa Cruz 95061, 338-2366.

Live Oak Senior Ctr Singles, Capitola Rd. & 17th Ave, 423-8468. Sundays, 8:30-10am. For senior citizens.

SANTA ROSA

Enjoy Life, Box 2593, Santa Rosa 95405, 575-1006. Monthly seminars and social get-togethers. Also matchmaking service. Violet Young. Publishes magazine that lists singles events for Sonoma County.

SANTA ROSA (continued)

Friendship First Singles, Box 5155, S.R. 95402, (707) 579-5282. All ages.

Over 50 Club, 320 W. 3rd St. #199, S.R. 95401, (707) 762-8517 (Ann). Potlucks, bridge, dinners.

Santa Rosa Help Support Group, 579-1666/576-4300. Support grp & social for those with herpes, 2nd Thursdays, Community Hospital.

Sierra Singles, Box 466, SR 95401, 544-7651. Outdoor activities.

Singles Connection, Box 2593, Santa Rosa 95405, 575-1006. Guest speaker/dancing, Tuesdays, 8pm, El Rancho Tropicana Hotel, $2.

Singles Outdoor Activities & Recreation (SOAR), Box 5196, Santa Rosa 95402, (707) 539-3795. 30+.

Single Outdoor Living Experience (SOLE), Box 6374, Santa Rosa 95406, (707) 769-0834.

Singularity Benefit Events, Box 5462, Santa Rosa 95402. Carol Walsh, Director. Large fundraising events for local charities. All ages.

Social Singles, Box 511, Santa Rosa 95402, 528-8632. Ballroom dancing, live music, 3rd Saturdays, 9pm, Veterans Memorial Bldg. 40+.

SCOTTS VALLEY

Singular Focus, 1050 Lockhart Gulch Rd., Scotts Valley 95066.

SOLANO COUNTY

The Professionals Guild, (800) 992-1166. Occasional mixers. Coat & tie.

SONOMA COUNTY

Singles Information Line, (707) 575-1006.

SUNNYVALE

Sunnyvale Singles, 837 Mulberry, Sunnyvale 94087, (408) 739-6862 (F. Lorimer). Square dancing, Thursdays.

Sunnyvale Singles Squares, (480) 997-2653 (Jim) or 227-2162 (Gary). Thursdays, 8-10:30pm, Blackford Ave., San Jose. 30+.

Trellis, 1260 Persian #6, Sunnyvale 94089, (415) 941-2900 or (408) 747-1455. Daily lectures, discussions, dance parties, live big band dances, comedy, primarily Peninsula & South Bay. Mainly 30s and 40s. Paul Reese, Director.

TIBURON

The Progressive Dinner, Belvedere-Tiburon Recreation Dept., 1920 Paradise Dr., Tiburon 94920, (415) 435-4355. Dinner & dancing for singles every month. Also singles cruises on the Bay.

UKIAH

Ukiah Singles, Box 264, Ukiah 95482, 485-7200. Socials. 21+.

VACAVILLE

Bereavement Recovery Club, Vacaville Community Ctr, 1100 Alamo, 448-6620 (Olga Chanda) or 642-7148 (Stanley Cornils).

New Beginnings, (707) 446-2184. 1st & 3rd Fridays, 8pm, at 480 Buck St., Vacaville. For mature singles.

VALLEJO

Friendly Singles, (707) 642-6751 or 648-4630. Mondays, 7:30pm, Dan Foley Park in Vallejo. For singles only. 40+.

Singles Outdoor Activities & Recreation (SOAR), 837 Keats Dr., Vallejo 94591, (707) 643-0489.

WALNUT CREEK

Ballroom Dance Classes for Singles, (415) 687-5270. Classes are held at Veterans Hall in Walnut Creek. Monthly dance party.

Cancer Society Singles League, 1250 Springbrook, Walnut Creek 94596, 934-7640. Fund-raising & socials. Mainly 40+.

Diablo Singles, Box 5067, Walnut Creek 94596, 820-4299. Ballroom dancing, live music, 3rd Saturdays, Civic Park Community Ctr. 40+.

Divorce Classes, Patricia Padgett, M.F.C.C., 1844 San Miguel Dr. #317, Walnut Creek 94596, (415) 937-5131.

5th Wheelers, Box 4569, Walnut Creek 94596, 676-7129. Ballroom dancing, live music, even Saturdays, Veteran's Hall, 1250 Locust, $4. 40+.

New Orinda Club, Box 31642, Walnut Creek 94598, 946-1313. Promotes arts. Also tennis, water skiing, travel, parties, dinners. Mainly 30s & 40s.

Personal Growth Groups for Single Men & Women, 2940 Camino Diablo, #250, Walnut Creek, 94596, 946-9449. Led by Tom Grimm.

Rusty Bindings Singles Ski Club, Box 3096, Walnut Creek 94598, 724-3093 (Mariell Jaren). Tuesdays, El Papagallo Rest., 2995 Ygnacio Valley.

Single Again Workshops, 1200 Mt. Diablo Blvd., #107, Walnut Creek, 94596, (415) 254-5754. Led by Jean Wight.

Young Exciting Singles (YES), Box 3765, W.C. 94598, (415) 746-6999. Coat & tie dance parties. Also travel.

Young Unattached Professionals (YUPS), Box 31533, W.C. 94598, 947-6700. Tom Coop, Director. Large coat & tie dances at elegant hotels.

WATSONVILLE

Monterey Bay Singles, 724-9406 (Marty). Coffee, discussion, Tuesdays.

MISCELLANEOUS

Advanced Degrees, Box 455, Woodland Hills 91365, (800) 333-4937. For singles with master's, doctoral, or professional degrees.

International Club Elite (ICE), Box 241512, Los Angeles 90024, (415) 330-8166. Elegant parties throughout California.

March of Dimes Bid for Bachelors, (415) 468-7400. Charity auction of eligible bachelors with a prearranged date package going to the highest female bidder.

Who's Who International sponsors elegant parties for singles by invitation only. Mainly 40+. In Alameda, Contra Costa, Marin, San Francisco, & N. San Mateo counties contact Alyce Dunn, 111 E. Court, Foster City, (415) 570-6847. In Monterey, Santa Clara, S. San Mateo, and Santa Cruz counties contact Joy Smith at 6412 Camden, San Jose 95120, (408) 997-3141.

DATING SERVICES

Suppose you hate going to lectures, classes, dances, and parties, and you don't like outdoor sports? What do you do? Why not join a dating service? They're usually more expensive than the non-profit singles clubs, but you get a professional organization working for you to increase your chances of meeting someone special.

There are many dating services to choose from ranging from the very inexpensive (often as little as $30 for a three month membership) to the ones requiring thousands of dollars. You can find out about them by reading the Introductions or Business Personals sections of your daily newspaper. Or you can contact the dating services listed below. There are two categories of dating services: Matchmaking & Self-Service.

MATCHMAKING DATING SERVICES

Matchmaking Dating Services do not allow you to directly choose from membership files. Instead, the service goes through the files looking for a match for you. These services may be divided into two types: Computer Dating Services and Personal Introduction Services.

Computer Dating Services

With computer dating you fill out a questionnaire describing yourself and the man you want to meet. The computer matches you with several men whom you can telephone. If you prefer, you can wait for your "match" to telephone you.

The main advantage of computer dating is that it is usually quite cheap (often only $30 for three months). Ideally, this enables the service to enroll a vast membership. The computer then can go through the membership files efficiently to find the one man who has all the qualities you seek. Of course, in real life this doesn't always happen. Some computer dating services have so few members that the computer is only a joke. You could personally thumb through the files in minutes without a computer.

"Garbage in, garbage out" is an old computer adage. In the case of computer dating, it means that frequently people lie when they fill out the questionnaires. Don't blame the computer if it matches you up with someone 5 foot 3 when you wanted someone over 6 feet tall. The computer doesn't administer a lie detector test.

The most common lies from men pertain to their height and occupation. Men know that women like to date tall men who have a status job and a high income.

Personal Introduction Services

Many matchmaking services scoff at their competitors who use computers. They claim that you can't program a computer to find a person for you to spend the rest of your life. That takes the "human touch". Personal Introduction Services claim to have an intimate knowledge of their members and suggest they can do a better job of matching than a computer. Unfortunately, these Personal Introduction Services charge a great deal more than Computer Dating Services for using a "personal touch" (from $200 to thousands of dollars).

Think of dating a man through this kind of service as being similar to a blind date, except instead of a friend matching you up for free you are paying a professional to do that for you. Here you are relying on the intuition of the matchmaker who interviews you personally and then makes recommendations on who you should meet.

SELF-SERVICE DATING SERVICES

Self-Service Dating Services are often critical of matchmaking services. They argue that it is ridiculous to expect someone else to find the right person for you for a romantic relationship. How can the matchmaker or computer know what turns you on? Self-service dating services allow you to go through their membership files to find the right person. There are three types of Self-Service Dating Services:
Profile Dating Services
Photo Dating Services
Video Dating Services

Profile Dating Services

Profile dating services are usually the least expensive of the self-service dating services. As a member you will receive a collection of profiles of the men. You decide which men you wish to contact and the men have the same opportunity to contact you. One word of caution: some of the information in profiles may be fictitious. As with computer dating, members sometimes lie about age, height, weight, looks, and occupation.

Photo Dating Services

Wouldn't it be nice if you could see a photo of each man next to his profile before deciding to meet him? That's the logic behind the photo dating services. They allow you to go through photo albums of the male members. Alongside the photo is a full page of information about the man. When you see someone you'd like to meet, the club contacts him on your behalf so he can come down and view your photo and profile sheet. If there is mutual attraction the telephone numbers are released so the two of you can arrange to meet one another.

As with profile dating and computer dating, be prepared for members of photo dating to occasionally lie about themselves. The added dimension of deception in photo dating pertains to the photo.

Often it is not current. The handsome fit man you think you're going to meet may now be bald with a pot belly.

Video Dating Services

With Video dating you have all the advantages of photo dating plus the opportunity to see and hear your prospective date on television before you go out. There are many advantages. For one thing, you have more than a snapshot to base your decision. Even the Hunchback of Notre Dame would look good if you photographed him properly! With video dating you get the opportunity to watch the man for five minutes from many different camera angles. You also get to view his body language, hear his voice, and get a feel for his personality. You are more likely to choose the right person through video dating than through photo dating. The catch is that you have to pay more for this added dimension.

HOW TO CHOOSE A DATING SERVICE

There are many things to consider when choosing a dating service:
1. How long have they been in business? Most small businesses in the United States fail in their first year. This is also true for dating services. Joining a brand new dating service can be risky. **Warning:** you may find that many of the dating services listed in this book have gone under since publication.
2. How many active men do they have? Some dating services claim to have hundreds or thousands of men, but many of these may be unavailable due to marriage, committed relationships, heavy work schedule, or moving out of the area.
3. How many active men do they have in the geographical area you prefer? It does you no good to join a service with thousands of men if none of them live close enough to you to facilitate meeting them. Local dating services usually have a preponderance of members in the immediate vicinity of their offices. The further away you live from their offices the less likely they are to have many potential partners for you. With the matchmaking services you will frequently find that if you limit them to a small geographical radius they will not be able to find even one man who has the qualities you seek in a romantic partner. They will pressure you to "expand your horizons" and date people outside of your immediate area.
4. What percentage of the members are in the age range you prefer? Most dating services have a surplus of young men in their 20s and women over 40. Dating services are usually good investments for women in their 20s and early 30s and for men over 40, because those are the age categories in shortest supply. Many dating services offer free or reduced price memberships for women in their 20s-early 30s.
5. What is the cost of the service? There is often a wide difference in prices from one service to the next.

6. How long is the membership? Are there alternative membership plans? What are the privileges and limitations of each plan?
7. If it is a photo or video dating service, are **you** committed enough to go down to their office each time someone selects you in order to view their photo or video? If the answer is no, save your money.
8. Do you feel comfortable with the process employed and the people working at the dating service office?
9. Does the dating service have a good reputation? If you don't know any of the members and therefore don't have any testimonials, what does the Better Business Bureau or local Chamber of Commerce have to say about the dating service?

An additional question is, "Do I want to have the opportunity to see what the man looks like before I go out with him?" If so, you would best join a photo dating or video dating service. Usually computer dating and profile dating services do not provide a photo of the man you are to meet. Often matchmakers do not provide a photo either.

Of course the flip side of the coin is, "Do I want the man to see what I look like before we meet?" If you are not photogenic, you may not get your money's worth joining a service where a photo or videotape of yourself is seen **before** the man decides whether or not to meet you. If you have a "heart of gold" and communicate well through the mail or over the phone, you might be better off joining a service where external beauty is not a factor before the initial meeting.

Many singles fail to properly investigate and analyze the dating services they join. They end up feeling "ripped off". If you take the precautions listed above you can make a wise choice and get your money's worth. Shopping for a dating service is no different than shopping for a used car. Caveat emptor!

NATIONWIDE DATING SERVICE DIRECTORY

Please note: even though the services in this section are nationwide, they will introduce you to men in your geographical area.

Astromatch, (800) 64-ASTRO. Matchmaking through astrology.
Datique, 1347 Divisadero, San Francisco 94115. Low cost profile dating.
Dateline, 1-800-727-3300. Low cost matchmaking. Many offices:
    Northeast, 132 W. 24th, NY, NY 10011
    Southeast, 4801 E. Independence Bl #1000, Charlotte, NC 28212
    East Central, 18055 James Couzens Hwy, Detroit, MI 48235
    North Central, 39 S. LaSalle St., Chicago, IL 60603
    South Central, 3540 Summer Ave #307, Memphis, TN 38122
    Midwest, 7001 N. Locust #102, Kansas City, MO 64118
    Northwest, Seattle 1st Natl Bank Bldg #3618, Seattle, WA 98154
    Southwest, 8609 NW Plaza #300, Dallas, TX 75225
    West Coast, 256 S. Robertson Bl, Beverly Hills 90211

NATIONWIDE DATING SERVICES (continued)

Fields Dating Service, 41 E. 42nd St. #1600, NYC 10017. (212) 391-2233. For religious singles, 18-30.

International Society of Introduction Services, 1028 E. Juneau Ave #5, Milwaukee 53202, (414) 272-5595. Bob Aldrich. Non-profit.

Jewish Introductions International, 264 H ST #8110, Dept 113, Blaine, WA 98230, (800) 442-9050. Barry Turner. Jewish only.

Matchline USA, (516) 933-1320. Computer dating.

Someone for Everyone, Tod House, Box 4769, Chicago 60680. Profiles.

Zipcode Date Club, Box 84, St. Ann, MO 63074. Matchmaking.

LOCAL DATING SERVICE DIRECTORY

ANTIOCH

Connections, Box 3241, Antioch 94531, (415) 778-6883. Matchmaking after psychological testing.

CAMPBELL

Big Hearts USA, Box 110581, Campbell 95011, (408) 929-9042. Matches large people and slim people.

CAPITOLA

Compatibility Plus, Box 1235, Capitola, CA 95010, (408) 462-1457. Computer dating. Allan Gleicher.

Connections, 720-D Capitola Ave., Capitola 95010.

New Friends, Box 1235, Capitola, CA 95010, (408) 462-5662. Computer dating for singles with herpes.

CONCORD

Matters of the Heart, 3015 Grant St., Concord 94520, (415) 676-7542. Matchmaking. Maria Isola.

Video Introductions, 1950-D Market, Concord 94520, (415) 676-2399. Video dating. Norm Mickey.

CUPERTINO

Dinner Introduction & Networking Group, Box 1510, Cupertino 95015, (408) 257-1450. Matchmaking and dinner club.

FREMONT

Unique Encounters, 39120 Argonaut Way #531, Fremont 94538, (415) 745-9898. Matchmaking.

HAYWARD

Photointroductions, 928 Snowberry Ct., Hayward 94544.

Select Introduction Service, 24032 Hesperian #161, Hayward 94545. Matchmaking.

MONTEREY

Foto Date, (408) 372-2280. Photos of your matches are mailed to you.

Your Match, 284 Foam #1, Monterey 93940. Video dating.

MOUNTAIN VIEW

Great Expectations, 2065 Landing, M.V. 94043, (415) 964-2985. Video.

NAPA

Confidential Dating Service, Napa, (707) 255-0414. Matchmaking.
Patricia Moore Group, (707) 579-3037. Matchmaking.
Reliable Singles, Box 3706, Napa, (707) 252-2002.

OAKLAND

Opposites, Box 3845, Oakland 94609, (415) 654-6565. Matchmaking (interracial) and parties. 9 months/$150. Chandler Fairchild.
Something in Common, 484 Lake Park Av. #272, Oakland 94610, 530-6903. Partners and pals for every interest: theater, single parent outings, hiking, movies, symphony, skiing, musicians. All ages.

OCCIDENTAL

Stargazers, Box 272, Occidental 95465, (707) 874-3165. Matchmaking based on astrological compatibility. Janice Barsky, Director.

PLEASANT HILL

Big Alternatives, 363 Gladys Dr., Pleasant Hill 94523, (415) 676-3635. Matchmaking for overweight singles.

REDWOOD CITY

Sunrise Dating Service, 368-2446. Self service photo dating.

SAN FRANCISCO

Amicus, 1347 Divisadero, S.F. 94115, (415) 359-6900. Photo dating.
Datique, 1347 Divisadero, San Francisco 94115, (415) 359-6900 or (408) 295-8600. Profile dating. Marty Siders, Linda Simmons.
Foto Date, (415) 937-2203. Photos of your matches are mailed to you.
Have I Got a Friend for You, 15 Gerke Place #1, S.F. 94133, (415) 399-0695. Profile dating service.
The Jewish Connection, 3569 Sacramento, San Francisco 94118, (415) 221-5683. Matchmaking.
John Wingo & Associates, 44 Montgomery St., San Francisco 94104, (415) 955-2722. Matchmaking.
May-December Introduction Svc, 2940 16th St. #308, SF 94103, Matches younger men with older women. Women pay no fee. C. Polk.
New Partners, SF Jewish Community Center, 3200 California, S.F. 94118, (415) 346-6040. Matchmaking. $125 fee. Barrett Moore.
The Original Matchmaker, 887-1010.
The Patricia Moore Group, Box 31130, San Francisco 94131, (415) 337-1551 or 321-9655. Matchmaking.
Perfect Strings, Box 22277, San Francisco 94122, (415) 566-7774 or 566-6800 (info on parties). Matching by similar musical interests for attending symphony, opera, ballet or for playing and singing your favorite classical music.
SelectraDate of Northern California, Box 11149, S.F. 94101, (800) 232-3283. Computer dating. $55. Minimum of 5 matches.
Singles & Sidekicks, 285-0843. Introductions for single parents.
Yellow Phone, 870 Market #428, S.F. 94102, (415) 765-4321 (S.F.) (408) 737-7770 (Sunnyvale), (415) 944-0744 (Walnut Ck), (800) 538-7289. Computer dating & personalized matchmaking. Telephone personal ads with personalized attention, (900) USA LINK.

SAN JOSE

Amicus, (408) 295-8600. Matchmaking.

Ananda Astrological Matching Service, 99 Wilson, S.J. 95126, (408) 947-5958.

Brown Sugar Soul Singles, Box 32595, San Jose 95152. $35. Black dating service. 21-45.

The Dating Center, (408) 479-9635. Photo matchmaking.

Foto Date, 913 Willow #101, S.J. 95125, 286-7000 (24 hrs). Matchmaking. Photos of your matches are mailed to you.

More to Love, 395-7417. Big men & women and those who love them.

2010 Singles Club, (408) 253-6200. Self-service photo dating.

SAN MATEO

Venus Computer Matchmaking Service, 2228 S. El Camino #80, S.M. 94403.

SAN RAFAEL

American Singles, 4 Highland Ave., San Rafael 94901, (415) 456-5683. Non-profit, free profile dating.

SANTA ROSA

Enjoy Life, Box 2593, S.R. 95405, 575-1006. Matchmaking, seminars.

SAUSALITO

New Connections, (415) 421-8222. Linda Sampson, Director.

Great Expectations, 2330 Marinship Way #105, Sausalito 94965, (415) 332-2353. Video dating.

SUNNYVALE

John Wingo & Associates, 1250 Oakmead Parkway, Sunnyvale 94086, (408) 730-6806. Matchmaking.

UNION CITY

Kings & Queens, 4719 Loretta, U.C. 94587, (415) 489-4395. Jo Ann Larez.

WALNUT CREEK

Foto Date, 1615 Bonanza #207, W.C. 94596, (415) 937-3283. Photos of your matches are mailed to you.

Great Expectations, 1280 Civic Dr., 1656 Oakland Bl #200, Walnut Creek 94596, (415) 944-4900. Video dating.

John Wingo & Associates, 1990 N. California Blvd., Walnut Creek 94596, (415) 932-7057. Matchmaking.

Marriage Minded, Box 4313, Walnut Creek 94596. Matchmaking.

Successful Singles International, 2175 N. California #150, W.C. 94596. Matchmaking.

The Professional Connection, 778-6883. Martin Schaaf. Matchmaking with psychological screening.

MISCELLANEOUS

The Activity Connection, American Meeting Svc, 976-3283. Computer matching by 130 activities, via telephone. $2 + toll, if any.

Ethnic Connections, (415) 778-6883. Matchmaking for Black, Asian, Hispanic singles.

Introphoto, 796-1706. Photos mailed to your home.

New Age Connections, 861-3554, x26. Matchmaking.

Part Three:

OTHER PLACES

TO MEET SINGLES

PERSONAL ADS

Are you the adventurous type? If so you might try placing or responding to a personal ad. According to US Magazine, June 1, 1987, "each year at least 10,000 people who meet through personals get married" in the United States each year. It is now socially acceptable to both place and respond to personal ads. According to the US article, "2 million men and women run personal ads each year, and over 10 million answer them."

Most newspapers accept personal ads, as well as many magazines. A number of singles publications are listed below which are also ideal for personal ads.

Should you place an ad or respond to one? Assuming you can afford it, the ideal way to use the personal ad columns is to place an ad yourself. The reason for this is that if you only respond to ads, you may be one of dozens of people responding to a particular ad. The odds are against your being selected by the person placing the ad. If you place the ad however, you're in the driver's seat. You can choose from the many different types of people who will hopefully be responding to your ad.

What should you say in your ad? Honesty is the best policy. Tell who you are and who you are looking for. Be aware, however, that a price has to be paid for honesty. Dishonest people who exaggerate their attractiveness are going to get many more responses than you. The advantage of being honest, however, is that the people who respond to your ad won't be disappointed when they meet you.

Try to be original, clever, and funny if possible. You'll get many more times the responses than if your ad is serious and similar to others. Make your ad stand out.

Avoid being too specific about who you are looking for. Remember, each characteristic or quality that you require diminishes the number of responses. The fewer singles from which you choose the less likely you are to find someone who is right for you.

On the other hand, if you're too vague (e.g., "I want to meet someone nice"--who's going to admit they're not nice?) you'll get a lot of responses that are totally unsuitable for you. So try to strike a happy medium.

If physical appearance is important to you, request that responding letters include a recent photograph. Ask them to describe themselves physically, emotionally, educationally, etc. as thoroughly as possible. Be sure to send them a photo of yourself also.

If you would like professional help in writing your ad, contact Leigh Roth at 2910 Newbury St., Berkeley 94703, (415) 548-2792; James Frank, M.S., at (415) 571-1888; or Jay Wiseman, author of **Personal AdVentures**, Box 1261, Berkeley 94701, (415) 386-5762.

How do you select who to meet from those who respond to your ad? Some people keep an open mind and meet everyone who responds to their ad. They enjoy meeting potential new friends and are willing to take a chance. Others are very selective. They correspond through the mail and converse over the phone to the point that they feel fairly confident that they're going to like the person before they schedule a face-to-face meeting. Either method works.

Where should you meet? That depends on how cautious you are. If you're afraid of meeting a weirdo you might want choose a public place during the day. This is obviously a lot safer than giving a man your home address and telephone number. Do what feels comfortable to you.

What kind of people are you liable to meet through personal ads? The same kind you'll meet anywhere else. Some will be winners and some will be losers. Your job is to choose wisely so you wind up with someone appropriate for you.

Hopefully you will approach personal ads in a spirit of fun. Here's your opportunity to meet a lot of nice people like yourself who are looking to meet someone special for a romantic relationship. So don't be too serious. And don't be disappointed if you don't meet Mr. or Ms. Right. Just have a good time and keep trying.

The newest rage is Voice Personals. You can record your ad over the phone and people can respond to your ad using voice mail. Your phone number is kept confidential.

Request a sample copy of some of the publications listed below and compare them with your local newspaper. Determine which publication has the most ads of people you'd like to meet at the most reasonable cost. That's the publication that's right for your personal ad.

RECOMMENDED PUBLICATIONS

Call of the Wild Radio Reporter, KORK Radio, 127 E. Napa St., Sonoma 95476, (707) 996-9125. Free personal ads.

Coast Singles Magazine, Box 3097, Salinas 93912, (408) 449-8243. For Santa Cruz & Monterey County.

The Dating Magazine, Box 1357, Marina 93933, (408) 646-0717 publishes low cost personal ads for Monterey & Santa Cruz Counties.

Dollar Saver, 37365 Centralmont, Fremont 94536, (415) 792-4052, publishes a low cost "Companions Column" each week.

East Bay Guardian, 520 Hampshire, San Francisco 94110, (415) 255-7600. Monthly printed ads. Voice Personals, (900) 844-5555. 99 cents per minute.

Fairfield Daily Republic, Box 47, Fairfield 94533, (707) 425-4646. Singles Connection section daily.

Goodtimes, Box 1139, Santa Cruz 95061, (408) 426-8430, publishes personal ads weekly.

In Marin, 640 Mission, San Rafael 94901, (415) 453-9824. Monthly magazine.

Lifestyle, 421 W. MacArthur Blvd., Oakland 94609, (415) 420-1381. David Sawle, Publisher.

Metro, 410 S. 1st St., San Jose 95113, (408) 298-8000. Weekly.

Personal Ads

97-Match, (415) 976-2824. Voice personal ads only. $2 plus toll, if any.
976-Date, Voice personal ads only. $2 + toll charge if any.
Oakland Tribune, Box 24424, Oakland 94623, (415) 645-2000. Printed ads. Also LINX Voice Personals.
Open Mind, 5271 Dry Creek Rd., Napa 94558, (707) 255-5022. Single File section. Quarterly. Free ads.
Pacific Sun, 21 Corte Madera Ave., Mill Valley 94941, (415) 383-4500.
Photointroductions, 928 Snowberry Ct., Hayward 94544. Publishes personal ads with passport photo.
San Francisco Bay Guardian, 520 Hampshire, San Francisco 94110, (415) 255-7600. Weekly.
San Francisco Weekly, 230 Ritch St., San Francisco 94107, (415) 541-0700.
San Francisco Focus, 680 8th St., San Francisco 94103, (415) 553-2821.
San Francisco Magazine, 45 Belden Pl., San Francisco 94104, (415) 982-2700.
Selections, (415) 391-0757. Voice personal ads only. Dial 1-900-999-3700. 89 cents per minute.
Single Again, Box 384, Union City 94587, (415) 656-0322.
Singles Network, 1-900-844-6600. Voice personal ads only. 95 cents per minute.
Trellis Singles Magazine, 1260 Persian Dr. #6, Sunnyvale 94089, (408) 747-1455 or (415) 941-2900. Bimonthly. Publishes more personal ads per issue than any other periodical in Northern California. Paul Reese, Publisher. Also voice personal ads, (900) 844-4445. 89 cents per minute.
Whole Valley Catalogue, 2801 Ygnacio Valley Rd., Walnut Creek, (415) 939-3777.

CLASSES

Classes are a great place to meet singles. Almost every city in the Bay Area has a recreation department that offers non-credit classes. The same holds true for most community colleges. In addition, some of the school districts also offer adult classes. Finally, organizations such as The Learning Annex also sponsor these "personal enrichment" classes.

These classes usually meet in the evenings and Saturdays. You will find that a large percentage of the people attending these classes are singles, since married people usually stay home with their families.

A national survey revealed that the number one reason people take "lifelong learning" classes is not to learn anything! 40% stated that their motivation was "to meet new friends". In other words, a high percentage of people who take adult education classes are singles hoping to meet other singles.

Some classes are aimed exclusively at singles. They concentrate on such topics as how and where to meet other singles or how to be happily single.

Call up the listings below that are in your area and ask for a current catalog of courses. If you want to save yourself a lot of time why not ask the person in charge to recommend the class that has the most single men or the most single women? Whatever the class is, take it! The point isn't to learn something, it's to meet someone for a romantic relationship! Classes that tend to attract men deal with such "masculine" subjects as sports, building things, automotive repair, and investments. Women usually prefer classes concerning arts and crafts, relationships, psychology, or metaphysics.

I know a man who took a class on PMS. Out of 40 in the class, he was the only man. Now that's courage. He confessed that he initially feared that some of the women would be snide about his presence. He was surprised by how friendly the women were.

The following publications list classes and seminars throughout the Bay Area:

Bay Guardian, 520 Hampshire, San Francisco 94110, (415) 255-7600.
Common Ground, 9 Mono Ave., Fairfax 94930, (415) 459-4900.
Lifestyle, 419 W. MacArthur Blvd., Oakland 94609, (415) 420-1381.
Open Exchange, Box 5905, Berkeley, 94705, (415) 526-7190/527-4273.
You may also wish to consult the calendar sections of your local newspapers and magazines for class listings.

CLASS DIRECTORY

ALAMEDA COUNTY

Alameda Recreation Dept., City Hall, Rm. 201, Santa Clara Ave. & Oak, Alameda 94501, (415) 522-4100.
Albany Recreation Dept., 1100 San Pablo Ave., Albany, (415) 528-5740.

ALAMEDA COUNTY (continued)

Dublin Recreation Dept., Box 2340, Dublin 94568, (415) 829-4932.
Fremont Community Services, Box 5006, Fremont 94537, (415) 791-4320.
Fremont Adult School, 4700 Calaveras Ave., Fremont 94538, (415) 793-6465.
Hayward Adult School, 2652 Vergil Ct., Hayward 94546, (415) 537-4203.
Hayward Area Recreation District, 1099 E St., Hayward 94541, (415) 881-6735.
Livermore Area Recreation & Park Dept., 71 Trevarno Rd., Livermore 94550, (415) 447-7300.
Oakland Recreational Services Dept., 1520 Lakeside Dr., Oakland, (415) 339-8919.
Ohlone College, Community Services, 43600 Mission Blvd., Box 3909, Fremont 94537, (415) 659-6215.
Piedmont Recreation Dept., 358 Hillside Ave., Piedmont, (415) 420-3070.
Pleasanton Recreation Dept., 200 Old Bernal Ave., Pleasanton 94566, (415) 484-8160.
San Leandro Recreation Dept., 835 14th St., San Leandro, (415) 577-3462.
Separation & Divorce Workshop, Marilyn G. Denn, Ph.D., Berkeley and Alameda, (415) 644-0124.
Union City, Holly Community Center, 31600 Alvarado Blvd., Union City, (415) 471-6877; or Charles Kennedy Community Center, 1333 Decoto Rd., Union City, (415) 489-0360.

CONTRA COSTA COUNTY

Acalanes Adult Center, Walnut Creek, (415) 935-0170.
Antioch Leisure Services, 213 F St., Antioch 94509, (415) 757- 0900.
Brentwood Recreation Dept., 724 3rd St., Brentwood 94513, 634-1044.
Concord Leisure Services, 2885 Concord Blvd., Concord 94519, 671-3498.
Contra Costa College, Community Services Dept., 2600 Mission Bell Dr., San Pablo 94806, (415) 235-7800 x3303.
Diablo Valley College, Community Services, 321 Golf Club Rd., Pleasant Hill 94523, (415) 685-1230.
El Cerrito Community Services, 10890 San Pablo Ave., El Cerrito 94530, (415) 234-7445.
Hercules Community Services, 111 Civic Dr., Hercules, (415) 799-8230.
Lafayette Recreation Dept., 500 St. Mary's Rd., Lafayette 94549. (415) 284-2232.
Martinez Adult School, 600 F St., Martinez, (415) 228-3276. Sponsors classes that are predominantly attended by singles.
Martinez Leisure Services, 525 Henrietta, Martinez 94553, (415) 372-3510.
Moraga Recreation Dept., 2100 Donald Dr., Moraga 94556, 376-2520.
Pinole Recreation Dept., 2131 Pear, Pinole 94564, (415) 724-9004.
Pittsburg Leisure Services, 340 Black Diamond, Pittsburg 94565. (415) 439-3440.

CONTRA COSTA COUNTY (continued)

Pleasant Hill Adult School, Pleasant Hill, (415) 937-1530. Sponsors classes that are predominantly attended by singles.
Pleasant Hill Recreation Dept., 320 Civic Dr., P.H. 94523, (415) 676-5200.
Richmond Recreation Dept., (415) 620-6792.
San Pablo Community Services, (415) 236-7373.
San Ramon Recreation Dept., 2222 Camino Ramon, San Ramon 94583, 275-2300.
San Ramon Valley Community Services Group, 545 Sycamore Valley Rd. W., Danville 94526, (415) 837-8235.
Walnut Creek Leisure Services, Box 8039, W.C. 94596, (415) 943-5858.

MARIN COUNTY

Belvedere-Tiburon Recreation Dept., 1920 Paradise Dr., Tiburon 94920, (415) 435-4355.
Corte Madera Recreation Dept., 498 Tamalpais Dr., Corte Madera 94925, (415) 924-2901.
Fairfax Recreation Dept., 142 Bolinas Rd., Fairfax, 94930, (415) 453-1584.
Larkspur Recreation Dept., 400 Magnolia Ave., Larkspur 94939, (415) 924-4777.
Marin Community College, Community Education Dept., Kentfield 94904, (415) 485-9657.
Marin County Recreation Dept., Marin County Civic Center, San Rafael 94903, (415) 499-6387.
Mill Valley Recreation Dept., 180 Camino Alto, Mill Valley 94941, (415) 383-1370.
Novato Recreation Dept., 917 Sherman Ave., Novato 94947, (415) 897-4323.
Ross Recreation Dept., Lagunitas Rd., Ross, (415) 453-6020.
San Anselmo Recreation Dept., 1000 Sir Francis Drake Blvd., San Anselmo 94960, (415) 453-9055.
San Rafael Recreation Dept., 1400 5th Ave., San Rafael 94901, (415) 485-3333.
Sausalito Recreation Dept., 420 Litho, Sausalito 94965, (415) 332-4520.

MONTEREY COUNTY

Carmel Recreation, 15th Ave. & Monte Verde Blvd., Carmel 93923, (408) 625-2252.
Hartnell College, 156 Homestead Ave., Salinas 93901, (408) 755-6700.
King City Recreation, 411 Division, King City 93930, (408) 385-3575.
Marina Recreation, 211 Hillcrest Ave., Marina 93933, (408) 384-3715.
Monterey Peninsula College, Community Services, 980 Fremont Blvd., Monterey 93940, (408) 646-4051.
Monterey Recreation, 546 Dutra, Monterey 93940, (408) 646-3866.
Pacific Grove Recreation, 515 Junipero Ave., P.G. 93950, (408) 372-2809.

MONTEREY COUNTY (continued)

Salinas Recreation, 200 Lincoln Ave., Salinas, (408) 758-7306.
Seaside Recreation, 986 Hilby Ave., Seaside 93955, (408) 899-6270.

NAPA COUNTY

Calistoga Recreation Dept., 1232 Washington, Calistoga 94515, (707) 942-5188.
Napa College, Community Education Dept., 2277 Napa-Vallejo Hwy., Napa 94558, (707) 253-3095.
Napa Recreation Dept., 1100 West, Napa, (707) 252-7800.
St. Helena Recreation Dept., 1360 Oak Ave., St. Helena 94574, (707) 963-5706.

SAN FRANCISCO

A Good Relationship Class, Isadora Alman, M.F.C.C., (415) 386-5090.
Ft. Mason Art Center, Building B, Laguna & Marina Blvd., San Francisco 94123, (415) 776-8247.
The Learning Annex, 2500 Clay St., San Francisco 94115, (415) 922-9900.
National Center for Financial Education, Ft. Mason Center, Bldg C, Room 218, San Francisco 94123, 415) 567-5290.
San Francisco Community College, Adult Learning Center, 33 Gough St., San Francisco, (415) 239-3070.
San Francisco Recreation Dept., McLaren Lodge, Golden Gate Park, San Francisco 94117.

SAN MATEO COUNTY

Belmont Recreation Dept., 1225 Ralston Ave., Belmont 94002, (415) 573-3561.
Burlingame Recreation Dept., 850 Burlingame Ave., Burlingame 94010, (415) 344-6386.
Canada College, Community Education, 4200 Farm Hill Blvd., Redwood City 94061, (415) 364-1221.
College of San Mateo, Community Education, 3401 College of San Mateo Dr., San Mateo 94402, (415) 574-6563.
Daly City Recreation Dept., 111 Lake Merced Blvd., Daly City, (415) 991-8004.
East Palo Alto Community Services, 2415 University Ave., East Palo Alto, (415) 853-3144.
Foster City Recreation Dept., 650 Shell Blvd., Foster City, (415) 345-5731.
Half Moon Bay Recreation Dept., 501 Main, Half Moon Bay, (415) 726-1617.
Menlo Park Recreation Dept., 700 Alma, Menlo Park 94025, (415) 858-3470.

SAN MATEO COUNTY (continued)

Millbrae Recreation Dept., 477 Lincoln Circle, Millbrae 94030, (415) 697-7426.
Pacifica Recreation Dept., 170 Santa Maria Ave., Pacifica 94044, (415) 875-7380.
Redwood City Recreation Dept., 1400 Roosevelt Ave., Redwood City, (415) 780-7251.
San Bruno Recreation Dept., 567 El Camino Real, San Bruno 94066, (415) 877-8863.
San Carlos Recreation Dept., 666 Elm St., San Carlos 94070, (415) 593-8011.
San Mateo Recreation Dept., 330 W. 20th Ave., S.M. 94403, (415) 377-4700.
Skyline College, 3300 College Dr., San Bruno 94066, (415) 574-6563.
South San Francisco Recreation Dept., 33 Arroyo Dr., South San Francisco 94080, (415) 877-8560.

SANTA CLARA COUNTY

Campbell Recreation Dept., 70 N. 1st St., Campbell 95008, (408) 866-2105.
Cupertino Recreation Dept., 22221 McClellan Rd., Cupertino 95014, (408) 253-2060.
De Anza College, Community Education Dept., 21250 Stevens Creek Blvd., Cupertino 95014, (408) 864-8966.
Evergreen Valley College, Community Education & Services, 3095 Yerba Buena Rd., San Jose 95135, (408) 288-3720.
Foothill College, Community Services Dept., Los Altos Hills 94022, (415) 948-2588.
Gavilan College, 5055 Santa Teresa Blvd., Gilroy, 95020, (408) 848-4771.
Gilroy Recreation Dept., 7351 Rosanna St., Gilroy 95020, (408) 842-0221.
Gourmet Cooking for Singles, Palo Alto, (415) 321-0388. Barbara Millin, Instructor.
Los Altos Recreation Dept., 97 Hillview Ave., Los Altos 94022, (408) 941-0950.
Los Gatos Recreation Dept., 123 E. Main, Los Gatos, (408) 354-8700.
Mission College Community Education, 3000 Mission College Blvd., Santa Clara 95054, (408) 727-7584.
Milpitas Community Services, (408) 942-2470.
Morgan Hill Recreation Dept., 17666 Crest Ave., Morgan Hill 95037, (408) 779-7283.
Mt. View-Los Altos Adult Education, 415 E. Middlefield, M.V. 94043, (415) 967-7986.
Mountain View Recreation Dept., Box 7540, M.V. 94039, (415) 966-6331.
    Palo Alto, Mitchell Park Center, 3800 Middlefield Rd., Palo Alto, 329-2487; Lucie Stern Center, 1305 Middlefield Rd., 329-2261.
San Jose City College, Community Education & Services, 2100 Moorpark Ave., San Jose 95128, (408) 288-3720, 288-3755.

SANTA CLARA COUNTY (continued)

San Jose Recreation Dept., 151 W. Mission, San Jose, (408) 277-4000.
Santa Clara Recreation Dept., 1500 Warburton Ave., Santa Clara, (408) 984-3223.
Saratoga Community Center, 19655 Allendale Ave., Saratoga 95070, (408) 867-3438.
Sunnyvale Recreation Dept., 550 E. Remington Dr., Sunnyvale 94087, (408) 730-7350.
West Valley College, Community Development Dept., 14000 Fruitvale Ave., Saratoga 95070, (408) 867-0440.

SANTA CRUZ COUNTY

Cabrillo College Community Education, 6500 Soquel, Aptos 95003, (408) 479-6229.
Capitola Recreation, 4400 Jade, Capitola 95010, (408) 475-5935.
Santa Cruz County Cultural Services, 701 Ocean, Santa Cruz, (408) 425-2079.
Santa Cruz Recreation, 307 Church, Santa Cruz, (408) 429-3663.
Watsonville Recreation, 20 Maple, Watsonville 95076, (408) 728-6081.

SOLANO COUNTY

Benicia Recreation Dept., 250 E. L St., Benicia 94519, (707) 746-4285.
Fairfield Civic Arts, 1000 Webster, Fairfield 94533, (707) 428-7465.
Solano Community College, Community Services Dept., 4000 Suisun Valley Rd., Suisun City 94585, (707) 864-7115.
Vacaville Recreation Dept., 1100 Alamo Dr., Vacaville 95688, (707) 449-1830.
Vallejo Recreation Dept., 395 Amador, Vallejo 94590, (707) 648-4600.

SONOMA COUNTY

Healdsburg Recreation Dept., 126 Matheson, Healdsburg 95448.
Petaluma Recreation Dept., Box 61, Petaluma 94953, (707) 778-4380.
Rohnert Park Recreation Dept., 5401 Snyder Ln., Rohnert Park 94928.
Santa Rosa Junior College, Office of Community Services, 1501 Mendocino Ave., Santa Rosa 95401, (707) 527-4371.
Santa Rosa Recreation Dept., 415 Steele Ln., S.R. 95401, (707) 576-5116.
Sebastopol Recreation Dept., 7120 Bodega Ave., Sebastopol 95472, (707) 823-1511.

MISCELLANEOUS

Human Awareness Institute, 1720 S. Amphlett Blvd. #128, San Mateo 94402, (415) 571-5524. Stan Dale, Director. Sex, Love & Intimacy Workshops are held at Harbin Hot Springs. Evening symposiums, 1st Fridays, 8-10:30pm, Lone Mountain College, 2800 Turk St., San Francisco. Monthly Moonlight in Marin parties. Also Sunrise Parties and Foothill Parties throughout Bay Area.

Improvisational Theater Classes for Singles, (415) 626-4229 (Rita Shimmin) or 420-1230 (Merry Ross).

SPORTS

While sports are a great place to meet new friends of both sexes, I particularly recommend sports for women hoping to meet men. The odds will be heavily in your favor, since most men love sports and women often hate them. Some women make the mistake of stereotyping sportsmen. Supposedly they are all brainless hunks, exciting to be with until they open their mouths.

Nothing could be further from the truth. Studies reveal that a wide cross-section of men are fanatical about sports. Corporate executives with advanced degrees are just as likely to watch the Super Bowl as high school dropouts.

One objection I often hear is, "What's the use of meeting a man at a sporting event? I won't have anything in common with him." There are four answers to this objection.

1. Few men are uni-dimensional. Clearly a man who is so obsessed with sports that he is totally uninterested in anything else would make a poor romantic partner (unless **you** are equally enamored with sports). In the vast majority of cases, however, you will find that sports fans also enjoy other activities, some of which are hopefully your favorites.
2. If you can't beat 'em, why not join 'em? What's wrong with learning to enjoy sports? If you're a woman who loves sports that gives you tremendous advantage in competing for men. You automatically have something in common with them.
3. Participation in sports is one of the healthiest things you can do in life. Just ask your physician. Many women spend endless hours on the exercycle or in aerobics classes in order to maintain fitness. Why not improve your health in an equally effective manner and gain the added benefit of meeting men on their own turf?
4. Sports are fun. Even if you don't meet Mr. Right on the tennis court or during the Monday Night Football Game telecast, you can still have a great time.

HOW TO LEARN TO ENJOY SPORTS

1. Become proficient in sports. Just as it's hard to enjoy cooking if you always burn the casserole, you can't enjoy tennis or baseball if you miss the ball each time you swing. As your skill improves so does your enjoyment.
2. Understand them. Mothers often complain to finicky young eaters: "How do you know you don't like it if you haven't tasted it?" The same is true for women who hate sports. How can you say you dislike sports if you haven't tried them or don't understand them? A common woman's complaint is that "football is stupid". Nothing could be further from the truth! Football is an immensely

complicated game. That's why Bill Walsh, the former coach of the San Francisco 49ers, was commonly referred to as "the Genius". It's difficult to enjoy watching sports unless you understand the fine points of the game.

3. Learn the jargon of each sport. You'd probably find a foreign film without subtitles to be boring. The same is true of watching a sporting event without knowing the meaning of such phrases as "southpaw", "on-sides kick", "in the paint", "bogie", and "switch hitter". If you can speak the language of a sport you'll enjoy conversing more with men who love sports (and they'll enjoy you a whole lot more as well).

4. Start reading the sports section of your local newspaper. Learn the names of the top athletes and teams. Also the rules.

A good place to start getting involved with sports is your neighborhood. First check your local parks. That's where you'll find baseball, football, rugby, softball, and tennis. Next, check your gyms for basketball, gymnastics, and table tennis. Then turn to your health clubs for weightlifting, racquetball, and swimming. Health Clubs are listed in the yellow pages of your telephone directory.

This chapter has 3 sections listing places for meeting sports-minded singles: Recreation Departments, YMCA's, and Individual Sports.

RECREATION DEPARTMENTS

Your local recreation department is likely to sponsor competitive sports teams and activities, many of which are coed.

ALAMEDA COUNTY

Alameda Recreation Dept., Santa Clara Ave. & Oak, Alameda 94501, (415) 522-4100.
Albany Recreation Dept., 1100 San Pablo Ave., Albany, (415) 528-5740.
Berkeley Recreation Dept., 2180 Milvia, Berkeley, (415) 644-6530.
Dublin Recreation Dept., 6500 Dublin Blvd., Dublin, (415) 829-4932.
Fremont Community Services, 3375 Country Dr., (415) 791-4320.
Hayward Area Recreation District, 1099 E St., Hayward 94541, 881-6735.
Livermore Recreation Dept., 71 Trevarno, Livermore 94550, 447-7300.
Oakland Recreational Services Dept., 1520 Lakeside Dr., 273-3092.
Piedmont Recreation Dept., 358 Hillside Ave., Piedmont, 420-3070.
Pleasanton Recreation Dept., 200 Bernal, Pleasanton 94566, 847-8160.
San Leandro Recreation Dept., 835 14th St., (415) 577-3462.
Union City Recreation, Holly Community Center, 31600 Alvarado Blvd., Union City, (415) 471-6877; or Charles Kennedy Community Center, 1333 Decoto Rd., Union City, (415) 489-0360.

CONTRA COSTA COUNTY

Antioch Recreation Dept., 213 F St., Antioch 94509, (415) 757-0900.
Brentwood Recreation Dept., 724 3rd St., Brentwood 94513, 634-1044.
Concord Recreation Services, 2885 Concord Blvd., Concord, 671-3270.
El Cerrito Community Services, 10890 San Pablo Ave., El Cerrito 94530, (415) 234-7445.
Hercules Community Services, 111 Civic Dr., Hercules, (415) 799-8230.
Lafayette Recreation Dept., 500 St. Mary's Rd., Lafayette 94549, (415) 284-2232.
Martinez Recreation Dept., 525 Henrietta, Martinez 94553, 372-3510.
Moraga Recreation Dept., 2100 Donald Dr., Moraga 94556, 376-2520.
Pinole Recreation Dept., 2131 Pear, Pinole 94564, (415) 724-9004.
Pittsburg Recreation Dept., 340 Black Diamond, Pittsburg 94565, (415) 439-3440.
Pleasant Hill Recreation Dept., 320 Civic Dr., (415) 676-5200.
Richmond Recreation Dept., (415) 620-6792.
San Pablo Community Services, (415) 236-7373.
San Ramon, Shannon Community Center, (415) 829-4932.
Walnut Creek Recreation Dept., 1650 N. Broadway, (415) 943-5858.

MARIN COUNTY

Corte Madera Recreation Dept., 498 Tamalpais Dr., C.M. 94925, 924-2901.
Fairfax Recreation Dept., 142 Bolinas Rd., Fairfax, 94930, (415) 453-1584.
Larkspur Recreation Dept., 400 Magnolia, Larkspur 94939, 924-4777.
Marin County Recreation Dept., Marin County Civic Center, S.R. 94903, (415) 499-6387.
Mill Valley Recreation Dept., 180 Camino Alto, M.V. 94941, 383-1370.
Novato Recreation Dept., 917 Sherman Ave., Novato 94947, 897-4323.
Ross Recreation Dept., Lagunitas Rd., Ross, (415) 453-6020.
San Anselmo Recreation Dept., 1000 Sir Francis Drake Blvd., S.A. 94960, (415) 453-9055.
San Rafael Recreation Dept., 1400 5th Ave., S.R. 94901, (415) 485-3333.
Sausalito Recreation Dept., 420 Litho, Sausalito 94965, (415) 332-4520.
Tiburon Recreation Dept., 1155 Tiburon Blvd., Tiburon 94920, 435-4355.

MONTEREY COUNTY

Carmel Recreation, 15th Ave. & Monte Verde, Carmel 93923, 625-2252.
Gonzalez Recreation Dept., Box 647, Gonzalez 93926, (408) 675-2321.
King City Recreation, 411 Division, King City 93930, (408) 385-3575.
Marina Recreation, 211 Hillcrest Ave., Marina 93933, (408) 384-3715.
Monterey Recreation, 546 Dutra, Monterey 93940, (408) 646-3866.
Pacific Grove Recreation, 515 Junipero Ave., P.G. 93950, (408) 372-2809.
Salinas Recreation, 200 Lincoln Ave., Salinas, (408) 758-7306.
Seaside Recreation, 986 Hilby Ave., Seaside 93955, (408) 899-6270.

NAPA COUNTY

Calistoga Recreation Dept., 1232 Washington, Calistoga 94515, (707) 942-5188.
Napa Recreation Dept., 1100 West, Napa, (707) 252-7800.
St. Helena Recreation Dept., 1360 Oak Ave., S.H. 94574, (707) 963-5706.

SAN FRANCISCO

Adult Sports Leagues, Jewish Community Center, 3200 California, S.F. 94118, (415) 346-6040 (Danny Schwager).
San Francisco Recreation Dept., McLaren Lodge, Golden Gate Park, S.F. 94117.

SAN MATEO COUNTY

Belmont Recreation Dept., 1225 Ralston, Belmont 94002, (415) 573-3561.
Burlingame Recreation Dept., 850 Burlingame Ave., Burlingame 94010, (415) 344-6386.
Daly City Recreation Dept., 111 Lake Merced Blvd., (415) 991-8004.
East Palo Alto Community Services, 2415 University Ave., 853-3144.
Foster City Recreation Dept., 650 Shell Blvd., (415) 345-5731.
Half Moon Bay Recreation Dept., 501 Main, (415) 726-1617.
Menlo Park Recreation Dept., 700 Alma, M.P. 94025, (415) 858-3470.
Millbrae Recreation Dept., 477 Lincoln Circle, Millbrae 94030, 697-7426.
Pacifica Recreation Dept., 170 Santa Maria, Pacifica 94044, (415) 875-7380.
Redwood City Recreation Dept., 1400 Roosevelt Ave., (415) 364-6060.
San Bruno Recreation Dept., 567 El Camino Real, S.B. 94066, 877-8863.
San Carlos Recreation Dept., 666 Elm St., S.C. 94070, (415) 593-8011.
San Mateo Recreation Dept., 2720 Alameda de las Pulgas, (415) 377-4704.
South San Francisco Recreation Dept., 33 Arroyo, S.S.F. 94080, 877-8560.

SANTA CLARA COUNTY

Campbell Recreation Dept., 70 N. 1st St., Campbell 95008, 866-2105.
Cupertino Recreation Dept., 22221 McClellan, Cupertino 95014, 253-2060.
Gilroy Recreation Dept., 7351 Rosanna St., Gilroy 95020, (408) 842-0221.
Los Altos Recreation Dept., 97 Hillview Ave., L.A. 94022, (408) 941-0950.
Los Gatos Recreation Dept., 123 E. Main, Los Gatos, (408) 354-8700.
Milpitas Community Services, (408) 942-2470.
Morgan Hill Recreation Dept., 17666 Crest Ave., M.H. 95037, 779-7283.
Mountain View Recreation Dept., 201 S. Rengstorff, 966-6331.
Palo Alto Recreation Dept., Mitchell Park Ctr, 3800 Middlefield, (415) 329-2487; Lucie Stern Center, 1305 Middlefield Rd., (415) 329-2261.
San Jose Recreation Dept., 151 W. Mission, San Jose, (408) 277-4000.
Santa Clara Recreation Dept., 1500 Warburton Ave., (408) 984-3223.
Saratoga Community Center, 19655 Allendale, Saratoga 95070, 867-3438.
Sunnyvale Recreation Dept., 550 E. Remington Dr., (408) 730-7350.

SANTA CRUZ COUNTY

Capitola Recreation, 4400 Jade, Capitola 95010, (408) 475-5935.
Santa Cruz Recreation, 307 Church, Santa Cruz, (408) 429-3663.
Watsonville Recreation, 20 Maple, Watsonville 95076, (408) 728-6081.

SOLANO COUNTY

Benicia Recreation Dept., 250 E. L St., Benicia 94519, (707) 746-4285.
Fairfield Recreation Dept., 1000 Webster, Fairfield 94533, (707) 428-7465.
Vacaville Recreation Dept., 1100 Alamo, Vacaville 95688, (707) 449-1830.
Vallejo Recreation Dept., 395 Amador, Vallejo, (707) 648-4600.

SONOMA COUNTY

Healdsburg Recreation Dept., 126 Matheson, Healdsburg 95448.
Petaluma Recreation Dept., (707) 778-4380.
Rohnert Park Recreation Dept., 5401 Snyder Ln., Rohnert Park 94928.
Santa Rosa Recreation Dept., 415 Steele Ln., Santa Rosa, (707) 576-5116.
Sebastopol Recreation Dept., 7120 Bodega, Sebastopol 95472, 823-1511.

YMCAs

ALAMEDA COUNTY
  Albany, 921 Kains Ave., (415) 525-1130.
  East Bay Headquarters - 2001 Allston Way, (415) 848-6800
  South Berkeley, 2901 California, (415) 843-4280/848-6800.
  West Berkeley, 2009 10th St., (415) 848-6800.
  Central Oakland Center, 2101 Telegraph, (415) 451-9622.
  Eastlake Center, 1612 45th Ave., Oakland, (415) 534-7441.
  Eden Center, 951 Palisade, Hayward, (415) 582-9614.
  Fremont Center, 41811 Blacow Rd., (415) 657-5200.
  M. Robinson Baker Center, 3265 Market, Oakland, (415) 653-7818.
  Tri-Valley Center, 400 Main, Pleasanton, (415) 462-0270.
CONTRA COSTA COUNTY
  Walnut Creek Center, 1855 Olympic Blvd., (415) 935-9622.
  Mt. Diablo Center, 350 Civic Dr., Pleasant Hill, (415) 687-8900.
MARIN COUNTY
  Marin Center, 1500 Los Gamos Dr., San Rafael 94901, (415) 492-9622.
SAN FRANCISCO
  Chinatown-North Beach Center, 965 Clay, (415) 397-6883.
  Downtown Center, 620 Sutter, 775-6500 (includes swimming pool).
  Embarcadero Center, 166 The Embarcadero, 392-2191.
  Central Y, 220 Golden Gate, 885-0460
  Mission Center, 1855 Folsom, (415) 552-6790.
  Stonestown Center, 333 Eucalyptus, (415) 759-9622.
  Western Addition Center, 1830 Sutter, (415) 921-3814.

Sports   89

SAN MATEO COUNTY
   Peninsula Family Center, 240 N. El Camino Real, San Mateo, 342-5228.
SANTA CLARA COUNTY
   Central Branch, 1717 The Alameda, San Jose, (408) 298-1717
   East Valley Branch, 1975 S. White Rd., San Jose, (408) 258-4419
   Milpitas Branch, 540 S. Abel, Milpitas, (408) 945-0919
   Northwest Branch, 20803 Alves Dr., Cupertino, (408) 257-7160
   Palo Alto Branch, 3412 Ross Rd., (415) 494-1883.
   South Valley Branch, 5632 Santa Teresa Blvd., (408) 226-9622.
SANTA CRUZ COUNTY
   Boulder Creek YMCA, 16275 Hwy. 9, B.C. 95006, 338-2128.
   Watsonville, 27 Sudden, Watsonville 95076, (408) 728-9622.
SOLANO COUNTY
   Vallejo Y, 401 Amador, (707) 643-3268 or 643-5858.
SONOMA COUNTY
   Santa Rosa Y, 1111 College Ave., (707) 545-9622.

INDIVIDUAL SPORTS

BASEBALL & SOFTBALL

There are coed softball leagues all over the Bay Area that are ideal for meeting both men and women. Contact your local city recreation department (see the listings earlier in this chapter).

Baseball and softball are particularly good for meeting single men, so consider visiting the local baseball diamond evenings and weekends during the Summer. In San Francisco, Golden Gate Park, Moscone Field (Chestnut & Buchanan), Sunset Field (39th & Pacheco) are examples. If you don't know how to play, don't worry. Just ask to play the outfield--the ball will seldom come to you out there. If you're not into playing baseball or softball just sit in the stands and find out where the team goes out drinking afterwards.

If you're more interested in watching the pros rather than amateurs, the ballpark is a great place to meet single men. Contact the San Francisco Giants, Candlestick Park, (415) 467-8000. You might also consider joining the San Francisco Baseball Club, 555 California, S.F., (415) 421-2357.

Concord Athletic League, 689-3217.
Pleasant Hill Baseball Association, 147 Gregory Ln., (415) 687-7422.
San Ramon Valley Adult Softball, (415) 828-4848.
South Alameda County Softball Association, Box 711, Hayward 94542.
Sunnyvale Coed Softball, (408) 446-1864 (Sparky). Softball clinics, group
   activities, parties, barbecues, ball games, wine tastings, and travel.
Walnut Creek Adult Softball Assoc., 301 N. San Carlos Dr., 943-1955.

BICYCLING

Contact your local bicycle shop for information about local bicycling clubs.

Backroads Bicycle Touring, Box 1626, San Leandro 94577, (415) 895-1783.

Berkeley Bicycle Club, Box 817, Berkeley 94701, (415) 653-4624

Bombay Bicycle Riding Club, 1107 Howard Ave., Burlingame, 342-8959.

Cherry City Cyclists, 20206 Lucot Ct, Hayward 94541

East Bay Bicycle Coalition, Box 1736, Oakland 94604, (415) 273-3941 or 452-1221.

Fremont Freewheelers Bicycle Club, Box 1089, Fremont 94538, (415) 489-1310.

Grizzly Peak Cyclists, Box 9308, Berkeley 94709, (415) 655-4221 or 953-0322.

Napa Bicycle Club, 2917 Pinewood Dr., Napa 94558, (707) 257-6344 or 224-3922.

Psychedelic Cyclists, San Mateo, (415) 344-7046.

Rhody Co. Productions, 2929 California, San Francisco 94118, (415) 387-2178. Bicycling events throughout Bay Area.

Santa Cruz County Cycling Club, 414 Soquel Ave., (408) 423-0829.

Single Cyclists, Box 684, Kentfield 94904, (415) 258-8067. Bike trips. 25+.

Total Race Systems/The Schedule, 627 Galerita Way, San Rafael 94903, (415) 472-7223.

Valley Spokesman Bicycle Touring Club, Box 2630, Dublin 94568, (415) 828-5299.

Western Wheelers Bicycle Club, Box 518, Palo Alto 94302.

BOATING

Cal Sailing Club of Berkeley, (415) 527-7245.

Fremont Sailing Club, Box 793, Fremont 94537, (415) 792-0341.

Lake Merced Sailing Club, Boat House, Skyline & Harding, S.F. 94132, (415) 753-1101.

Marina Sailing Society, San Francisco, (415) 368-1718.

Napa Boat Club, Box 134, Napa 94559, (707) 255-5290

Oceanic Society, Fort Mason, San Francisco, (415) 441-5970. Activities include sailing, classes, lectures, films, and parties.

Olympic Circle Sailing Club, 1 Spinnaker Way, Berkeley Marina 94710, (415) 843-4200.

Treasure Island Sailing Club, Treasure Island Rd., S.F. 94130, 397-7827.

Yacht Racing Association, Fort Mason, S.F. 94123, (415) 771-9500.

See Yacht Clubs in the yellow pages of your phone directory for information about boating activities.

BOWLING

Coed bowling leagues start up every few months at the various bowling alleys (listed in the yellow pages of your phone book). It's easy to meet people and get to know them since you run into them each week at the bowling alley. Look up the BOWLING section of the yellow pages of your telephone book.

5th Wheelers, Box 4569, Walnut Creek 94596, 676-7129. 40+. For singles only.
Palo Alto Bowling Association, 4329 El Camino Real, Palo Alto, (415) 941-5098.
Peninsula Bowling Association, 735 Industrial Rd., San Carlos 94070.
San Francisco Bowling Association, Inc., 1485 Bayshore Blvd., San Francisco 94128, (415) 467-8937.
Santa Clara Valley Bowling Association, 90 E. Gish Rd., San Jose, (408) 453-5080.

BOXING

Not too many women hang out at the gym to watch men exercise and practice beating each others brains out, so you'll have all the men to yourself.

Fremont International Boxing Club, 5773 Butano Park Dr., Fremont, (415) 651-0271.
Newman's Gym, 312 Leavenworth, SF, (415) 775-7020.

CAMPING

American Camping Association, Box 3017, San Rafael 94912.
Tri-Valley Sundowners, (415) 449-7293.

DARTS

British pubs usually feature dart boards. Dart leagues often meet at these pubs on a regular basis. Check the COCKTAIL LOUNGE section of the yellow pages of your phone book.

Barnacles Saloon, 3243 Pierce, SF, (415) 346-6824.
Edinburgh Castle, 950 Geary, (415) 885-4074. British pub. Bagpipes on Saturdays.
Mad Dog in the Fog, 530 Haight, (415) 431-0630. Irish bar.
Mayflower Inn, 1533 4th St., San Rafael 94901, (415) 456-1011. Wednesday night is Darts night.
Penny Farthing Club, 679 Sutter, San Francisco, (415) 771-5155.
San Francisco Dart Association, 1416 Bush, San Francisco, (415) 885-6918.

FENCING

Halberstadt Fencers' Club, 621 S. Van Ness, San Francisco, 863-3838.
Pacific Fencing Club, 1249 34th Ave., Oakland, (415) 436-3800.

FISHING & FLYCASTING

Anglers' Lodge, Golden Gate Park, San Francisco.
Captain Al, San Francisco, (415) 878-4644.
Captain George's Boating Centers, Pier 39, Box CAP, San Francisco 94133, (415) 956-2628.
Captain Joe, San Francisco, (415) 673-9815
Crab Boat Owners Association, 2907 Jones St., San Francisco 94109, (415) 885-1180.
Crockett Striped Bass Club, Box 58, Crockett 94525, (415) 787-9976.
Diablo Valley Fly Fishermen, Box 4988, Walnut Creek 94596.
Trout Unlimited, 1024-C Los Gamos, San Rafael 94903, (415) 472-5837.

FOOTBALL

49ers Entertainment, 2133 Leghorn St., Mt. View 94043.
San Francisco 49ers, Candlestick Park, San Francisco, 468-2249.

GOLF

One place to meet people is at the driving range, where you can buy a bucket of golf balls and practice teeing off. Ask the most attractive person there for tips.

Meeting singles on the golf course is more expensive and requires an investment in a complete set of clubs as well as the time needed to master their use. The alternative is to just wait in the clubhouse for the golfers to tire out on the greens and come in for a snort. You are permitted to sit in the clubhouse of public golf courses without being a member. Private golf courses may require that you be accompanied by a member. Both public and private courses are listed in the yellow pages of your phone book.

California Golf Club, 844 W. Orange Ave., South San Francisco 94080, (415) 761-0210.
Fairway Singles Golf Club, 830 Rigel, Foster City 94404, 349-8191, 349-5822. Meets at golf courses throughout the Bay Area Saturdays & Sundays. Ron Gabel, Director.
Golf Club of Vallejo, Box 5207, Vallejo 94590, (415) 642-0247.
San Francisco Golf Club, Junipero Serra Blvd & Brotherhood Way, San Francisco 94132, (415) 469-4100.
Tri-Valley Singles Golf Association, 2558 Derby Dr., San Ramon 94583, (415) 830-4527 or 833-7014.

GUNS

Chabot Gun Club, Box 2246, Castro Valley, (415) 569-0213.
Eagle Rock Gun Club, Empire Grade Rd., Santa Cruz, (408) 426-0623.
Green Lodge Gun Club, Cygnus Station, Suisun, (707) 864-0533.
Livermore-Pleasanton Rod & Gun Club, 4000 Dagnino Rd. Livermore, (415) 449-9810.
Los Altos Rod & Gun Club Range, 14750 Skyline Blvd., Los Gatos, (408) 867-3106.
Marin Rod & Gun Club, San Quentin, (415) 459-9845.
Napa Rifle & Pistol Club, (707) 226-6624.
Pacific Rod & Gun Club, 520 John Muir Dr., San Francisco, 239-9750 or 239-9613. Check the bulletin board or call for info on social events.
Pajaro Valley Rod & Gun Club, Lakeview, Watsonville 95076, 724-7311.
San Bruno Rod & Gun Club, 732 7th Ave., San Bruno 94066, 952-3774.
Santa Clara Valley Rifle Club, 1580 S. 10th St., San Jose, (408) 275-1738.

GYMNASTICS

Gymnastic Association, (SOKOL), 1306 Elmer St., Belmont 94002, (415) 591-8734.
Napa Valley Gymnastics Club, 1836 Soscal Ave., Napa 94559, (707) 224-5140.
Sunnyvale Gymnastics Club, (408) 358-3525. Odd Wednesdays, 10am, Sunnyvale Community Center.

HANG GLIDING

Hang Gliders can usually be found near the beach. One popular Bay Area spot is at Fort Funston on Skyline Blvd. near the ocean in southern San Francisco.

HIKING

Green Earth Singles, Box 7933, Santa Cruz 95061, 338-2366.
Hayward Hiking & Backpacking Club, 1308 Skokie, Hayward 94545, (415) 886-4877 or 792-3299
Monterey Outdoor Singles Society (M.O.S.S.) Box 51416, Pacific Grove 93950, (408) 445-1850. Mainly 30-60. Dancing, beach parties, hikes.
Sierra Singles
  Bay Area Chapter, 6014 College, Oakland 94618, 548-0591 (Phil Gale). 21-40.
  Loma Prieta Chapter, Box 391775, Mountain View 94039. 21+.
Solo Sierrans, Sierra Club, 568 Fairmount Ave., Oakland 94624, 658-9977, or 654-4163 (Joe Dorst). 40+.
Singles Outdoor Activities & Recreation (SOAR)
  Napa - (707) 255-8610 (Rosemarie).
  Fairfield - (707) 422-4694.

HIKING (continued)

Singles Outdoor Activities & Recreation - SOAR (continued)
  Santa Rosa - Box 5196, Santa Rosa 95402, (707) 539-3795 (Gladys) or
  539-5016 (Carolyn). 30+.
  Vallejo - 837 Keats Dr., Vallejo 94591, (707) 643-0489
Single Outdoor Living Experience (SOLE), Box 6374, Santa Rosa 95406,
  (707) 795-2609 (Jim) or 538-8271 (Carl).

HORSEBACK RIDING

California Horsemens Association, 2838 Emerald Dr., Walnut Ck 94598.
Carmel Valley Trail & Saddle Club, E. Garzas Rd., Carmel Valley 93924,
  (408) 659-9987.
Concord Mt Diablo Trail Ride Association, 1601 Russelman Park Rd.,
  Clayton, (415) 672-7557.
Contra Costa County Horsemens Association, 3119 Grant, Concord,
  (415) 680-9713.
Horsemen's Association of Vallejo, 2100 American Canyon Rd., Vallejo
  94589, (707) 644-0626.
Napa Valley Horseman Association, 1200 Foster Rd., Napa 94558, (707)
  255-9627.
San Mateo Horsemen, 239 Scenic Dr., Redwood City 94062.
Santa Clara County Horsemens Association, 20350 McKean Rd., San
  Jose, (408) 268-6155.
Santa Cruz County Horseman's Association, Graham Hill Rd. & Sims
  Rd., Santa Cruz, (408) 458-3198.
Trail Riders of the North Bay, 111 Lorene Cir., Vallejo 94590, 642-8672.

HORSE RACING

Many singles love to take off for a day at the races. Just make sure
that the people you meet at the track aren't addicted. That means they're
liable to be penniless. Also find out at which bars horse racing fans tend
to socialize afterwards.

Bay Meadows, San Mateo, (415) 574-7223.
Golden Gate Fields, 1100 Eastshore Highway, Albany, (415) 526-3020.

KAYAKING

Kayaking/Sea Trek, 85 Liberty Shipway, Sausalito 94965, (415) 332-4456.

LAWN BOWLING

Berkeley Lawn Bowling Club, 2270 Acton, Berkeley, (415) 841-2174.
Martinez Bocce Federation, Box 642, Martinez 94553, (415) 229-2157,
  671-4300.

LAWN BOWLING (continued)

Oakland Lawn Bowling Club, Lakeside Park, Oakland, (415) 832-9236.
Palo Alto Lawn Bowls Club, 474 Embarcadero Rd., Palo Alto, (415) 323-2575.
Sunnyvale Lawn Bowls Club, (408) 739-1293 (James Worwood).
Mondays, Wed-Th., Sat-Sun., 12:30-3pm, Murphy Park, Sunnyvale.

MARTIAL ARTS

Check the yellow pages of your phone book for local studios.

Napa Judo Club, Box 2175, Napa 94558, (707) 255-7407.
Palo Alto Judo Club, (415) 329-0615.
Sunnyvale Judo Club, (408) 739-3389 (David White).

MOTORCYCLING

If you get turned on by leather and the sound of loud engines revving, here's a sport that is ideal for meeting singles. For more information on motorcycle clubs and events read City Bike, 1126 Kearny St., San Francisco 94133, (415) 982-7242.

Marin County Motorcycle Association, (415) 456-0335.
Napa Motorcycle Club, 2453 Rigdon St., Napa 94558, (707) 255-0458.
North Bay Motorcycle Club, Fulton, (707) 526-7699.
Oakland Motorcycle Club, 742 45th Ave., Oakland, (415) 534-6222.
Sadistics Motorcycle Club, 2727 Milvia, Berkeley, (415) 548-4895.
San Jose Dons Motorcycle Club, 523 Columbia, San Jose, (408) 294-5434.
Soul Brothers Motorcycle Club, 1861 Bay Rd., E. Palo Alto, (415) 853-8850.
Wicked Wheels Motorcycle Club, 5816 Foothill Blvd., Oakland, 638-9659.
Zodiac Motorcycle Club, 9500 E. 14th, Oakland, (415) 638-9188.

ORIENTEERING

Orienteering is the Scandinavian sport of hiking. The ratio is four men for every woman.

Bay Area Orienteering Society, (415) 652-7851.
Bay Area Orienteering Club, 3015 Holyrood Dr., Oakland 94611.
    Livermore - (415) 422-4266 (Mark Blair, work)
    Marin - (415) 383-4429 (Gary)
    Pleasanton - (415) 846-1062 (Gerry)
    San Carlos - (415) 365-4275 (Nancy)
    San Jose - (408) 729-1960 (Dan)
Orienteering, 3151 Hollywood Dr., Oakland 94611, (415) 530-3059.

RACQUETBALL

Look up racquetball clubs in the yellow pages of your phone book. Many health clubs also feature racquetball, so check that section of the phone book as well.

ROWING

North Bay Rowing Club, 2390 I St., Petaluma 94952, (707) 762-1832. South End Rowing Club, 500 Jefferson, San Francisco 94109, (415) 441-9523 or 885-9564.

RUGBY

Marin Rugby Club, 410 Pinewood, San Rafael 94903, (415) 499-8777. No. Calif. Rugby Union, Box 15157, San Francisco 94115. Socializing afterwards at local bars.

RUNNING

Running is the great American obsession. Millions jog regularly. Many claim to experience "runner's high", which is caused by the release of endorphines (pleasure causing hormones) into the brain while exercising. Along with improving your health and feeling better emotionally, running can also improve your social life. The same holds true for walking and striding.

Below are listed some competitive events for runners and walkers. Many of them are fundraisers for good causes, so you will also be meeting charitable singles. For a running & walking calendar read **The Northern California Schedule**, 80 Mitchell Blvd., San Rafael 94903, (415) 472-7223.

American Heart Association, 120 Montgomery #1650, San Francisco 94104, (415) 433-2273.
April Showers Fun Run & Walk, Lois Koenig, 535 Darrell Rd., Hillsborough 94010, (415) 342-9328.
Big Sur International Marathon, Box 222620, B.S. 93922, (408) 625-6226.
Blind Date Relays, San Francisco, (415) 668-2830. 1 man/1 woman teams.
Brickyard Run, Martinez, Luka Sekulich, 1485 Darlene Dr., Concord 94520, (415) 685-5185.
Center for Living Skills, Box 1145, Lafayette 94549, (415) 284-4871.
Change of Pace, 1260 Lake Blvd. #248, Davis 95616, (916) 757-2012. Events throughout Northern California.
Charlie Wedemeyer Classic 10K Run, Tom Zades, 1230 Ridge Oak Ct., San Jose 95120, (408) 268-6693.
Chinatown Run, 855 Sacramento, San Francisco 94162, (415) 982-4412.
Christmas Classic, 528 Larch Ave., South San Francisco 94080, 583-6268.

Dash for Diabetes, Sunnyvale Medical Clinic, 596 Carroll, Sunnyvale 94086, (415) 328-1110 or (408) 287-3785.

Devil Mountain Run, Pleasanton, Box 93, Pleasanton 94566.

Dipsea, Box 30, Mill Valley 94942, (415) 381-DIPC.

DSE Lake Merced Single & Double Runs, San Francisco, (415) 668-2830.

Eden Hospital, Ellen Kushner, 20103 Lake Chabot Rd, Castro Valley 94546, (415) 889-5061.

ESL Runaway 10K, Dori Wilson, 495 Java #M-503, Sunnyvale 94088, (408) 743-6399.

Fleet Feet, 2086 Chestnut St., San Francisco 94123, (415) 921-7188.

Fujitsu 5M Classic, San Jose, (408) 922-9118.

Golden Gate Race Walkers, 130 Graystone Terr., S.F. 94114, 863-0479.

Golden Gate Vista Run, San Francisco, (415) 668-2830.

Gonzalez Recreation Dept., Box 647, Gonzalez 93926, (408) 675-2321.

Good Samaritan Hospital League, 2425 Samaritan Dr., Los Gatos 95124, (408) 559-2555.

Human Race 10K/5K, Lois Koenig, 535 Darrell Rd., Hillsborough 94010, (415) 342-9328.

Irish Sprint & Stride, Jeff Benes, 347 Keeler Ct., San Jose 95139. Events throughout the Bay Area.

Kennedy Drive Run, Golden Gate Park, San Francisco, (415) 668-2830.

Kiwi Running Club (for women), Santa Rosa, (707) 526-2940.

Lake Merritt Joggers & Striders, Elvyn Blair, 3136 California, Oakland 94602, (415) 530-9151. Fourth Sundays.

Los Altos Hills Country Climb, Box 1286, L.A. 94022, (415) 949-5415.

Monterey Bay Academy, 783 San Andreas Rd., Monterey 95076, (408) 728-1481 x371.

Monterey Rape Crisis, Box 2630, Monterey 93942, (408) 373-3389.

Mulberry Great Escape 5K/10K, Rae Dorough, 6154 Escondido Cir., Livermore 94550.

Napa Valley Marathon, 1325 Imola W., Napa 94559, (707) 255-2609.

Options for Women Over 40, 3543 18th St., S.F. 94110, (415) 431-6944.

Pacific Sun 10K, TRS, 80 Mitchell Blvd., San Rafael 94903.

Palo Alto Park & Recreation Dept., 750 N. California, P.A. 94304, (415) 329-2381.

Pamakid Runners, Box 27557, San Francisco 94127, (415) 681-2323.

Pleasant Hill Recreation Dept., 147 Gregory Lane, P.H. 94523, 827-2255.

Quadruple Dipsea, Mill Valley, Jim Skophammer, 666 Orange St., Daly City 94014, (415) 994-6218.

Race/Fun Walk 1.5M, Pam Lambert, Napa Valley Bank, 940 Adams St., Benicia 94510, (707) 746-7820.

Rhody Co. Productions, (415) 387-2187. Running events throughout the Bay Area.

Rio Resolution Run, Simon & Deborah Treadmill, Carmel, 624-4112.

Run & Walk for Open Space 5K, J.A. Harmes, 8 Ivy Ln., San Anselmo 94960, (415) 774-2554.

RUNNING (continued)

Run for the Seals, CMMC, GGNRA, Marin Headlands, Sausalito 94965, (415) 331-SEAL.

Run for the Health of It, Washington Hospital, 2000 Mowry Ave., Fremont 94538, (415) 797-1111 x4730.

Run for the Roof, Joan Runyeon, Box 13434, San Rafael 94913, 453-1063.

Run for Your Life, Joel B. Doss, 358 Searidge #1, Aptos 95003.

Runners Factory, 51 University Ave., Los Gatos 95030, (408) 395-4311.

Runner's Feet, 1004 Oak Grove, Burlingame 94066, 343-4242 or 579-7881.

Run Your Axe Off, UC Development Office, CSF, 2440 Bancroft Way, Berkeley 94720, (415) 643-7001.

Ruth Anderson 100K, San Francisco, Dick Collins, 1015 Hollywood Ave., Oakland 94602, (415) 530-6634.

San Francisco Marathon, 1233 Taraval, S.F. 94116, (415) 681-2324.

San Francisco Zoo Society, Sloat Blvd. at Pacific Ocean, S.F. 94132, (415) 753-7080.

Santa Cruz Recreation Dept., Lisa McGinnis, 307 Church St., S.C. 95060, (408) 429-3477.

Serra Residential Center, Jane Bell, Box 3296, 650 Washington Blvd., Fremont 94539, (415) 657-2002.

Serra's Run, Will Franke, 2992 Lausen, Carmel 93923, (408) 375-2661.

Shoreline Run 10K, 3K, Ted Swenson, 835 E. 14th, San Leandro 94577, (415) 577-3469.

Sonoma State Intramural Office, 1801 E. Cotati Ave., Rohnert Pk 94928, (707) 664-2753.

South San Francisco Parks & Recreation Dept., Box 711, S.S.F. 94080, (415) 877-8560.

Team Challenge, Box 963, El Sobrante 904803, (415) 841-1190. Running events throughout the Bay Area.

Tri-Sports, 21 Live Oak, Berkeley 94705 (415) 540-7008. Running events throughout the Bay Area.

West Coast Knights, Box 23731, San Jose 95153, (408) 281-4599. Events throughout the Bay Area.

West Valley Track Club, Marc Lund, 1433 Norman Dr., Sunnyvale 94087, (415) 387-7172 (Flory) or (415) 482-4355 (Laury).

Windsor Whale Run, Box 237, Occidental 95465, (707) 829-9493.

SAILING

Monterey Outdoor Singles (M.O.S.) Box 51416, Pacific Grove 93950, (408) 624-0202. Mainly 30-60.

Sierra Singles
Bay Area Chapter, 6014 College, Oakland 94618, 548-0591. 21-40.
Loma Prieta Chapter, Box 391775, Mountain View 94039. 21+.

SCUBA DIVING

Alacosta Divers, 50 Entrada, Oakland 94611.
Alameda Divers, 3551 Joaquin Miller Rd., Oakland 94611.
Amphibians, 759 Lundy, Pacifica 94044 (415) 355-7776.
Aqua Tutus, Box 494, San Lorenzo 94580.
Bamboo Reef, 584 4th St., San Francisco, (415) 362-6694.
Barbara Coast, 2334 Fulton, San Francisco 94118.
Bay Area Divers, 1178 Euclid, Berkeley 94708. Underwater hockey team.
Blue Coral Dive Club meets the 2nd Wednesday of each month at Whistle Stop North, on Grant Ave., Novato.
Bottom Watchers, Box 1244, Fremont 94538.
Bud Davis School of Scuba Diving, 1550 Bay, San Francisco, 921-3676.
California Sport Divers, Box 4008, Mt. View 94403.
Conquestadores del Mar, Box 29356, San Francisco 94129.
Diablo Sea Bears, 4955 Boxer Blvd., Concord 94521.
East Bay Barnacles, 210 N. San Tomas-Aquino Rd., Campbell 95008.
Hydro Knights, Box 75, San Carlos 94070.
Kahunas, 1130 Deanna Ct., Morgan Hill 95067.
Lera Scuba Knights, 6150 Joaquin Murieta Dr., Newark 94560, meet 2nd Saturday of each month at LERA Auditorium in Sunnyvale.
Lera Underwater Club, 4766 Bannock Circ., San Jose 95130.
Los Altos Aquatic Club, Box 1269, Los Altos, (415) 941-5133.
Livermore Aquatics, (415) 443-9666.
Martinez Blue Fins, 112 Cotton Wood Dr., Vallejo 94590.
Nor Cal Club, 215 Los Altos 94590.
North Bay Dive Club, (707) 573-9007. 1st Tuesdays, 7:30pm, at 1625 Hill St., Novato.
Outrigger Dive Club, 14291 New Jersey, San Jose. 1st Mondays, Round Table Pizza, Hamilton & Darryl, Campbell.
Pinnacles Dive Center, 875 Grant Ave., Novato 94947, 897-9962. Classes.
Richmond Pelicans, 1196 Arch Ct., Concord 94520. 2nd & 4th Tuesdays, month, Pinole Sportsmens Club, Pinole.
Salt Water Revival, Box 573, Rodeo 94572. 1st Wednesdays, Memorial Park Club House in Albany.
San Francisco Cormorants, 22 Lee, San Francisco 94112. Diving, trips, and parties.
San Francisco Flipper Dippers, 10 Woodside, San Anselmo 94960. 3rd Wednesdays, Round Table Pizza, 16th & Geary, San Francisco. Diving, trips, and parties.
San Francisco Hammerheads, Box 1387, Pacifica 94044.
San Francisco Reef Divers, 1230 Broadway #3, San Francisco 94109.
San Jose Flipper Dippers, Box 6205, San Jose 95150.
San Jose Skin Divers, 350 Quinnhill Rd., Los Altos 94022.
San Ramon Valley Aquatics, (415) 820-9362.
Santa Cruz County Aquatic Team, (408) 476-5620.
Sonoma State University Scuba Club, 180 Valpariso #2, Cotati 94928.
Suisun Sea Spirits, 1035 Pintail Dr., Suisun 94585.

SCUBA DIVING (continued)

Tritonians, 840 Coleman, Menlo Pk 94025. 3rd Wednesdays, Stanford Research Institute in Palo Alto.
Underwater Photo Society (UPS), 2708 Laramie Gate Cir., Pleasanton 94566. 1st Fridays, Fort Mason Bldg C, 3rd Floor, San Francisco.
Vacqueros del Mar, Box 882, Livermore 94550. 1st Wednesdays, Lawrence Livermore Lab So. Cafeteria.

Please note: For an up-to-date listing of scuba diving clubs in Northern California, contact Central California Council of Diving Clubs (CEN-CAL), Box 779, Daly City 94017, (415) 583-8492. Activities include diving, hockey, underwater photography, classes, spear fishing.

SKATING

Diablo Figure Skating Club, 1774 Lucille Ln., Pleasant Hill 94523.
Marin Figure Skating Club, 233 W. Baltimore, Larkspur 94939.
Palomares Figure Skating Club, 33157, Palmetto, Union City 94587.
Peninsula Figure Skating Club, 1110 Tuolumne Rd., Millbrae 94030.
Santa Rosa Figure Skating Club, 16678 W. Steele, Santa Rosa 95404.
The Skating Club, Ice Arena, 1557 48th Ave., S.F. 94118, (415) 681-6430.
St. Moritz Ice Skating Club, 11753 Silvergate, Dublin.

SNOW SKIING

All-Seasons, (415) 236-1471 (Michael).
Alpineer Ski Club, 450 Hearst Ave., San Francisco 94112, (415) 334-3732.
Apres Singles Ski Club, Box 1027, Mountain View 94042, 377-5966 or 259-5142. Even Thursdays, 8pm, Sunnyvale Elks Club, 375 N. Pastoria.
Bear Valley Ski Club, 3100 Mowry #401, Fremont, (408) 379-4849 (France) or (415) 797-1368.
Berkeley Ski Club, Box 758, Berkeley 94701, (415) 236-1127 (Bob).
Bladerunners, (415) 792-3010 (Elaine).
Bota Baggers Singles Ski Club, Box 772, Pleasanton 94566, 443-4451 (tape) or 275-0317. Tuesdays, 8pm, Velvet Turtle, Sheraton Hotel.
California Adventures, UC Berkeley, 642-4000. Young singles.
California Alpine Club, 870 Market, San Francisco 94102, (415) 334-4619.
Cal State Hayward Ski Club, 848 South M St., Livermore 94550, (415) 443-5363 (Kari)
Camber Ski Club, Box 1043, Salinas 93902, (408) 663-4616 or 757-6301. 1st Thursdays, 7pm, Lord Byron's Pizza, Northridge Mall.
Castro Valley Ski Club, Box 2032, C.V. 94546, 483-7782 or 786-3026.
Chi Ski Club, Box 5596, San Francisco 94101.
Concord Ski Club, Box 27-213, Concord 94527, (415) 932-2191, 676-9551 (Fred), or 671-3408.

SNOW SKIING (continued)

Fall Line Singles Ski Club, Box 2367, San Rafael 94912, (415) 492-9293. Odd Tuesdays, Strawberry Joe's, Strawberry Shopping Center, Mill Valley.

Flexy Flyers Ski Club, 25200 Carlos Bee #94, Hayward 94542, (415) 889-6146 (Val)

Gatebusters, (408) 923-0962 (David).

Inskiers Singles Ski Club, Box 5065, San Mateo 94402, 494-8243 (Bonnie Soeas) or 364-5490 (Sandy). Tuesdays, 8 pm, Sand Bar Cocktail Lounge, San Mateo Municipal Golf Course. Also potlucks, happy hours.

Marin Ski Club, Box 334, San Rafael 94915, (707) 745-3462 (Shelly).

National Ski Club, (408) 732-9104 (Josip).

Nisei Ski Club, 1233 Taylor #1, San Francisco, (408) 371-1451 (Alice).

Oakland Ski Club, Box 12541, Oakland 94604, (415) 283-1127 (Laura).

Pacific Ski & Trail Club, 235 Montgomery #860, San Francisco 94104, 398-7372. Dances, skiing, sports, flea markets, matchmaking.

Palo Alto Ski Club, 135 Commercial, Sunnyvale, (415) 967-5841 or (408) 738-0160.

Parallelers, (415) 422-9136.

Peninsula Ski Club, Box 305, San Mateo 94401, (415) 574-4981 or 591-1809.

Powder Hounds Singles Ski Club, Box 12763, Oakland 94604, (415) 769-7669. Tuesdays, 8pm, Sheanigans, Jack London Square. Volleyball, Thursdays. Also baseball & camping.

Rusty Bindings Singles Ski Club, Box 3096, Walnut Creek 94598, 724-3093 (Mariell Jaren). Tuesdays, El Papagallo Rest., 2995 Ygnacio Valley.

Rut Riders Ski Club, Box 32706, San Jose 95152, (408) 729-9262 or (415) 641-4541.

San Francisco Singles Ski Club, Box 421765, San Francisco 94101, (415) 337-9333. Tuesdays, 7pm, Duffy's Tavern, 451 Pine St. at Kearny.

Saratoga Ski Club, 13 Sorrel Ln., San Carlos 94070.

Sierra Ski Club (Division of Sierra Club), Jerry Abad, 6454 Valley View, Oakland 94611, (415) 339-2961.

Skoalers Ski Club, 99 Crestview Dr., Orinda 94563.

Skyline Ski Patrol, 1028-D Middle Ave., Menlo Park 94025.

Sno-Ball Express Ski Club, 729 Peekskill Dr., Sunnyvale 94087, (408) 730-9623.

Snowchasers Ski Club, Box 6171, Concord 94524, (415) 930-8424.

Snow Drifters Singles Ski Club, Box 396, Mountain View 94042, 265-4206. Odd Wednesdays, 8pm, at The Bold Knight, 769 N. Mathilda Ave.

SnoFlakes Ski Club, 1684 Spruce St., Livermore 94550

South Bay Ski Club, Box 1431, San Jose 95109, (408) 267-0802/593-7692.

Sundancer Ski Club, Box 390636, Mt. View 94039, (415) 323-4941. 40+.

SOCCER

Alameda Soccer Club, Box 426, Alameda 94501, (415) 865-1551.
California Soccer Association, Box 12066, San Francisco 94112, (415)
    586-5800 or 467-1881.
Fremont City Soccer Club, 3755 Washington Blvd., (415) 659-8150.
Livermore Soccer Club, Box 881, Livermore, (415) 449-1155.
Marina Soccer Association, 122 Belle Dr., Marina, CA, (408) 384-4330.
Newark Soccer Club, (415) 797-6502.
San Carlos Soccer World, 1144 Holly, San Carlos, (415) 595-2190.
Sunnyvale Alliance Soccer Club, 442 Leota Ave., Sunnyvale, (408) 738-
    0989 or (415) 967-6184/733-5425.
Walnut Creek Soccer Club, Box 3057, Walnut Creek, (415) 930-0210.

SWIMMING

Most cities in the Bay Area have neighborhood pools, which are listed
under the Recreation Dept. listing for each city in the white pages of
your phone book. YMCA's often have pools as well. (See that section
of this chapter). Best time to meet single people is early mornings, during
the lunch hour, and after work.

Dolphin Swim & Boat Club, Foot of Hyde, San Francisco, (415) 441-9329.
Montclair Swim Club, 1901 Woodhaven Way, Oakland, (415) 339-2500.
Napa Swim Club, Box 2515, Napa 94558, (707) 252-7244.
Oak Hill Swim Club, 7624 Olive, Pleasanton, (415) 846-8822.
Palo Alto Swim Club, 777 Embarcadero, Palo Alto, (415) 327-7459.
Petaluma Swim Club, 3 English, Petaluma 94952, (707) 763-8140.
Santa Clara Swim Club, 2625 Patricia Dr., Santa Clara, (408) 246-5050.
Sunnyvale Swim Club, (408) 244-3618. Mon-Fri, 3:45-6:30pm, Mango
    Pool, Sunnyvale.
Vacaville Swim Club, 447-1676.
Valley Swim Association, San Ramon, (415) 820-4182.

TENNIS

You can meet singles at no cost by going to any public tennis court.
An alternative is to join private tennis clubs, which are listed in the
yellow pages of your phone book.

California Tennis Association, 2455 Bush, S.F. 94118, (415) 346-3611.
East Bay Tennis Matchmakers, (415) 548-6240. Mixed doubles, dinners,
    dancing at Blackhawk Tennis Villas, Danville and Amador Valley
    Athletic Club, Pleasanton.
Fairfield Tennis Club, Box 604, Fairfield 94523.
Napa Valley Tennis Association, 1375 Trower, Napa 94558, 257-8361.
Northern California Tennis Association, 645 5th St., San Francisco 94107,
    (415) 775-5683.

TENNIS (continued)

San Ramon Valley Tennis Club, (415) 837-1643.
Sunnyvale Tennis Club, (408) 736-7006.
Tennis Matchmakers, (415) 548-6240. 30+.
Tuesday Night Tennis, (415) 521-0440. Mixed doubles for single people, Tuesdays during summer, 6:30-8pm, at Golden Gate Park Tennis Courts. Dinner afterwards at a member's home. Another group meets at Golden Gate Park on Wednesdays.

VOLLEYBALL

Apres Singles Ski Club, Box 1027, Mountain View 94042, 377-5966 or 259-5142.
Bota Baggers Singles Ski Club, Box 772, Pleasanton 94566, 443-4451 (tape) or 275-0317. Tuesdays, 8pm, Velvet Turtle, Sheraton Hotel.
Fall Line Ski Club, Box 2367, San Rafael 94912.
Green Earth Singles, Box 7933, Santa Cruz 95061, 338-2366. Mondays, 7-9pm.
Inskiers Ski Club, Box 5065, San Mateo 94402, 494-8243 (Bonnie Soeas) or 364-5490 (Sandy).
Monterey Outdoor Singles (M.O.S.) Box 51416, Pacific Grove 93950, (408) 624-0202. Tuesday nights. Mainly 30-60.
Powder Hounds Singles Ski Club, Box 12763, Oakland 94604, (415) 769-7669. Thursdays.
Rusty Bindings Ski Club, Box 3096, Walnut Creek 94598, 724-3093 (Mariell Jaren).
San Francisco Ski Club, Box 421765, San Francisco 94101, (415) 337-9333.
Sierra Singles
   Bay Area Chapter, Sierra Club, 6014 College, Oakland 94618, 548-0591 (Phil Gale). 21-40.
   Loma Prieta Chapter, Box 391775, Mountain View 94039. 21+.
Snow Drifters Ski Club, Box 396, Mountain View 94042, 265-4206 (Bill Turner).

WEIGHT-LIFTING

Here's a sport that is ideal for meeting single men. If you are a woman, go down to your local gym, health club, or Y.M.C.A. and start pumping iron.

WRESTLING

Professional wrestling events are quite popular nowadays.
Many are held at the Cow Palace in Daly City.

Bay Area Triathlon Club, (415) 282-4491.

Berkeley Water Ski Club, Aquatic Park at Bolivar Dr., Berkeley (415) 540-9396.

Chinese Sportsmen Club, 773 Sacramento, San Francisco 94108, (415) 362-9786.

Concord Athletic League, Box 58, Concord 94520, (415) 687-6750.

Concordia Sport Club, 2355 Ocean, San Francisco 94132, (415) 239-9602.

Indoor Sports Club for Physically Disabled, 391 17th Ave., San Francisco 94121, (415) 751-4300.

Menlo Polo Club, 2070 Manzanita Ave., Menlo Park, (415) 854-4211.

Menlo Sportsmen Social Club, 2110 Dumbarton Ave., East Palo Alto, (415) 326-6803, 853-8923.

Outdoors Unlimited, 500 Parnassus, San Francisco 94143, (415) 666-2078, is a cooperative resource center for outdoor adventures for all skill & experience levels. Also offers skills clinics, reasonably priced equipment rental, cooperative outings, and trip planning information in the following areas: day hikes, nature study, backpacking, mountaineering, cross-country skiing, bicycling, canoeing, kayaking, white water rafting, windsurfing, sailing, safety & first aid. You will receive a free quarterly newsletter if you send a stamped, self-addressed envelope.

Peninsula Sportsmens Clubs, 1600 Rutgers, East Palo Alto, (415) 853-8889.

Sportsmatch, 2966 Diamond St. #103, San Francisco 94131, (415) 467-9955. Matches sports partners.

Squash Club of San Francisco, 525 Harrison, 957-0400.

Sunnyvale Badminton Club, (408) 735-8484.

DANCING

Many women complain that they get involved with men they meet at dances who never take them out dancing. That's because most men don't really like to dance. The only reason they attend dances is because walking up to someone on the street is a tough way to meet women. It takes guts. At a dance, on the other hand, it's socially acceptable to walk up to a complete stranger and ask for three minutes of her time. At the end of the dance either of you can say thank you and move on. Or, if you like each other, you can continue to dance or sit down and chat. Easy in, easy out.

What do you do if you don't like to dance? Learn! It's difficult to enjoy an activity unless you have some proficiency at it. If you still don't enjoy dancing after taking lessons, go out dancing anyway. You're going to be hard-pressed to find an easier method for meeting the opposite sex.

A few of the best dance schools are included in this chapter. The dance instruction section of the yellow pages of your phone book lists many others. Choose one that caters primarily to single adults. Usually at these dance lessons you will automatically meet many different partners of the opposite sex, even if you're shy!

Some singles complain that dances are "meat markets". They are. The correct spelling, however, is "meet markets". Dances are the most popular social activity in America to meet a romantic partner.

Many nightclubs feature dancing. The most popular ones are listed in the next chapter. What do you do if you hate the bar scene? Attend a dance sponsored by one of the organizations listed below. Choose one that specializes in your favorite type of dancing, be it ballroom, swing, square, folk, rock, or disco.

Also listed below are regular dances throughout the Bay Area that are open to both singles and couples. Of course these dances are always subject to change. For up to date information on what's going on in the Bay Area dance scene, subscribe to the **Ballroom Dancer's Rag**, a monthly magazine that lists numerous dances and dance clubs throughout the Bay Area. Send $1.45 per copy or $11.65 per year to 1448 Montego Dr., San Jose 95120 or call (408) 268-6042 or 252-4940.

Another valuable resource is the **Dance Directory** by Marge Gabbert, with suggestions on where to go dancing in the Bay Area, including ballroom, swing, and Latin/salsa. Contact Fascinating Rhythm Dance School, 28 Prague, San Francisco 94112, (415) 334-9914.

BALLROOM & SWING DANCING

ALAMEDA
Alameda Theater, 2317 Central. Ballroom, Sundays, 6-10pm.
Mecca Ballroom Dance Party, 2305 Alameda Ave., Alameda.

BERKELEY
Ballroom Dancing in Berkeley, Charlene Van Ness, 2600 Bancroft, Berkeley, (415) 848-6370.
Berkeley Ballroom Dancers, 2525 8th. Sundays, 4-6; Fridays, 7-10pm.
Berkeley Singles, Box 456, Berkeley 94710, (415) 236-8840. Ballroom dancing to live music, even Fridays, 8:30pm-12:30am, Cerrito City Club, Potrero & Kearney, El Cerrito. Mainly 40+.
University of California, Chris Williams, (415) 527-1486. Wednesdays, Ballroom Dancing.
University YWCA Dance & Fitness Classes, 2600 Bancroft Way, Berkeley 94704, (415) 848-6370. Flamenco, salsa, jazz, Polynesian, ballroom classes.

BURLINGAME
Guys & Dolls, Box 5, Burlingame 94010, (415) 342-8471 (Laverne Parker). Live music, Fridays, Burlingame Women's Club, 241 Park Rd., Burlingame. Mainly 40+. For singles only.

CAMPBELL
Men-Gals, Box 1145, Campbell 95009, 298-6391. Odd Fridays, 9pm, American Legion Hall, 1344 Dell. 40+. For singles only.

CONCORD
Merry Mixers, Box 993, Concord 94522. Odd Fridays, Sportsman Club, Evora Rd., Concord. Mainly 40+. For singles only.

DANVILLE
Dance America, 268 S. Hartz Ave., Danville, (415) 838-DANCE.
Tea Dancing, 120 S. Hartz Blvd., Danville. Thursdays, 1-3pm.

DUBLIN
Shannon Seniors Dance Club, 1600 Shannon. Tuesdays, 1-4pm.

EL CERRITO
Dancing for Fun, Belinda Ricklefs, El Cerrito, (415) 893-1519. Swing, Ballroom, Latin, Jitterbug dance lessons for beginners.

FAIRFAX
Dance Spirit, Fairfax Health Club, 711 Center Blvd, (415) 453-1613.

FREMONT
Choices, 5399 Farwell Pl., Fremont, (415) 791-1660. Tea Dances, Sundays, 5-9:30pm.

GREENBRAE
Body & Soul, 208 Bon Air Shopping Ctr, Greenbrae 94904, 459-0832.

LOS GATOS
Villa Felice, 15350 Winchester, Los Gatos. Ballroom.

MARIN
Dance Extravaganza, 625-6240. Classes in, Mill Valley/Larkspur.

MORGAN HILL
Flying Lady, 15060 Foothill Rd., Morgan Hill.

BALLROOM & SWING DANCING (continued)

NAPA

Ballroom Dancers, Inc., Box 3081, Napa 94558, (707) 255-7697 (John) or (707) 224-0834 (Burl) or 253-0890.

Napa Town & Country Fairgrounds, Arts & Crafts Bldg., (707) 255-3330 or 255-7697. Fridays, 8:30 pm.

Senior Center, 1500 Jefferson St., (707) 255-1800. Tuesdays & Saturdays, 8-11 pm. 50+ age group.

OAKLAND

Ali Baba Dance Club, Scottish Rite Temple, 1547 Lakeside, 465-0669. Ballroom, big band jazz, Latin. Fridays, 8pm-12, $7.

Grand Dance, 3501 Grand Ave. (at Mandana), Oakland, (415) 835-94960. West Coast Swing, Saturdays, 8-11pm.

National Smooth Dancers, Oakland, (415) 989-2473 (Carl). 4th Saturdays.

Romantic Ballroom, John & Cynthia Bilorusky, 473 Hudson, Oakland, (415) 547-1069.

PACIFIC GROVE

Chatauqua Club, Pacific Grove, 394-0270 (Harry). Dancing, Saturdays.

PALO ALTO

Garfield's, 3901 El Camino Real, Palo Alto. Big Band.

Los Amigos, YMCA, 3412 Ross, Palo Alto, (408) 494-1883. Thursdays, 8pm, Sundays, 8pm, & even Saturdays, 8:30pm. Also bridge.

Pavilion, 4000 Middlefield, Palo Alto, (415) 489-9368 (Robin). Fridays, 8pm (lessons), 9pm-12 (dance). $4.

Palo Alto Masonic Temple, 461 Florence, (415) 856-8044 (Stan). Vintage Ballroom, Mondays, 8-10pm (lesson & dance).

TGA Singles, YWCA, 4161 Alma St., Palo Alto, 494-0972 or 969-9772 (Antonio Fernandes). Ballroom Dancing, odd Saturdays & dance classes, Tuesdays, 7-8pm, followed by dancing.

Viennese Waltz Seminars (held in Palo Alto), Robin Rebello, 4932 Casper St., Union City 94587, (415) 489-9368.

PLEASANTON

Pleasanton Hotel, 855 Main, Pleasanton 94566, (415) 846-8106. Big Band, 1st Sundays, 5-9pm.

Popis, 3059 Hopyard, Pleasanton. Tuesdays, 9-1, and Wednesdays, 7:30-10:30pm, Veterans Memorial Bldg, 301 Main St.

REDWOOD CITY

Imperial Dance Club, 822 Cassia St., Redwood City 94063, (415) 366-0504 (Rex Lewis & Denise Jourdaine). Classes in ballroom & Latin dance. Ballroom dance, Saturdays.

RICHMOND

Hacienda, 12020 San Pablo, Richmond. Dancing/lessons, Sundays, 4-9pm.

SAN ANSELMO

Dance-It Together, Knights of Columbus Hall, 167 Tunstead Ave., (415) 459-0983. Frank & Nancy Flores.

Marin Solos, Box 335, Novato 94948, 479-3827. Live music, 1st Saturdays, 9pm, $6, Isabel Cook Recreation Ctr, 1000 Sir Francis Drake Bl, San Anselmo. Dress code. Mainly 40+. For singles only.

SAN FRANCISCO

Avenue Ballroom, 603 Taraval, 681-2882. Sundays, 8-11pm.

Bay Swingers Dance Club, Box 4410, S.F. 94101 (415) 994-2856/351-9296 or 957-0177 (Joe). Free dance lessons before dancing starts.

The Boat House, Skyline Blvd. Swing dancing, Tuesdays, 8-12.

Dancers Unlimited, Arthur Calandrelli, (415) 282-3195. Ballroom & Latin lessons.

Golden Gate Swing Club, (415) 626-1004 (Jim). Sundays.

International Ballroom, 50 Oak St., (415) 863-7676.

International Latin & Smooth & Rhythm Dance Lessons, Dan Santiago, (415) 752-5658 or 755-7548.

Kimball's, 300 Grove. Swing Fever, Wednesdays, 8-12.

National Smooth Dancers, (415) 989-2473 (Carl).

Pick School of Ballroom Dancing, 380 18th Ave., (415) 752-5658. Ballroom dance lessons Tuesdays, Wednesdays, & Thursdays, 7 pm. Dance Party, even Saturdays, 8pm-12.

Renaissance School of Dance, 285 Ellis, (415) 474-0920 (Teddy Leigh). American smooth, Latin, ballroom lessons. Dance Party, Fridays, 9-11:30pm.

Roll up the Carpet with Cynthia Glinka, 5214-F Diamond Hts Blvd. #F, S.F. 94131, (415) 469-0422. Tea dancing, mainly singles.

Ruvano Dance Studio, 1290 Sutter. Ballroom, Fridays, 8-11pm.

S.F. Dance Hall, 827 Hyde, (415) 771-5600. Ballroom, Fridays, 8pm-1. Swing, Saturdays, 8pm-1.

S.F. Samba Club, Studio Brasil, 50 Brady St., (415) 863-8291. Josephine Morada & Chalo Eduardo.

S.F. School of Ballroom Dancing, 63 Onondaga, (415) 333-5570. 4th Sundays.

Slavonic Cultural Center, 60 Onondaga, (415) 585-6282 (Michelle). Swing, 2nd Sundays, 5pm (lesson), 6-10pm (dance).

Vintage Dance Club, 1885 Mission St., (415) 826-1914. Swing & ballroom lessons.

SAN JOSE

California Dance Club, 938 The Alameda, San Jose 95126, (408) 297-9772. Ballroom.

Cypress Senior Center, 403 S. Cypress Ave., San Jose. Ballroom.

National Smooth Dancers, San Jose, (408) 739-8869 (Charlene). Mondays.

Over 40 Singles, Box 9593, San Jose 95157.

SAN LEANDRO
San Leandro Library, 300 Estudillo. Senior Swing Dances, 1st, 4th, & 5th Wednesdays, 1-4pm.
SAN LORENZO
Eden Singles, 21455 Birch St., Hayward 94541. 3rd Saturdays, San Lorenzo Community Center, 377 Paseo Grande, San Lorenzo.
SAN MATEO
Beau'n Belles Dance Club, St. Bartholomew's Gym, Alameda de las Pulgas, San Mateo.
Dance Connection sponsors ballroom dancing Mondays at Crystal Springs Hall, Alameda de las Pulgas, San Mateo.
Peninsula Ballroom Dance Club, (415) 490-0479 (Henry). Fridays.
Peninsula Social Club, Top of Beardsleys, 1010 N. B St., (415) 659-1740 or 886-3487. Wednesdays, 7-9pm (lessons), 9-12 (dance).
SAN RAFAEL
DanceArts Studio, Montecito Plaza, 361 3rd St., (415) 459-1020. Dance Party, Odd Fridays, 8pm-12.
SANTA CLARA
Single Ballroom Dancers, (408) 268-6042 (Dick Wilson). Thursdays, 8-11pm, Senior Ctr, Fremont & Monroe, Santa Clara.
SANTA CRUZ
Ballroom Classes, Thursdays, 7-8pm, German/American Hall, 230 Plymouth, Santa Cruz.
Santa Cruz Ballroom Dance Club, 1214 1/2 Pacific Ave., Santa Cruz.
West Coast Swing, Becky Adams, Box 1204, Soquel 95073, (408) 475-4427. Tuesdays, Santa Cruz,
SANTA ROSA
Arthur Murray Studio, Cleveland Square Shopping Center, 3401 Cleveland Ave. #7, Santa Rosa, (707) 575-9226. Dance parties.
Bill & Juanita Robinson, Santa Rosa, (707) 542-6066.
Dancetime Dance Studio, 320 W. 3rd St #H, Santa Rosa, (707) 575-0606. Swing & Ballroom, Fridays, 7pm (lesson), 8:30-12 (dance). Redwood Empire Swing Dance Club, (707) 579-0339. 2nd Sundays.
Flamingo Hotel, Santa Rosa, Swing, 1st Sundays, 1:30-6pm.
Social Singles, Box 511, Santa Rosa 95402, 528-8632. live music, 3rd Saturdays, 9pm, Veterans Memorial Bldg. 40+.
West Coast Swing Dance Club, Santa Rosa, (707) 575-7633.
Vets Club, Santa Rosa, (707) 545-7340 (Porter).
SEBASTOPOL
Continentalaires, Sebastopol, (707) 528-4829.
SONOMA
Cabaret Sauvignon, 478 1st St. E. Ballroom, Sonoma. Sundays, 5-8pm.
SOUTH BAY
Christian Singles Ballroom Dancing. Judy Walter at (408) 736-7211.

BALLROOM & SWING DANCING (continued)

SUNNYVALE
  Belleswingers, 297-3947. Wednesdays, 7:30pm, Cumberland School.
  Hai Yuan, 711 Town & Country Village, Sunnyvale.
  Starlite Ballroom, 1160 N. Fair Oaks, Sunnyvale, (408)745-STAR.
  Ballroom, Fridays ($6) & Saturdays ($8), 8pm (lesson), 9-12 (dance).
  Ballroom (80s music), Sundays, 7pm (lesson), 8-11pm (dance), $7.
  Sunnyvale Ballroom Dance Club, 248-0304. 1st Fridays, 8:30pm, TRI-
VALLEY
  Phran Turner's Dance Classes, 635 Hemlock Ct., Livermore.
VACAVILLE
  Vacaville Senior Center, 411 Kendal St., (707) 449-5192.
VALLEJO
  Friendly Singles, (707) 642-6751 or 648-4630. Mondays, 7:30pm, Dan
  Foley Park in Vallejo. For singles only. 40+.
WALNUT CREEK
  Acalanes Adult Center, 1963 Tice Valley Blvd., W.C. 94595, 935-0170.
  Ballroom Dance Classes for Singles, (415) 687-5270. Classes are held
  at Veterans Hall in Walnut Creek. Monthly dance party.
  Dance World, 15 Sage Ct., W.C. 94596, (415) 938-1434. Ballroom &
  social dance. 2nd Saturdays, 7-10:30pm, Dance & Lesson, $8.
  Diablo Singles, Box 5067, Walnut Creek 94596, 820-4299. Live music,
  3rd Saturdays, Civic Park Community Ctr. 40+.
  5th Wheelers, Box 4569, W.C. 94596, 676-7129. Live music, even
  Saturdays, Veteran's Hall, 1250 Locust, $4. 40+. For singles only.
YOUNTVILLE
  Yountville Veterans Home, (707) 944-4534 or 944-8158. Grant Hall,
  Sundays, 1:30-3:30 pm. No charge. All welcome.
MISCELLANEOUS
  Carousel Dance Club, (415) 468-4499 (Fred). 2nd Saturdays.
  Debonairs, (415) 656-6660 (Ed).
  Phil Riservato, (415) 487-7802 or 487-6287. Private or group lessons.
  Social Dance for Shy People & Klutzes, (415) 530-4019. L. Lepoff.

FOLK DANCING

BERKELEY
  Ashkenaz, 1317 San Pablo, Berkeley, (415) 525-5054. Folk dance lessons
  and dances, Tues-Wed., 9:30pm. African, reggae, swing, square
  dance, Latin, Thur-Sat., 9:30pm.
  Berkeley Folk Dancers, Box 9091, Berkeley 94709, 845-1905/525-5851.
  International House Folk Dancing, 2299 Piedmont Ave., Berkeley
  94720, (415) 642-9490.
  University of California Folk Dancers, (415) 642-3288.
COTATI
  Folk Dancing, Cotati, (707) 823-0526.

LAFAYETTE
Scottish Country Dancing, (415) 934-6148/837-9483.
MILL VALLEY
Able Steppers of Marin, 81 Montford Ave., M.V. 94941, 388-4332.
Almonte Dancers, 40 Glen Dr., Mill Valley 94941, (415) 383-1014.
Bay Area Scandia Dancers, 40 Glen Dr., M.V. 94941, (415) 383-1014.
Kopachka Dancers, 40 Glen Dr., Mill Valley 94941, (415) 383-1014.
Mill Valley Scottish Country Dancers, 745 Alta Vista Rd., MV 94941, (415) 388-7031.
NAPA
International Folk Dance Classes, 1025 Napa Rd., Napa, (707) 938-2226 (June Schaal). Mondays and Thursdays, 7pm.
Napa Valley Folk Dance Club, (707) 944-2069. Tuesdays, catch-up class, 7-8 pm; intermediate folk dancing, 8-10pm. Kennedy Park Multi-Purpose Bldg., 2296 Streblow Dr., Napa.
PALO ALTO
Stanford Folkdancers, (415) 723-1234.
PETALUMA
International Folk Dancing, Petaluma, (707) 892-9405.
SAN FRANCISCO
Rikudom Israeli Folk Dancers, Bethany Church, Clipper & Sanchez, 647-2483. Sundays, 7-10pm, $2.50 (includes one-hour lesson. After 10pm the group goes out for ice cream.
SANTA ROSA
Santa Rosa Folk Dance Club, (707) 546-8877.
Santa Rosa Folk Dancers, 5430 Hutchison Rd., Sebastopol 95472, (707) 823-3826.
ST. HELENA
Robert Louis Stevenson Gym, 1316 Hillview Park Place, St. Helena, (707) 963-5706 or 965-9372. Country Dancing, Saturdays, 8pm.
MISCELLANEOUS
Folk Dance Federation of California, 1275 A St. #111, Hayward 94541, (415) 581-6000.
Greater East Bay Folk Dance Council, 24013 Fairlands Rd., Hayward 94541 or 6200 Alhambra, Martinez 94553.
Scottish Country Dancing, (415) 333-9372.

SQUARE DANCING

BENICIA
Old Capitol Squares, 189 Carlisle, Benicia 94510.
BERKELEY
Solos & Pairs, 1799 Euclid, Berkeley, (415) 848-7041.

CONCORD
  Square Dance Information, 1033 E. Shary Cir., Concord 94518, (415) 687-4092.
  Yellow Rock Singles, 1844 Clayton, Concord 94520, 671-0730 (Mervin).
HAYWARD
  Square Dance Club, 28293 Applegate, Hayward 94545.
LAFAYETTE
  Walnut Whirlers, 1542 Pleasant Ln., Lafayette 94549, (415) 939-2430 or 757-9033.
MARTINEZ
  Diablo Singles, 26 Lagunitas Ct., Martinez 94553, 228-3654 or 798-5797. Thursdays, 7:30pm, Fair Oaks Sch.
NAPA
  Boots & Belles, Welcome Grange Hall, 3275 Hagen Rd., (707) 224-8207 (days) or 255-3538 (eves). Square Dancing, Wednesdays, 8 pm.
  Boot Heel Ramblers, Welcome Grange Hall, 3275 Hagen Rd., (707) 224-9046 or 552-9462. Square Dancing, Fridays, 7:30-10:30pm.
  5 Star Squares, Welcome Grange Hall, 3275 Hagen Rd., (707) 224-2001. Square & Round Dancing, Tuesdays, 7:30-10pm.
  Napa Buzzsteppers, Welcome Grange Hall, 3275 Hagen Rd., (707) 224-5883 or 255-2180. Mainstream Plus Square Dancing, Thursdays.
NOVATO
  Novato Sidekicks, 124 Marin Valley Dr., Novato 94947, (415) 897-1298, 883-6084 or 456-1621.
  Novato Stump Jumpers, Box 123, Novato 94947, 897-9489 or 883-7072.
PALO ALTO
  Bay Area Country Dance Society, Palo Alto, (415) 321-2773.
  Bows & Beaus, 3631 Evergreen, Palo Alto, 494-8236 (M. West). Mondays, Monta Loma Sch.
  Stanford Quads, 3280 Ross Rd., 494-0603 (P. Curtis). Sundays, Old Union Clubhouse.
PENINSULA
  Peninsula Federation of Square Dancers, 730 Ulloa, San Francisco 94127, (415) 661-9788.
PENNGROVE
  Question Marks Square Club, Penngrove, (707) 546-3430.
PETALUMA
  Adobe Squares, Box 372, Petaluma 94953, (707) 762-2445.
PLEASANTON
  Pleasanton Singles, Camp Parks, RFTA, Bldg. 790, Dublin 94568, (415) 484-3513 or 449-7015.
SAN FRANCISCO
  Bachelors 'n' Bachelorettes, 55 Garcia 94127, 566-3563/681-4843. S.F.
  Bay Area Dance Coalition, Ft. Mason, (415) 673-8172 or 333-5570.

SAN JOSE
Bachelors 'n' Bachelorettes, Bill Gates, 965 Katherine, San Jose 95126, 249-1609, or Mike, (408) 374-6148. Mainly 40+. For singles only.
Single Squares, 720 Laguna Seca Ct, San Jose 95123, 227-2162 (G. Carnes). Thursdays, Mt. View H.S.
SAN LORENZO
San Lorenzo Singles, 16871 President, S.L. 94578, 278-6957 (Eldon) or 490-4096. Square & round dancing Tuesdays, 7:30-10pm, Ashland Community Ctr, 167th Ave., in San Leandro. Mainly 40+.
SAN MATEO
Bachelors 'n' Bachelorettes, Marvin G. Smith, 3633 Colegrove #12, San Mateo 94403, (415) 345-9853, or Ben, 278-3290. For singles only.
SANTA CLARA
Santa Clara Square Dancers, 170 W. Rincon Ave. #8, Campbell 95008.
Single Clara, 1802 Amelia #2, S.C. 95050, (408) 244-1668 (M. Wyman). Square dancing, Fridays, Kinderwood Pre-Sch.
SANTA ROSA
Circle & Squares Dance Club, Santa Rosa, (707) 546-1623.
Markwesterners' Square Dance Club, Santa Rosa, (707) 528-4829.
Singles & Pairs Square Dance Club, Santa Rosa, (707) 545-1513.
SEBASTOPOL
Sebastopol Spinners (Square Dance), (707) 829-1944.
SUNNYVALE
Sunnyvale Singles, 837 Mulberry, Sunnyvale 94087, (408) 739-6862.
Sunnyvale Singles Squares, (480) 997-2653 (Jim) or 227-2162. 30+.
VALLEJO
Pioneer Square Dances, (707) 648-4640. Vallejo Community Center, 225 Amador. Mondays, 7-10pm.
MISCELLANEOUS
Northern California Square Dancers Association, 7044 Corinth Ct., Dublin 94568, (415) 826-6071
San Francisco Bay Area Dance Coalition Information & Referral, 2141 Mission, (415) 255-2794.

MISCELLANEOUS DANCING

LIVERMORE
Country & Western Dance Classes, 1467 Wagoner Dr., Livermore 94550, (415) 443-9254. Nora Wilt.
Phran Turner's Dance Classes, 635 Hemlock Ct., Livermore. Western Dance Classes, Wednesday nights, Livermore.
MT. VIEW
Reach, 1495 El Camino Real, (415) 965-3018. 50s & 60s music and swing dance lessons in a smoke-free, alcohol free environment. Cappucinos, juices, hot coco, colas, and snacks are served.

OAKLAND

Caribee Dance Center, 1408 Webster St., Oakland, (415) 835-4006. Reggae, Wednesdays & Fridays. Salsa, Thursdays. Caribbean, Saturdays. Variety Sundays. Dance lessons begin at 5:30pm. Dancing begins at 9pm.

Dance Jam, 2822-A Union St., Oakland, (415) 526-0964. Fridays, 9pm-12:30. $5.

Oakland Theatre of Dance, 4226 park Blvd., Oakland 94602.

SAN BRUNO

Dance Party, 444 San Mateo, San Bruno. Tuesdays, 8-11:30pm; Saturdays, 8pm-12:30.

SAN CARLOS

Los Danzeros, 1617 Belmont Ave., San Carlos 94070, (415) 593-4977.

SAN FRANCISCO

Dance Action, Studio 101, 101A S. Van Ness, San Francisco 94103, (415) 621-8820/968-5959.

The Dance Art of Isadora Duncan, Maria Villazana-Ruiz, 3435 Army St. #240, (415) 587-0730.

SAN JOSE

South Bay Dance & Social Club, 516 El Paseo de Saratoga, 370-6961.

SAN LORENZO

Checkmates, 1st Christian Church, 15661 Washington, 278-0517.

SANTA CLARA

Josetta School of Dance, 3280 El Camino, Santa Clara, (408) 296-3245.

SANTA CLARA COUNTY

Coronets, (408) 736-4255 (Paul). Thursdays.

Mates & Dates Stardancers Club, (408) 226-5493 (Dan).

Nite Outers, (408) 267-4569 (Diane).

Sea & Tree Dance Club, (408) 724-2502 (Bob).

Stardusters Club, (408) 377-9365 (Dale). 4th Saturdays.

SANTA ROSA

Nostalgia Dance Club, (707) 585-1859 or 538-1647.

Traditional Jazz, (707) 542-3973 (Tom). 1st Mondays.

MISCELLANEOUS

Bach Dancing & Dynamite Society, (415) 726-3839. Dinners, dancing, and concerts.

Berkeley Morris Dancers, 3437 Birdsall, Oakland 94619, 536-4081.

Choreographers Performance Alliance, 1442-A Walnut #390, Berkeley 94709, (415) 268-1940/398-6700.

Dance Time Studios, 1015 Camelia.

Los Olmecas Ballet Folklorico, 33129 Great Salt Lake Dr., Fremont 94536, (415) 489-6579.

South Indian Dance, Karen Elliott, (415) 845-3431.

Wallflower Order Dance Collective, Box 2962, Berkeley 94704, (415) 848-5824.

NIGHTCLUBS

Everybody hates singles bars. Or so they say. That's despite the fact that singles bars are loaded with single people who want to meet someone nice for a romantic relationship. So why don't we all love singles bars?

Go to a singles bar on a Friday or Saturday night and you'll find out the answer. Have you heard of the 80-20 Rule? It means that 20% of baseball players hit 80% of the home runs and 20% of fishermen catch 80% of the fish. At singles bars, 20% of the people get 80% of the action. The rest go home without having met anybody nice. No wonder they hate singles bars.

You can be one of the 20% who meet nice people in bars. You just have to follow the rules. Here are **three suggestions for men:**

1. Don't drink. Women are paranoid about meeting an alcoholic in a bar. The more you drink the less attractive you'll be. Furthermore, the more time you spend drinking the less time you'll have to meet women, which is the purpose of going to the bar in the first place. After all, you can drink at home for a fraction of the cost and not have to worry about being picked up for drunk driving. So drink at home and meet women at bars.
2. Skip the bar area and go straight out to the tables in the dark corners of the bar. That's where all the women are hiding. Most of the men will be too shy to approach them. That means that no matter how crowded the bar may be, there really isn't all that much competition. Ask a woman to dance (or if you're in a quiet bar, introduce yourself and ask if you can join her for some conversation.)
3. Don't give up until you meet someone attractive. The 80% of men who don't get their needs met in singles bars give up after one or two rejections. They rush back to the bar and order a double. If you get turned down by a woman go on to another table on the other side of the bar. Keep asking until you meet someone who finds you attractive. Most of the women who go to singles bars aren't there to talk to their friends, get drunk, or listen to the music. They are there to meet men. Do them and yourself a favor. Make contact.

Likewise, you can meet many fine men if you follow these suggestions for **three suggestions for women:**

1. Go alone. If you go with your friends you'll spend all night talking to them instead of meeting men. If you need a ride then enter the bar separately once you arrive. There's no reason why you can't leave together with your friends later in the evening, but don't sit with them while you're supposed to be meeting men.

2. Sit or stand at the bar, not the tables in the dark corners of the bar. The bar is where all the men are. You'll be approachable. You'll meet more men than any other woman in the singles bar.
3. Stand up for your rights and your needs. If a man is obnoxious, tell him. If he won't take a hint, then move away from him. Also, don't allow yourself to be cornered for the rest of the evening by some nice guy who is inappropriate for you. Tell him you enjoyed meeting him and would like to meet other men as well. Or, if you don't have the guts to be honest, tell him you have to powder your nose and then return to a different part of the room.

If you don't feel comfortable in bars, that's fine. There are plenty of better places to meet people. But if you do decide to go to a singles bar, do it right. Follow the rules so that your experience will be a happy, satisfying one.

Which bars should you frequent? That depends on personal taste. There are two main types of singles bars: conversation bars and dance bars. **Conversation Bars** are places where you can easily carry on a conversation. The music is for background, not dancing. This is ideal for getting to know someone. There's only one catch. At a conversation bar it's difficult for people to meet. There's no easy, socially acceptable way to introduce yourself by asking someone to dance. So if you're a man and know you won't have the nerve to engage anyone in conversation, skip the conversation bars. If you're a woman, sitting at a table is the kiss of death. Very few men will have the guts to initiate contact.

The second type of singles bars, **Dance Bars**, are the most popular because it easier to meet people. The disadvantage, of course, is that it's next to impossible to carry on a conversation with the music blaring in your ears. What's the solution? Go to a place with live music, rather than a disk jockey. Every 45 minutes the band will sit down and you'll be able to converse with new friends.

What do you do if you don't like to dance and have a hard time making contact at a conversation bar? I've heard of one single woman who goes to a different bar every Monday night during the football season. She couldn't tell you the difference between a touchdown and a home run. All she does is sit in a corner and balance her checkbook. The men come over to meet her during breaks in the action because she's more interesting to them than the beer commercials.

Another option is to go to bars that feature free hors d'oeuvres (usually 5-6pm). When you see someone attractive of the opposite sex in the food line, stand behind them and ask that them what's good to eat. Even if you don't meet anybody special at least you're getting a free meal!

What do you do if you don't drink? Order club soda or a soft drink. Nowadays a good percentage of men and women who go to bars don't drink alcohol. If you hate being around alcohol go a cafe that features espresso.

ALAMEDA

Beltline Station, 1700 Clement, 523-4668. Hors d'oeuvres, M-F, 4-7pm.

Croll's Bar & Grill, 1400 Webster, 522-8439. Live music, Fridays. DJ, Saturdays. No cover.

Top 4 Club, Bldg 585, Naval Air Station, 869-4441.

Twilight Zone, Alameda Theater, 2317 Central Ave., (415) 769-0198. Modern rock, Fri-Sat. Swing/ballroom, Sundays, 6-10pm. Cover charge.

BERKELEY

Au Coquelet, 2000 University Ave., (415) 845-0433. Conversation bar.

Berkeley Square, 1333 University, 849-3374. Live music & DJ. Cover.

Blake Street Garage, 2029 Blake.

Cafe Bistro, 2271 Shattuck, 9415) 848-3081. Live jazz every night.

California Dream Cafe, 2041 Center, 843-9343. Rap & funk, Fri-Sat.

Freight & Salvage, 1827 San Pablo, 548-1761, Live music.

Gilman Street, 924 Gilman, 525-9926. Rock music.

H's Lordship's, 199 Seawall Dr., 843-2733.

Kesha's Inn, 2618 San Pablo, 486-9157.

La Pena, 3105 Shattuck, 849-2568. Live Latin, Brazilian dance music, Fri-Sat. Cover charge.

Larry Blake's, 2367 Telegraph, 848-0888. Blues music, Mon-Sat. Cover charge.

La Val's Subterranean, 1834 Euclid, 540-7743. Folk & country music.

Roaring Rock, 1920 Shattuck, 843-2739. Good place to meet shuffleboard players.

Starry Plough, 3101 Shattuck, 841-2082. Live rock music, Thur-Sat. Irish dancing, Mondays. Variety of music on Sundays. Cover charge.

Windsurf Bar & Grill, 235 University, 845-7656. DJ, Fri-Mon. Cover charge.

Your Place Too, 5319 Martin Luther King Jr. Way. Live blues music.

CASTRO VALLEY

Krayon's Gallery, 3477 Castro Valley Blvd, 581-4186. TGIF.

Muggy's, 20920 Redwood, 582-8200.

DUBLIN

Jimmy O'Gills, 11873 Dublin Bl, 833-2613. Music every night.

EMERYVILLE

Carrara's, 1290 Powell, (415) 547-6763. Cafe. No alcohol.

Carlos Murphy's, 5901 Frontage Rd., 547-6766.

Kimball's East, 5800 Shellmound, 658-2555. Live jazz, salsa music, dancing. Cover charge.

Townhouse, 5862 Doyle, 652-5336. Live music. Cover charge.

FREMONT

Black Angus, 3101 Walnut, 794-8222. DJ every night. Young crowd.

Choices, 5399 Farwell, 791-1660. DJ every night. Huge, elegant singles bar. Mainly 20s & 30s age group. Cover charge varies.

FREMONT (continued)
  Fremont Inn, 46845 Warm Springs Blvd.
  King's Inn, 41025 N. Trimboli, 657-2324.
  Niles Station, 37501 Niles Blvd., 794-7797. Live rock music, Tue-Sun.
    Cover charge.
  Sergio's Supper Club, 3890 Mowry, 797-7970. Live dance music every
    night.
  Sheila's Cage, 4500 Peralta, 796-8072.
  South 40 Club, 46850 Warm Springs, 657-8935. Live country music
    Wed.-Sat. and free country dance lessons Wed.-Thu., 7:30-9pm.
HAYWARD
  Amador West, 253 W. Jackson 785-5677. Dancing.
  The Beat, 24744 Mission, 881-4789.
  Calhoun's, 18974 Meekland, 276-5121. Live dance music Thu.-Sun.
  Casa Carlita's, 24041 Southland Dr., (415) 782-8100. DJ, Tue-Sat. Top
    40, reggae. No cover.
  Catrina's Lounge, 225 W. Winton, 782-4030.
  Detton's, 939 B St, 537-6770.
  Garden Inn, 22821 Mission, 538-2717.
  Green Lantern, 22580 Grand, 886-6565.
  Images, 29097 Mission, 581-5393.
  La Plaza Nightclub, 22164 Mission, 889-0997.
  Le Club Moderne, 22626 Main, 581-0264.
  West 40, 871 W. A St., 783-1882. Live country music.
LIVERMORE
  The Hideaway, 2293 1st St., 455-4141. Live music every night.
  Rock House Saloon, 1840 Portola, 455-5878.
NEWARK
  Bobby McGee's, 5995 Mowry, 794-7481, DJ every night. Mainly singles
    in their 20s & 30s.
  Ike's Cocktail Lounge, 81 Lewis Ctr., 792-5455. Top 40 (DJ), Thur &
    Sun. Live music Fri-Sat.
OAKLAND
  The Cantina, 4239 park, 482-3663. Folk & country music.
  Caribe Dance Center, 2424 Webster, 835-4006, Live Brazilian, Congo,
    and Trinidad music Fri.-Sat.
  Claremont Hotel Terrace Lounge, Ashby & Domingo, 843-3000. Live
    light rock music every night of the week.
  Club Bella Napoli, 2330 Telegraph, 893-5552. Top 40 & rap music,
    Wed-Sun. Cover charge.
  Coffee Mill, 3363 Grand Ave., Live dance music Fri.-Sun.
  The Complex, 10 Hegenberger. Live dance music Fri.-Sat.
  Court Lounge, 132 14th, 452-1496. Live music.
  Cozy Den, 1524 Peralta, 836-9842. DJ every night. Oldies, Sunday
    afternoons.
  Eli's Mile High Club, 3629 Martin Luther King Jr. Way, 655-6661. Live
    West Coast Blues, Wed-Sun. Cover charge.
  Escovedo's, 3285 Lakeshore, 893-7670. Live music.

Nightclubs   **119**

OAKLAND (continued)
5th Amendment, 3255 Lakeshore. Live dance music Tue.-Sun.
The Hill, 4100 Redwood Rd., 530-7260. Live rock music.
Larry Blake's, Oakland City Center, 12th & Broadway, 839-4163. Live comedy and rock music. Cover charge.
Manyatta, 10-B Hegenberger, (415) 568-9282. African-Caribbean music, Fri-Sun. Cover charge.
The Old Warehouse Cabaret, 577 18th St., 268-0591. Live music. Cover charge.
Omni, 4799 Shattuck. Live rock music Thu.-Sat. Cover charge.
Pacific Coast Brewing Company, 906 Washington, (415) 836-2739. Conversation bar for beer-lovers.
Til Two, 6573 Shattuck, (415) 652-6204. Blues music. Dancing on Monday nights.
Uptown Nite Klub, 1803 Webster, 832-8282. African, reggae music Thur-Sun. Cover charge.
Yoshi's, 6030 Claremont, 652-9200. Live jazz.. Cover charge.
Your Place Keesee's Lounge, 6528 Telegraph, 652-4040. Live music. Cover charge.
Your Place, Too, 5319 Martin Luther King Jr. Way, (415) 652-5837. Live blues & rock music every night. Cover charge.
PLEASANTON
Black Angus, 5930 Stoneridge Mall Rd., Pleasanton, (415) 463-0990. DJ every night. Young crowd.
Pleasanton Hotel, 855 Main, 846-8106. Live dance music. No cover.
Sunshine Saloon, 1807 Santa Rita, 846-6108.
SAN LEANDRO
Bogie's, 101 Parrott, 357-7333. Live top 40 dance music Wed-Sun.
SAN LORENZO
Black Angus, 15800 Hesperian, 276-1400. DJ every night. Young crowd.

CONTRA COSTA COUNTY

ANTIOCH
Delta Holiday Restaurant & Lounge, 1500 W. 10th, 778-6141.
Ugly Duck Bar & Grill, 992 Fitzuren Rd., 778-5267.
BETHEL ISLAND
Billeci's Ristorante, 6200 Bethel Island Rd, 684-3223. Live music, Fri-Sat.
CLAYTON
Clayton Club, 6096 Main St., (415) 672-4333. Country & Western dance, Fri-Sat., 9pm-1. No cover.
CONCORD
Fatt's, 1731 Monument, 687-6101.
Hobie's Roadhouse, 2045 Mt Diablo, 676-4417. Top 40 every day, 9pm. $2 cover Fri-Sat.
The Old Hangout, 1970 Concord, 682-4760.

CONCORD (continued)

The Ranch, 1450-A Monument Blvd., (415) 689-1235. Country & Western dancing every day. Dance lessons, Wednesdays, 7-9pm. $3 cover.

Sheraton Hotel, 45 John Glenn Dr., 825-7700. Dancing to live top 40 music or DJ. No cover charge.

TR's, 2001 Salvio St., (415) 827-4660. Top 40 & rock dancing, Thur-Sun. No cover.

DANVILLE

Bottom Line, 103 Town Country Dr, 837-5463. Live rock Fri-Sat. DJ, Thursdays. Cover charge.

The Club, 519 San Ramon Valley Bl, 831-0963.

EL CERRITO

Ayers Chapter 11, 10753 San Pablo. Live dance music.

The Downtown, 10582 San Pablo. Live music Fri.-Sat. Tea dancing, Sundays.

EL SOBRANTE

Capri Club, 4156 Appian, 223-9938.

LAFAYETTE

Cape Cod House, 3666 Mount Diablo, Lafayette, 283-8288. Piano bar.

PLEASANT HILL

Black Angus, 3195 N. Main, P.H., (415) 938-9900. D.J. every night. Young crowd.

Knights Inn, 1250 Contra Costa Bl, 682-4868.

PT. RICHMOND

The Point, 2 W. Richmond. Live jazz.

RICHMOND

Sho Gun Restaurant, 3044 Hilltop Mall, 222-8282. Dancing.

SAN PABLO

El Gallero, 1472 Rumrill, 234-2645.

Esquire Club, 2022 23rd, 237-0133. Live music Thu-Sat.

Star Club, 14273 San Pablo, 620-9546. Live Western music Thu-Sun.

SAN RAMON

Bobby McGee's, 3110 Crow Canyon Place, 831-1101. DJ every night. Mainly singles in their 20s & 30s.

Canyon Lakes Sports Bar & Grill, 500 Bollinger Canyon, 735-1806.

Charms, Marriott Hotel, 2600 Bishop Dr, 867-9200. DJ, Mon-Sat. No cover.

Rusty Pelican, 2323 San Ramon Valley Blvd., 820-6160. Live rock music. No cover charge. Mainly 20s & 30s age group.

WALNUT CREEK

After Dark, 1251 Arroyo, 933-2312.

Crogan's Bar & Grill, 1387 Locust, 933-7800. Singles often meet here Fridays (after work) & Saturday nights.

Devil Mountain Brewer, 850 S. Broadway, (415) 935-2337. Live rock, blues, Wed-Sat. $2 cover Fri-Sat.

El Papagayo, 2995 Ygnacio Valley, 939-6211. Live light rock. No cover charge.

WALNUT CREEK (continued)

HMS Endeavor, 2153 Oak Grove, 944-1844. Singles night, every Wednesday and Thursday. Live dance music.

Margaritaville, 1829 Mt Diablo Bl, 944-6595.

Max's Opera Cafe, 1676 N. California, 923-3434. Conversation bar. The waiters and waitresses sing opera.

Michael's, 1536 Newell. Dancing. 40+.

Musician's Coffeehouse, 55 Eckley, 229-2710.

Panache, 2355 N. Main, 935-8866. DJ, Mon-Sat.

WPLJ'S, 2112 N. Main, Walnut Creek, (415) 938-4140.

MARIN COUNTY

FAIRFAX

19 Broadway, (address is 17 Broadway), (415) 459-1091. Live music (mainly jazz) every night.

Perry's, 625 Redwood Highway, 383-9300. Conversation bar.

LARKSPUR

Baxter's, 601 Larkspur Landing Cir, 461-7022. DJ every night. $3 cover nightly, except Wednesdays. Mainly 20s and early 30s.

Marin Brewing Company, 1809 Larkspur Landing Cir, Larkspur 94939, (415) 461-HOPS. Live rock, no cover.

MILL VALLEY

All That Jazz, Howard Johnson's Motor Lodge, 160 Shoreline Hwy, (415) 332-5700. Live music Fridays & Saturdays.

La Bamba, 200 Shoreline Hwy. Live jazz.

Sweetwater, 153 Throckmorton, 388-2820. Live rock & blues music every night. Cover charge on weekends.

NICASIO

Rancho Nicasio, 1 Old Rancheria Rd, (415) 662-2219. Live country or swing dance music Fridays. Mainly ages 30-55.

NOVATO

Mr. Z's, Alvarado Inn, 6045 Redwood Highway, 883-5952. Rock & top 40 nightly (live and DJ). Young crowd.

T.J. On the Boulevard, 7110 Redwood, 892-3474. Live oldies, Thu-Sat.

SAN ANSELMO

Cafe Nuvo, 556 San Anselmo Ave., 454-4530.

Heartbeat, 100 Shaw, 258-0402. Smoke free.

Ted's, 218 Sir Francis Drake Blvd., 453-8600. Conversation bar.

SAN RAFAEL

Amadeus, 555 E. Francisco Blvd., (415) 453-0499. Live music daily. DJ from 1-4am. Jazz, blues, salsa music.

Andaron's, Holiday Inn, 1010 Northgate Dr., 479-8800. DJ every night. Cover charge, Fri.-Sat.

Bedroxx, 817 Francisco Blvd. W., 457-7697. Live rock music, Saturdays, $5. DJ every night except Saturdays, no cover. Young crowd.

Bobby McGee's, Embassy Suites Hotel, 101 McInnis Pkwy, 499-9222.

Fourth St. Tavern, 711 4th, 454-4044. Blues music.

SAN RAFAEL (continued)

Mayflower British Pub, 1533 4th, 456-1011. Live piano music with open mike, Fri.-Sat. Dart playing. No cover.

New George's, 842 4th, 457-8424. Live rock music Wed-Sat.

Royal Mandarin, 234 Northgate One Shopping Ctr, 472-5676. Dancing, live music, Fri-Sat. No cover charge. 40+ age group.

San Rafael Joe's, 917 4th, 456-2425. Live piano bar Thur-Sat. 40+.

Three Klicks Out, 555 E. Francisco, 454-3941. Dancing every night. Mainly 20s age group.

Trevor's, 927 Tamalpais, 456-7044. Live rock every night. No cover.

SAUSALITO

Bar With No Name, 757 Bridgeway. Live music Fri.-Sat. Jazz Sunday afternoons.

Zack's by the Bay, Bridgeway & Turney, 332-9779. Live rock music. No cover charge.

TIBURON

Amadeus Cafe, 20 Main, 435-3966. Live music every night.

Mr. Q's, 25 Main, 435-4550. Live music Fri-Sat nights & Sunday afternoons.

Christopher's, 9 Main, 435-4600. Live rock Fri-Sat. Cover charge.

MONTEREY COUNTY

CARMEL

Rio Grill, 101 Crossroads Blvd., (408) 625-5436. Conversation bar.

MONTEREY

The Club, 321 Alvarado, 646-9244. Dancing every night. Young crowd.

Carrera's, 414 Alvarado, 646-1415. Dancing.

Doc Rickett's, 95 Prescott, 649-4241. Live music every night.

Doubletree Hotel Lounge, 2 Portola, 649-4511. Live music. All ages.

Kalisa's, 851 Cannery Row, 372-8512.

Outrigger, 700 Cannery Row, 372-8543.

SALINAS

The Catalyst, 1011 Pacific. Live music.

The Paragon, 307 S. Main, 758-9800. Live piano music Wed.-Fri.

SEASIDE

Corral Club, 1153 Fremont, 899-2966. Live Western music every night.

NAPA

Collections, Clarion Inn, 3425 Solano, 253-7433. Live rock music Thu.-Sat. Cover charge.

Joe's Bar, Embassy Suites Hotel, 1075 California, 253-9540. Dancing to live music. No cover charge.

Junk Rock Cafe, 1017 Coombs, 224-5435.

O'Sullivan's Pub, 359 1st St., 224-5612. Live music, country swing dancing Fri.-Sat.

Tom Foolery Saloon, 600 Trampas, Napa, (707) 255-1688.

Abbey Tavern, 4100 Geary, 221-7767. Folk & Country music.
Ace Cafe, 1539 Folsom, (415) 621-4752. No alcohol.
A Classy Room, 32 9th, 861-2820. Dancing until 4am.
Albion, 3139 16th St., 621-9213. Folk & country music. Young group.
Amelia's, 647 Valencia, 552-7788. Disco Thur-Sat.
Bahia, 1600 Market, (415) 861-8657. Brazilian music.
Balboa Cafe, 3199 Fillmore,922-4595. Fern bar for conversation.
Bajone's, 1062 Valencia St., 282-2522. Live salsa, rhythm & blues, Brazilian music. Cover charge Fri-Sat.
Bentley's, Sutter & Kearny, 989-6895. Live music Tue-Sun.
Bix, 56 Gold St., (415) 433-6300. Piano bar.
Blue Lamp, 561 Geary, (415) 885-1464. Live rock music.
Blue Light, Fillmore & Greenwich. One of three bars in the "Bermuda Triangle" (along with Balboa Cafe & Pierce St. Annex). Conversation bar. Plenty of lawyers & secretaries.
Bo Grumpus, 561 Geary, 885-1464. Rock music.
Bopper's, 650 Howard, (415) 896-1950. 50s-60s music (DJ). Cover charge.
Bouncer's, 64 Townsend, 397-2480. Live music Tue-Sun.
Cafe International, 508 Haight, (415) 552-7390. No alcohol.
Cafe La Boheme, 3318 24th St., (415) 285-4122. No alcohol.
Cafe Picaro, 3120 16th St., (415) 431-4089. No alcohol.
Caffe Greco, 423 Columbus, (415) 397-6261. No alcohol.
Caffe Trieste, 601 Vallejo, (415) 392-6739. No alcohol.
California Cafe, 50 Broadway. Live music Mon-Fri.
Cal's, 2001 Union, (415) 567-3121. DJ or live top 40 music.
Camelot, 3231 Fillmore, 567-4004. Top 40, Fri-Sat.
Capurro's Pier 47, 300 Jefferson, 771-0377 Live music every night.
Caribbean Rose, 1039 Ocean. Live Caribbean & Jamaican music.
Cats, 48 Peter Yorke Way, 771-3309. DJ, Top 40 music. Cover charge.
Cesar's Latin Palace, 3140 Mission, 648-6611. Live Latin music, Fri.-Sat., 9pm-2. Cover charge.
Chatterbox, 853 Valencia, 821-1891. Live music Fri-Sat.
Chi Chi Club, 440 Broadway, 392-6213. Live music & DJ. Cover charge.
Clift Hotel Redwood Room, 495 Geary, (415) 775-4700. Older, wealthy crowd. Piano bar.
Club DV8, 55 Natoma, 777-1419. Live music Wed-Sat. Giant hall, dancing on two floors. Upscale. Mainly Asians.
Club 412, 412 Broadway, 391-8282. Live music Sat.
Club Metropolis, Market at 11th, 621-5001. Dancing Wed-Sat. Cover charge Fri-Sat.
Club Mirage, 2 Kansas, 431-9046. Top 40, Fri-Sat.
Coeur Samba, 1015 Folsom, 626-2899. Afro-Caribbean music, Fri.
Corona Bar & Grill, 127 Ellis, (415) 392-5500. Conversation bar.
Covered Wagon Saloon, 917 Folsom, 974-1585. Dancing every night.
Creativity Explored, 3245 16th St., 821-6210. Rock music.
Crystal Pistol, 842 Valencia, 695-7887. Dancing Thur-Sun.

Das Klub, 1015 Folsom. Live music Wed.-Sun.

DNA, 375 11th St., (415) 626-1409. Live music Sat.-Sun.

Edinburgh Castle, 950 Geary, (415) 885-4074. British pub. Bagpipes on Saturdays. Dart playing.

El Rio, 3158 Mission, 282-3325. Dancing Fri.

Fairmont Hotel, California & Mason, 772-5000. Live music every night in the New Orleans Room and Tonga Room. Wealthy, older crowd.

Farley's, 1315 18th St., (415) 648-1545. Magic shows, poetry readings, music. No alcohol.

The Farm, 1499 Potrero, 826-4290. Live music. Cover charge.

The Fillmore, 1805 Geary, 922-3455. Rock, new music, reggae, jazz, comedy.

Firehouse 7, 3160 16th St., 621-1617. Live world beat & reggae music and happy hour daily. All ages.

Full Moon Saloon, 1725 Haight, 668-6190. Live rock, reggae, blues. Cover charge.

Galleon, 718 14th St., (415) 431-0253. Live music.

Goat Hill Pizza, 300 Connecticut, 641-1440. Live music.

Gold Dust Lounge, 247 Powell, 397-1695. Live music every night.

Golden Grommet, 834 Irving, 564-6627. Blues music. Cover charge.

Grant and Green, 1401 Grant Ave., (415) 956-9065. Rock music.

Great American Music Hall, 859 O'Farrell, 885-0750. Live music. Cover charge.

Greek Taverna, 256 Columbus, 362-7260. Greek dancing.

The Hall, 827 Hyde, 771-5600. Ballroom dancing.

Hamburger Mary's, 1582 Folsom, (415) 626-5767. Conversation bar & restaurant.

Hard Rock Cafe, 1699 Van Ness, 885-1699. Loud rock music (taped), but no dancing. Plenty of singles in their 20s and 30s.

Harpoon Louie's, 55 Stevenson, (415) 543-3540. Conversation bar in financial district.

Harry's, 2020 Fillmore, (415) 921-1000. Elegant bar for up-scale businessmen.

Holiday Inn, Van Ness & Pine, 441-4000. Dancing, DJ, every night.

Horseshoe Cafe, 566 Haight, (415) 626-8852. No alcohol.

Hyatt Regency Hotel, 5 Embarcadero Ctr, 788-1234. Live big band dance music Fridays, 5:30-8:30 pm. Mainly 40+ age group.

I-Beam, 1748 Haight, 668-6006. Underground rock every night. Cover.

Ireland's 32, 3920 Geary, 386-6173.

John Barleycorn, 1415 Larkin, 564-1233.

Julie's Supper Club, 1123 Folsom, (415) 861-0707. Conversation bar.

Kimball's, 300 Grove, 861-5555. Jazz music.

La Terraza, 3472 Mission, 285-1236. North Mexican music every night.

Le Montmarte, 2125 Lombard, 921-9921. Live Latin & salsa music every night. Cover charge.

Last Day Saloon, 406 Clement, (415) 387-6343. Live music.

Lipps, 201 9th St., 552-3466. DJ. Cover charge.

The Little Shamrock, 807 Lincoln, 661-0060. Good place to meet softball players and bicyclists on Sunday afternoons.

Lost & Found Saloon, 1353 Grant, 397-3751. Rock music.

Lou's Pier 47, 300 Jefferson, 771-0377. Live rock music.

Mabuhay Gardens, 443 Broadway, 956-3315. Live music.

Mad Dog in the Fog, 530 Haight, (415) 431-0630. Irish bar. Darts.

Mangia, Mangia, 1 Embarcadero Center, 397-8799. DJ (rock & disco) and light show. No cover charge.

Mario's Bohemian Cigar Store, 566 Columbus, 362-0536. No alcohol.

The Mart, 32 9th St. DJ Fri.-Sat.

Maxwell's Restaurant, 900 North Point, 441-4140. Rock music.

Morty's, 1024 Kearny, 986-MORT. 50s & 60s music.

Mulhern's, 3653 Buchanan St., (415) 346-5549. Conversation bar. 35+ crowd.

Mumms, 2215 Powell, 433-3414. Private dinner-dance club. Non-members with reservations may stay for dancing. On weekends only members are allowed.

New Eagle Bar & Grill, 4 Embarcadero Center, 397-2056. Rock music, DJ.

New Tar & Feather's, 2140 Union, 563-2612. Rock music.

Nightbreak, 1821 Haight, 221-9008. Live underground rock music Wed.-Sun.

Nicki's Barbecue, 460 haight, (415) 621-0249. DJ. Young crowd.

Nine, 399 9th St., 863-9990. Live rock music. Cover charge.

Noc Noc, 557 Haight, (415) 861-5811. Conversation bar.

Oasis, 11th & Folsom, 621-8119. Rock music (live or DJ). Cover charge.

Onna No Shiro, 359 Grant, 398-6464. Piano bar.

Off Union Saloon, 2513 Van Ness, 928-1661. Live music.

Palladium, 1031 Kearny, 434-1308. After hours underground disco, 9pm-6am. Cover charge.

Paradise Lounge, 1501 Folsom, (415) 861-6906. Young crowd.

Park Bowl, 1855 Haight, 752-2366. Rock & oldies (DJ).

Passand, 1875 Union, 922-4498. Live music. No cover charge.

Pat O'Shea's Mad Hatter, 3rd & Geary, 752-3148. Rock music.

Paul's Saloon, 3251 Scott, 922-2456. Live country music every night.

Perry's, 1944 Union, 922-9022. Most famous singles bar in San Francisco. Conversation bar.

Pierce Street Annex, 3138 Fillmore, 567-1400. Top 40 music (DJ) every night. One of three bars in "Bermuda Triangle" (along with Balboa Cafe & Blue Light).

Pier 23 Cafe, The Embarcadero, 362-5125.

P.J. Montgomery's, Montgomery & Broadway. DJ on two dance floors every night.

Plough & Stars Irish Pub, 116 Clement, 751-1122. Live Irish folk music. Cover charge Fri.-Sat.

Rasselas, 2801 California, (415) 567-5010. Jazz music.
Regent Cafe, 952 Clement, 752-0354. Live Top 40 music Wed.-Sat. DJ,
Sundays. Cover charge Fri.-Sat.
Regina's, 490 Geary, (415) 885-1661. Conversation bar for the theatre
crowd.
Rockin' Robbins, 1840 Haight, 221-1960. Dancing every night. Cover
charge Fri-Sat.
Rockin' Robbins Downtown, 133 Beale, 543-1961. 50's & 60's music every
night. No cover charge.
Rocky Sullivan's Bar & Grill, 4737 Geary, 386-0909.
Roland's, 3309 Fillmore, 921-7774. Live jazz. Cover charge.
Sacred Grounds, Hayes & Cole, 387-3859. Rock music.
The Saloon, 1232 Grant, 989-7666. Blues music. Cover charge Fri.-Sat.
Silhouettes, 524 Union, 398-1952. 50's & 60's music.
Silhouettes at the Wharf, 155 Jefferson, 673-1954. 50's & 60's music.
690, 690 Van Ness, (415) 255-6900. Upscale conversation bar.
Slim's, 333 11th, (415) 621-3330. Blues & jazz music. Yuppie crowd.
16th Note, 3160 16th St., 621-1617. Dancing. Cover charge.
Sound of Music, 162 Turk, 885-9616. Live music.
The South Side, 1190 Folsom, (415) 431-3332. Top 40 music, DJ. Cover
charge Fri-Sat. 25-45.
Stan's Bar, 1401 Valencia, 826-3600. Talent Showcase, Thur-Sat. Music,
poetry, films, comedy, etc.
Starlite Roof, Sir Francis Drake Hotel, Powell & Sutter, 392-7755. Live
swing music, Mon-Sat. Mainly 40+. No cover. Expensive but classy.
St. Francis Hotel, Powell & Geary Streets, 397-7000. Top 40, pop, & disco
music (live & DJ) in the Compass Rose and Oz Club every night.
The Stone, 412 Broadway, 391-8282. After hours bar, Midnight-6 am
Fri.-Sat. Live rock music. Cover charge.
Studebaker's, 22 4th St., 777-0880. 50s-80s music Mon-Sat.
Tap Room Bar, 1151 Folsom, (415) 626-2388. Conversation bar.
Townsend, 177 Townsend, (415) 974-6020. Dance bar. Young crowd.
The Underground Club, 201 9th St., 552-3466. Live modern music.
VIS Club, 628 Divisadero, 567-0660. Live rock music. Cover charge.
Washington Square Bar & Grill, 1707 Powell, 982-8123. Conversation bar.
Insider crowd.
Wolfgang's, 901 Columbus, 441-4333. DJ. Cover charge.
Zuni Cafe, 1658 Market, (415) 552-2522. Upscale conversation bar.

SAN MATEO COUNTY

BELMONT
Iron Gate, 1360 El Camino, 592-7893. Live music Wed.-Thu.
BRISBANE
De Marco's 23 Club, 23 Visitation. Live swing and modern country
music.

BURLINGAME
Bobby McGee's, 150 Anza, 579-7807. DJ every night. No cover.
Fisherman Restaurant, 1492 Bayshore Hwy, 697-1490.
Hyatt Burlingame, 13333 Old Bayshore, 342-7741. Live music.
Mr. K's Cabaret, 1819 El Camino, 697-4042. Live music.
Route 66, 261 California, 347-3669. Live music Wed-Sat.
Safari Run, 1306 Bayshore Hwy, 347-8406.
Saluto's, 1600 Bayshore Hwy, 697-6565.

DALY CITY
R.V.'s Super Club & Bar, 6287 Mission, 991-4006.

FOSTER CITY
Black Angus, 1299 Chess, 345-9971. DJ every night. Mainly 20s & 30s age group.
Le Paradis, 1221 Chess, 570-5700. DJ.

HALF MOON BAY
Miramar Beach Inn, Highway 1. Live music Fri.-Sun.

MENLO PARK
British Bankers Club, 1090 El Camino, 327-8769.

MILLBRAE
Bit of Rhythm, 1741 El Camino, 588-6151. Live music, Fri-Sun.
Martinelli's Steak Pit, 1180 El Camino Real, (415) 588-6767. Live piano. 40+ crowd.

PACIFICA
Miramar Beach Inn, Magellan & Mirada, 726-9053.
Nick's Rockaway, 100 Rockaway Beach Ave., Pacifica. Live music.

REDWOOD CITY
Barney Steel's, 590 Veterans Blvd., 366-1238. Live music Fri.-Sat.
La Terrasse, Hotel Sofitel, 223 Twin Dolphin, 598-9000. Piano & Dance Trio, Thu-Sat.
Tommy's Club, 1794 Broadway, 368-8514.

SAN MATEO
Borel's, 2951 Campus, 341-7464.
Charlie Brown's, 3025 Clear View Way, 574-8330.
Club Ante, 223 S. B St., 348-2683.
Occa, 217-A Baldwin, 579-7282. Live music every night.
The Planet at Tingle's, Dunfey Hotel, 1770 S. Amphlett, 572-8400. DJ every night.
Villa Hotel, 4000 S. El Camino Real, (415) 341-0966. Live top 40 music Wed-Sat. No cover. All ages.

SOUTH SAN FRANCISCO
Railroad Station, 206 Grand, 588-0206.
Silver Dollar, 320 Grand, 589-0596. Live music Fri.-Sun.
3 Amigos Nightclub, 206 Grand, 588-7081.
Tony's Hofbrau Lounge, 151 S. Spruce, 583-8200.

CAMPBELL
Baja Cafe & Cantina, 499 E. Hamilton, 374-4290. DJ & cover nightly.
Boswell's, 1875 S. Bascom, 371-4404. Live rock nightly.
Fric n Frac's Cabaret, 1545 W. Campbell, 378-1121. Live rock, Thu.-Sat.
Kixx, 300 Orchard City, 374-4500.
L.A. Rocks, 300 Orchard City Dr., 866-5666. Live music Tue-Sun, 9:30pm. Cover charge varies.
Perrone's, 1777 S. Bascom, 377-6060. Live top 40 music.
Puma's Rock & Roll Club, 33 S. Central, 993-2697. Live music Wed-Sat, 9:30 pm. Cover charge.
Remington's, 1730 W. Campbell, 370-3280. Live music. Cover charge. Sundays, Singles night. Tuesdays, Parents Without Partners night.
Sebastian's, 1901 S. Bascom, 377-8600, Dance music (DJ), Wed-Sat., 9pm-1am. No cover charge.
Smokey Mountain, 33 S. Central, 866-8288. Live rock every night.
Southern Comfort, behind Hamilton House, 371-1861. Live music, Thu-Sat.
The Terrace, 750 The Pruneyard, 371-3801. Live music Thu.-Sat.
COYOTE
Coyote Inn, 102 Monterey Rd., 463-0452. Live country music, Fri-Sat., 9:15 pm. No cover charge.
CUPERTINO
Allstars, 10905 N. Wolfe, 725-8488. DJ every night, 9pm-1:30am. No cover charge.
Blue Pheasant, 22100 Stevens Creek Blvd., 255-3300. 50s & 60s music (DJ). Mainly 35+ age group.
Night Kap, 20020 Steven's Creek Blvd., 252-1100. Live music Mon-Sat. $2 cover charge Fri-Sat.
Peacock Bar & Grill, 19980 Homestead, 253-2141. Live music Fri-Sun. No cover charge.
P.J. Mulligan's, 19979 Stevens Creek, 255-0588.
Rusty Pelican, 10741 N. Wolfe, 255-6240. Live music, Thu.-Sat.
EAST PALO ALTO
Club Afrique, 583 O'Connor, (415) 322-3912. Live Caribbean and recorded music every night. Cover charge varies.
Collins Club, 1983 University, 329-1710.
Pena Moai, 1944 University, East Palo Alto, (415) 321-1944.
GILROY
Sandrino's, 420 1st St., 848-3811. Live rock, Fri-Sat. Mainly 20s-30s.
LOS ALTOS
Main Street Bar & Grill, 169 Main St., (415) 948-4332. Live music.
LOS GATOS
At the Hop, Old Town Center, 50 University, 354-4677. 50s & 60s & Top 40 dance music (DJ), Wed-Sun., 8pm-2am.
The Cats, 17533 Santa Cruz Hwy, 354-4020. Live rock music. No cover.
Il Nido, 170 W. Main, 354-8108. Live music Fri-Sat, 9pm-2am.

LOS GATOS (continued)
Johnny's, 14675 Winchester, 395-6888. Live top 40 music Tue-Sat, 9pm-1:30pm. Cover charge.
La Hacienda, 18840 Los Gatos/Saratoga Rd., 354-6669. Piano bar every night.
Los Gatos Lodge, 50 Saratoga, 354-3300. Live rock Tue-Sat.
Mountain Charley's, 15 N. Santa Cruz, 354-2510. Live music Tue-Sun, 9:30pm-1:30am. Cover charge varies.
#1 Broadway, 102 S. Santa Cruz, 354-4303. Live piano or quartet music Thu-Sat., 8pm-1am. No cover charge.
Scarlett La Rue's, 15940 Los Gatos, 356-2404. Live ragtime & dixieland jazz music, Fri & Sat., 9:30pm-1:45am. No cover charge.
University Club, 50 University, 354-5959. Live music Fri.-Sat., 8:30pm-12:30am. No cover charge.
MILPITAS
Brandon's, 1800 Barber, 432-6311. DJ Mon-Sat, 4pm-2am. Cover.
Holiday Inn, 777 Bellew, 945-0800. Live music every night. No cover.
Nino's, 1181 E. Calaveras, 946-4667. DJ, Fri.-Sat., 10pm-2am. No cover.
Riffs, 1801 Barber, 943-0600.
MOUNTAIN VIEW
Doug's, 1313 W. El Camino, (415) 940-9707. Live music, Fri-Sat.
J.J.'s Blues Cafe, 165 E. El Camino Real, (415) 968-2277. Live blues music every night. Cover charge.
No Jacket Required, 2540 California, (415) 949-1800.
Sports Page, 1431 Stierlin, (415) 961-1992. Live music Fri-Sat, 9:30-1:30am. No cover charge.
Wagon Wheel, 282 E. Middlefield, (415) 967-1244. 50s-70s music (DJ), Wed-Sat., 8:30 pm-1:30am. No cover charge.
PALO ALTO
British Bankers Club, 1090 El Camino Real, (415) 327-8769. Conversation bar.
City Lights, 575 High, 322-8731.
Chez Louie, 4170 El Camino Real, (415) 493-1660. DJ. Swing, big band, top 40, oldies. 40+ crowd.
Dinah's Shack, 4269 El Camino Real, (415) 493-9510. Live music Tue-Sat. No cover charge.
Fanny & Alexander's, 271 University, (415) 328-7700. Live piano & vocals, Tue.-Sat.
Gatehouse, 265 Lytton, Palo Alto, (415) 326-1330. Live music Thu-Sat., 9pm-1:30am. No cover charge.
The New Varsity, 456 University, (415) 321-1246. Live rock music Fri.-Sat.
Vortex, 260 California, (415) 324-1402. DJ, Thu.-Sat. After hours dancing until 4am, Fri.-Sat. Cover charge varies.

SAN JOSE

Almaden Feed & Fuel, 18950 Almaden Rd., 268-8950. Live music every Fri-Sat, 9:30 pm. No cover charge.

Barrington's Lounge, Ste. Claire Hilton, 302 S. Market, 295-2000. Live music Fri-Sat, 9pm-1am. No cover charge.

Beau's Annex, 35 N. San Pedro, 292-9277. Live music Mondays and Fri-Sat. Cover charge varies.

The Cabaret, 370 Saratoga Ave., 248-0641. Live rock music. Cover charge varies.

Calico Paints, 2250 Stevens Creek, 247-6050. Live rock music.

Cowtown, 3840 Monterey, 225-4277. Live country music, Tue-Sun. No cover charge.

D.B. Cooper's, 163 W. Santa Clara, 279-5867. DJ, Mon.-Sat., 9pm-2am. Also live rock. Cover charge.

El Rancho Grande, 301 S. Capitol, 259-7281. Live music.

El Tanampa, 1151 S. King, 258-8440. Disco dancing.

Essex Club, 510 El Paseo Shopping Ctr, 378-4433.

The Fairmont, 170 S. Market, (408) 998-3960. Live orchestra Tues-Sun. Cover charge.

Garden Alameda, 1520 The Alameda, 998-1415. Live piano music, 6-10:30pm, Tue.-Sat.

Garden City, 360 Saratoga Ave., 244-3333. Live piano, flute, vocals, bass, guitar, and jam sessions every night. No cover charge.

Ida's Fireside Inn, 2152 S. 1st, 297-4831. Live music Thu-Sat. No cover.

JJ's Lounge, 3934 Stevens Creek, 243-6441. Live blues music every night, 9:30 pm.

Joey's Lounge, 2058 N. Capitol, 263-3200. Country music Fri.-Sat., 9 pm. No cover charge.

Le Baron Hotel, 1350 N. 1st, 288-9200. Live light rock music every night, 6:30-10:30 pm. No cover charge.

The Loft, 951 Town & Country Village, 246-6672. Live music.

Lou's Village, 1465 W. San Carlos, 293-4570. Live piano music, Fri-Sat., 7-11 pm. No cover charge.

Marsugi's, 399 S. 1st, 286-8345. Live music Wed-Sat, 9:30 pm. Cover charge.

Miguelito's, 406 Blossom Hill, 226-0330. Live music Fri-Sat, 9:30pm-1:30am. No cover charge.

Mr. P's, 285 S. First, 295-8511. Live music Wed.-Sat.

Oasis, 200 N. 1st, 292-2212. Rock music (DJ) every night. Cover charge.

Pacific Fish Co., 177 W. Santa Clara, 298-7222. Live music. Usually no cover charge.

Paradise Beach, 175 N. San Pedro, 298-9283. Recorded music. 20s.

Ritz Pub & Pizzeria, 5180 Moorpark, 996-8870. Live music Wed-Sat, 8-11:30pm. No cover charge.

Saddle Rack, 1310 Auzerais, 286-3393. Live country music Tue.-Wed., 9pm. Also dance lessons. Usually no cover charge.

The Sanctuary, Calico Kate's, 4400 Stevens Creek, 296-2332. Live music every night, 9:30 pm. Cover charge.

Nightclubs   131

SAN JOSE (continued)

Spartan Pub, San Jose State University, 7th & San Carlos, 924-1855. Live music Tue-Thu. No cover charge.

Studio 47, 47 Notre Dame Ave., 279-3387. DJ. 20s age group.

3 Flames Restaurant, 1547 Meridian, 296-3133. Live music Tue-Sat, 9 pm. No cover charge.

3 Plus One, 675 E. Gish, 293-6289. DJ.

Time Out Sports Bar & Cafe, 111 N. San Pedro, 279-4330. Live music Thu-Sat.

Tony Roma's, 4233 Moorpark, 253-4900. Live music.

Tropicana Twin Ballroom, King & Story, 926-4321.

Village Retreat, 7028 Santa Teresa, 226-5424. Live music Fri. & Sat. DJ, Sun.-Thu.

Willows Lounge, Hyatt Hotel, 1740 1st, 993-1234. Live music, Thu-Sat. No cover charge.

Zorba's, 1850 S. Bascom, 293-7170. Live music & belly dancers, Tue-Sun, 9:15pm-1am. No cover charge.

SANTA CLARA

A.J.'s Cypress Lounge, 1031 Monroe, 243-0589. Live rock and top 40 music Fri-Sat., 9:30 p.m.

Arthur's, 2875 Lakeside, 980-1666.

Chips, Doubletree Hotel, 5101 Great America Pkwy., 986-0700. Top 40 music Tue-Sat., 8pm-2am, cover charge. Live jazz in the lobby, Fridays, 5pm, no cover.

Horseshoe Club, 2655 El Camino, 248-4100.

Lord John's Inn, 3190 The Alameda, 984-0475. Live music Tue-Sat., 9:30pm-1:30 am. Cover charge.

McNeil's, 800 Kiely, 244-4038. Live music Mon-Sat. Usually no cover charge.

One Step Beyond, 1400 Martin, 727-0901. Modern music, Thur-Sun. Cover charge.

SARATOGA

Crazy Horse Lounge, 14455 Big Basin, 867-4711. Live music. No cover.

Duke of Wellington, 14572 Big Basin, 867-7070. Live music Thu-Sat. No cover charge.

SUNNYVALE

Beefy's Cabin, 1028 W. Washington, 736-7141. Live music every Fri-Sat, 9 pm-1am. No cover charge.

Bold Night, 769 Mathilda, 782-4357.

Caribbean Cajun Restaurant, 172 Murphy, 737-7056. Live music Fri-Sat. No cover charge.

Donna's Dukes, 919 El Camino Real, 733-5575. Live country music, Wed-Sun. No cover charge.

Faces Cafe, 685 E. El Camino, 479-1288.

Hard Disk Cafe, Lawrence/Central Expwys., 733-2001. Live music Fri-Sat, 9 pm. No cover charge.

Jay Bird Lounge, 1102 W. Evelyn, 739-7939. Live country music, Fri-Sun. No cover charge.

SUNNYVALE

Michael's, 830 E. El Camino Real, 245-2925. Live piano music, Tue-Sat., 8:30pm-12:30am. No cover charge.

Odyssey Room, 799 El Camino Real, 245-4448. Live top 40 music every night, 8 pm. Cover charge.

Spot Cafe, 1010 Sunnyvale-Saratoga, 733-6000.

Stardust Lounge, 1183 W. El Camino Real, 732-5570, Oldies music (DJ) & dance lessons. Cover charge.

Starlite Ballroom, 1160 N. Fairoaks, 745-7827. Country dance music, Thursdays; top 40 music, Fri-Sat.

SANTA CRUZ COUNTY

APTOS

Aptos Club, 5 Post Office Dr, 688-9888.

Seascape, 610 Clubhouse Dr., 688-3254. Dancing.

Severino's, 7500 Old Dominion, 688-8987. Live rock music. No cover.

SANTA CRUZ

Bonny Doon Vineyard, 10 Pine Flat, 425-3625. Live music.

The Catalyst, 1011 Pacific, 423-1336. Live rock music, Thu-Sat. Cover charge.

Coconut Grove, 400 Beach, 423-5590. Live music.

Edgewater Club, 215 Esplanade, 475-6215. Dancing every night & Sunday afternoons.

Kuumbwa Jazz Center, 320-2 Cedar, 427-2227. Live music almost every night. Cover charge.

SOQUEL

O.T.'s, 3660 Soquel, 476-3939.

WATSONVILLE

Pasa Tiempo Club, 126 Main, 722-0605.

SOLANO COUNTY

BENICIA

Sundowner, 1401 E. 5th, 745-2600.

CORDELIA

Pure Energy, 364 Pittman, 864-0185. DJ. Young crowd.

FAIRFIELD

Duffy's, 150 Acacia, 425-7141.

Fairfield Landing, 2470 Martin, 429-2370. Live rock music. Mainly singles in their 20s and 30s.

Geronimo Room, 2030 N. Texas, 425-6413. Dancing Wed.-Sun.

Hickey's Brass Rail, 837 Texas, 425-4975.

Moon Room Lounge, Muffin Treat Restaurant, Hwy. 80 at N. Texas, 429-1519. Live music every night. Mainly 40+ age group.

SUISUN

Vista Club, E. Cordelia & Kellogg, 422-0584. Live music Wed.-Sun.

Zowie's Cafe Cabaret, 701 Main, 422-1613.

TRAVIS
Cecil's, 666 Parker, 437-3610. DJ every night.
VACAVILLE
Brigadoon's, 1591 E. Monte Vista, 448-8446. Live rock or country.
Monte Vista Pub, 1072 E. Monte Vista, 448-8173. Live country music.
VALLEJO
Harbor House, 23 Harbor, 642-8984. DJ. 35+ age group.
Jenicas Lounge, 1711 Solano, 554-1073.
Maritime Station, 117 Maritime Academy Dr, 643-2012.
Nitty Gritty Lounge, 2065 Solano, 642-4413. Dancing.
Outlaw Josie Wales, 1504 Sears Pt., 554-0107. Live country music.
Talk of the Town, 326 Virginia, 555-2600. Live music. After hours.
The Village, 732 Tuolumne, 648-9497. Live county music every night.
Vallejo Country Club, 1801 Solano, 552-8157. Live music.

SONOMA COUNTY

COTATI
Cotati Cabaret, 85 La Plaza, 795-7622. Dancing Thu.-Sun.
EL VERANO
Little Switzerland, Grove & Riverside, 938-9990. Waltz & polka, Sat-Sun. 50s & 60s music, Fridays.
HEALDSBURG
Skylark, 245 Healdsburg, 433-6789. Live music Fri-Sat.
PETALUMA
Aquarium Lounge, 1030 Petaluma Blvd., 762-9814. Live rock/country.
McNears, 23 Petaluma Blvd., 765-2121. Dixieland jazz Thu.-Fri. Live country Fri.-Sat.
Steamer Gold, 1 Water St., 763-6876. Live music every night.
ROHNERT PARK
Maxi's Lounge, Red Lion Inn, 1 Red Lion Dr., 584-5466. Live rock music. No cover charge. All ages.
Smitty's Bar & Grill, 5000 Commerce, 584-0235. Live music.
SANTA ROSA
Daily Planet, 578-0952. Dancing Wed-Sun. Mainly 20s-30s age group.
El Rancho Tropicana, 2200 Santa Rosa Ave., 542-3699. Live top 40 music Tues-Sat. No cover charge.
Magnolia's 107 4th, 526-1006. Live top 40 music Wed-Sat.
New Joe Frogger's, 527 4th, 526-0539. Live music every night.
Santa Rosa Inn, 4302 Santa Rosa Ave., 584-0345. DJ.
Studio Kafe, 418 Mendocino, 523-1971. Live music or comedy, Mon-Sat. Cover charge.
SEBASTOPOL
Marty's Top O' the Hill, 8050 Bodega, 823-5987. Live country music Thu-Sun. No cover charge.
Paradise Alley, 6930 Burnett, 823-3778. Live music.
SONOMA
Cabernet Sauvignon, 478 1st St. East, 996-3600. Live music Wed.-Sat.

SPECIAL INTEREST ORGANIZATIONS

ADVERTISING

Advertising Club of the Bay Area, Box 4966, Berkeley 94704, (415) 843-5323.

Greater East Bay Society of Communications & Advertising, Box 4966, Berkeley 94704, (415) 547-8854.

San Francisco Advertising Club, 150 Post St. #325, San Francisco 94108, (415) 986-3878. Social events for non-members.

San Francisco Creative Alliance, Box 410387, San Francisco 94141-0387, (415) 387-4040. Lectures, awards shows, socializing.

ALUMNI

Cal Singles, Alumni Association of UC Berkeley, 642-1945. Dances, speakers, trips. Mainly 40+. You do not have to have attended Cal in order to join.

Cal Alumni Association, Alumni House, Berkeley 94720, (415) 642-7026.

San Francisco State Alumni Association, 1600 Holloway, Office NAD 467, San Francisco 94132, (415) 338-2217.

San Jose State Alumni Association, 210 E. San Carlos 95129, (408) 227-3235.

Santa Rosa Junior College Alumni College, 1501 Mendocino Ave., Santa Rosa 95404.

Stanford Alumni Association, Bowman Alumni House, Stanford 94305, (415) 723-2021.

UC Club of Santa Clara County, 765 Harvard Ave., Sunnyvale 94087, (408) 736-7121.

University of San Francisco Alumni Association, Golden Gate & Parker, San Francisco 94117, (415) 752-6560.

AMATEUR RADIO

Amateur Radio Association of the North Bay, Box 1468, Vallejo 94590, (707) 642-8555.

Benicia Amateur Radio Club, Box 899, Benicia 94510, (707) 745-3738

CB Club, 247 Camellia, Fairfield 94533, (707) 426-6776

Marin Amateur Radio Club, Hamilton Air Force Base, Novato, 883-9789.

Nighttalkers, Box 2325, Dublin 94568, (415) 829-5330

South County Rebels CB Radio Club, Box 1176, Fremont 94538, (415) 657-2533.

ANIMALS

CATS
Cat Fanciers, 6107 Castle Knoll Dr., San Jose 95129, (408) 252-6252.
East of Eden Cat Fanciers, Box 783, Pacific Grove 93950, (408) 372-7018. Housecat Fanciers of the Bay Area, (415) 582-8067.

DOGS
Antioch - East Ridge Dog Club, 2309 Arthur Way, Antioch 94509, (415) 757-9038 or 757-8555.

Concord - Single Doglovers Association, Box 272245, Concord 94527. Showing, hunting, breeding of dogs. Also socials.

Del Valle Dog Club, Box 603, Livermore 94550, (415) 455-6900

Diablo Valley German Shepherd Dog Club, 113 Mazie Ln, Pleasant Hill 94523, (415) 689-9743.

Fremont Dog Training Club, 45581 Industrial, Fremont, (415) 490-9887.

Hayward Area Dog Training Club, 2551 W. Winton Ave., Hayward, (415) 782-1080.

Kennel Club, Box 101, Fairfield 94533, (707) 422-5039.

Napa Valley Dog Training Club, Box 253-8666.

Oakland Dog Training Club, (415) 339-3276.

Richmond Dog Fanciers, 1170 Roberts Ave., San Jose 95122, (408) 947-7812.

San Lorenzo Dog Training Club, 534 Lewelling Blvd., San Leandro, (415) 483-4546.

San Mateo Dog Training Club, Box 904, San Mateo, (415) 344-3240.

Santa Clara Dog Training Club, (408) 378-6030.

Santa Clara Valley Kennel Club, (408) 257-6400.

Santa Cruz Kennel Club, (408) 438-3647.

WHALES
Oceanic Society, Fort Mason, Bldg. E, San Francisco 94123, (415) 441-5970.

Whale Center, 3929 Piedmont Ave., Oakland 94611, (415) 654-6621.

Whale Conservation & Research Fund, 2062 Lincoln, Alameda 94501.

MISCELLANEOUS ANIMALS
Action for Animals, Box 20184, Oakland 94620, (415) 652-5603

Animal Legal Defense Fund, 333 Market St #2300, San Francisco 94105.

Animal Switchboard, Box 2087, San Francisco 94126, (415) 885-2679.

Animal Welfare Association, Box 178, Daly City 94016, (415) 771-1649.

Bay Area Amphibian & Reptile Society, Palo Alto Jr. Museum, 1451 Middlefield Rd., Palo Alto 94301

California Marine Mammal Center, Marin Headlands, Ft. Cronkhite 94965, (415) 331-0161

Concord Aquarium, 1585 Clayton Rd., Concord, 676-2626.

East Bay Zoological Society, 9777 Golf Links Rd., Oakland 94605.

Fund For Animals, Ft. Mason, San Francisco 94123, (415) 474-4020.

ANIMALS (continued)

Hayward Friends of Animals, Box 3986, Hayward, (415) 783-3685.
Hayward Homing Pigeon Club, 4250 Heyer Ave., Castro Valley 94546.
Humane Society of Marin, 171 Bel Marin Keys, Novato 94947, (415) 883-5837.
MartinezHomingPigeonClub,TheEmbarcadero,Martinez,228-8222.
Peninsula Humane Society, 12 Airport Blvd., San Mateo 94401, (415) 573-3720.
Pets Unlimited, 2343 Fillmore, San Francisco 94115, (415) 563-6700.
Progressive Animal Rights Alliance, Santa Cruz, (408) 426-5072.
San Francisco Aquarium Society, 2029 Palmetto, Pacifica, (415) 359-7916.
San Francisco Zoological Society, Skyline Blvd., San Francisco 94132, (415) 661-2023.
Society for the Prevention of Cruelty to Animals, (SPCA)
  San Francisco: 2500 16th St., San Francisco, (415) 554-3000.
  Solano County: (707) 642-3008
St. Francis Protective Society, Box 214, Corte Madera 94925, (415) 435-2097.
Valley Humane Society, Box 9001, Pleasanton 94566.

ARCHAEOLOGY

Santa Cruz Archaeological Society, Santa Cruz, (408) 425-7214.
Society for Historical Archaeology, Box 231033, Pleasant Hill 94523, (415) 686-4660.

ARCHITECTURE

Alameda Victorian Preservation Society, Box 1677, Alameda 94501, (415) 523-2877.
American Institute of Architects, (707) 576-7799. Contests, picnics.
Asian-American Architects & Engineers, 1670 Pine, San Francisco 94109, (415) 777-1818.
Berkeley Architectural Heritage Association, Box 1137, Berkeley 94701, (415) 841-2242.
Berkeley Design Advocates, (415) 893-6834 or 548-5700
Foundation for San Francisco's Architectural Heritage, 2007 Franklin St., San Francisco 94109, (415) 441-3000.
San Francisco Architectural Club, Fort Mason, (415) 441-1098.
Victorian Alliance Architectural Preservation Organization, 44 Peralta, San Francisco 94110, (415) 824-2666.

THE ARTS

Alamo-Danville Artists Society, 877 Richard Ln., Danville 94526.
American Federation of the Arts, 270 Sutter St., San Francisco 94108, (415) 392-9222.
Art Guild of Pacifica, Box 582, Pacifica 94044, (415) 359-6140. Mainly women.
Artisans, 78 E. Blithedale, Mill Valley 94941, (415) 388-2044.
Artists Equity Association, Box 460931, San Francisco 94146, (415) 626-6808.
Artist's Round Table, Santa Rosa, (707) 539-4170.
Arts of San Ramon, 30 Broadmoor Ct., San Ramon 94583, (415) 828-1568.
Association for Cultural Enhancement, 2 Shotwell, San Francisco 94103, (415) 553-4457.
Benicia Community Arts, Box 454, Benicia 94510, (707) 745-2787.
Berkeley Mural Group, 4701 San Leandro St., Oakland 94601, (415) 553-7416 or 849-0313.
Berkeley Potters Guild, 731 Jones, Berkeley 94710, (415) 524-7031.
Burlingame Art Society, 1515 Floribunda #109, Burlingame 94010, (415) 347-8432.
Business Volunteers for the Arts, 4 N. 2nd, San Jose 95113, (408) 948-2787.
California Lawyers for the Arts, Ft. Mason, San Francisco 94123, (415) 775-7200.
City Celebration, Ft. Mason, San Francisco 94123, (415) 474-3914.
Civic Arts Association, 1313 Civic Dr., Walnut Ck 94598, (415) 932-1731.
Coastal Arts League, Box 1322, El Granada 94018, (415) 726-7366 or 726-3949.
Danville Arts Council, 103 Bolla, Alamo 94507, (415) 837-9565.
Delta Art Association, 518 W. 6th, Antioch 94509, (415) 754-3565.
El Cerrito Art Association, 7768 Duke Ct., El Cerrito, 9415) 525-7711.
Exploratorium, 3601 Lyon St., (415) 563-3200.
Fremont Art Association, 37659 Niles Bl., Fremont 94536, (415) 790-9523. Classes, art demonstrations. Public invited.
Fremont Cultural Arts Council, Box 1314, Fremont 94538, (415) 794-7166.
Ft. Mason Foundation, Bldg A, Ft. Mason, San Francisco 94123, (415) 441-5706.
Hayward Area Forum of the Arts, 1015 E St., Hayward, (415) 581-4050.
Livermore Art Association, Box 216, Livermore 94550, (415) 484-1815/449-9927.
The Loring Club, 264 Fair Oaks, San Francisco 94110, (415) 648-6648.
Marin Arts Council, 251 N. San Pedro Rd., San Rafael 94903, (415) 499-8350.
Marin Arts Guild, Box 692, Belvedere 94920, (415) 435-5750.
Marin Society of Artists, Box 203, Marin Art & Garden Center, Ross 94904, (415) 454-9561.
Martinez Arts Association, Box 2304, Martinez 94553, (415) 228-0309.
Millbrae Arts Association, Box 87, Millbrae 94030, (415) 697-7471.

Mill Valley Art Club, 1 W. Blithedale, Mill Valley 94941, (415) 388-9237.
Napa County Arts Council, 101 Coombs, Napa 94558, (707) 257-2117.
Napa Valley Art Association, 1520 Behrens, Napa 94559, (707) 255-9616.
Neighborhood Arts Program, 45 Hyde, San Francisco 94102, (415) 558-3463.
Newark Arts Council, 5358 Port Sailwood, Newark 94560, (415) 792-1442.
North Bay Artists, (415) 883-7034.
North San Mateo County Center for the Arts, 699 Serramonte Blvd., Daly City 94015, (415) 994-5250.
Oakland Art Association, 3740 Grand Ave., Oakland 94610, (415) 839-9997.
Oakland Arts Council, 1520 Lakeside Dr., Oakland 94612.
Oakland Festival of the ARts, 678 13th St., Oakland 94612, (415) 444-5588.
Orinda Art Council, Box 121, Orinda 94563, (415) 254-8624.
Pacific Art League, 668 Ramona, Palo Alto, (415) 853-9608, 321-3891.
Palace of Fine Arts League, 3301 Lyon St., San Francisco 94123, (415) 563-6504.
Petaluma Art Assoc., Box 2623, Petaluma 94953, (707) 763-5662.
Pleasanton Art League, Box 23, Pleasanton 94566, (415) 846-3513 or 462-4722.
Redwood Empire Porcelain Artists, 152 W. Payran, Petaluma 94952, (707) 763-2716. Mainly women.
Society for Asian Art, Asian Art Museum, Golden Gate Park, San Francisco 94118, (415) 387-5675.
Sonoma County Yiddish Cultural Society, (707) 584-5612.
San Francisco Museum of Modern Art, Van Ness at McAllister, 863-8800.
San Ramon Arts Council, (415) 829-4562.
San Jose Art League, 482 S. 2nd, San Jose, (408) 294-4545.
San Mateo Performing Arts Center, 600 N. Delaware, San Mateo, (415) 348-8243.
Sunnyvale Art Club, (408) 745-7956. 3rd Mondays, 7pm, Senior Center.
Vacaville Art League & Gallery, 718 E. Monte Vista Ave., 448-8712.
Vacaville Arts Council, 618 E. Main, 447-0837.

AUTOS

Car enthusiasts are likely to be prosperous and male. Single women would be wise to attend car-related events. Read the San Francisco **Chronicle's** Sports section for lists of races and shows for cars.

Abingdon Rough Riders, 896 Gellert Blvd., Daly City 94015, (415) 878-4981.
Antique Auto Club, 830 Shary Ave., Mt. View 94041.

Cabrillo Region Antique Auto Club of America, Box 2755, Santa Cruz, (408) 475-7256.

Classic Car Club of America, Box 61078, Palo Alto 94306.

Classic Chevy Club, 2394 Norwood Rd., Livermore 94550, (415) 447-8224.

Diablo Valley Mustang Association, 3613 Hammond Pl, Concord 94519, (415) 687-7691.

Early Ford V-8 Club of America, Box 2122, San Leandro 94577.

Electric Auto Association, 1249 Lane St., Belmont 94002, (415) 591-6698 or 524-2242.

Electric Vehicle Association, 1460 Summit Rd., Berkeley 94708, (415) 848-1468.

Fremont Touring Club, Box 482, Fremont 94537.

Metropolitan Owners Club, 148 Garnet Ave., San Carlos 94070, (415) 591-0803.

Mid-Peninsula Old Time Auto Club, Box 525, Belmont 94002, (415) 366-0853.

Model A Clubs

Acorn A's Model A Ford Club, Box 2321, Castro Valley 94546, (415) 339-8257.

Napa Valley A's Auto Club, Box 2656, Napa 94558, (707) 255-9338 or 226-3413.

Sonoma County - 120 Suncrest Hill, Petaluma 94952, (707) 762-1204.

Morris Minor Registry, 2311 30th Ave., San Francisco 94116, (415) 566-6103.

National Hot Rod Association, Box 1343, Richmond 94802, (415) 232-0600.

North Bay Corvette Association, 27 Cove Rd., Belvedere 94920, (415) 435-1924.

Northern California MGA Register, 2628 Belmont Canyon Rd., Belmont 94002, (408) 739-0987.

Old Adobe Antique Car Club, 16 Volker Dr., Petaluma 94952, (707) 762-1051.

Sports Car Club of America, San Francisco Chapter, 1610 Pacific, San Francisco 94109, (415) 775-1010. Sponsors shows, races, and road rallies.

Team Sprint Sports Car Club, Box 341, Hayward 94543, (415) 278-4199.

BACKGAMMON

Backgammon Club, 777 Jones, San Francisco, (415) 474-7328.

The Backgammon Network, (415) 593-9433.

Campbell Bridge & Backgammon, 175 E. Campbell Ave., Campbell, (408) 378-3711.

BALLET

Ballet Arts Center, 2327 5th St., Berkeley 94710, (415) 486-8180.
Berkeley Ballet Theater, 2640 College Ave., Berkeley 94704, (415) 526-7833 or 526-7541.
Berkeley Conservatory Ballet, 1800 Dwight Way, Berkeley 94703, (415) 841-8913.
Friends of the Marin Ballet, 100 Elm St., San Rafael 94901, (415) 453-6705.
Oakland Ballet, 2700 MacArthur Blvd., Oakland 94602, (415) 530-7516.
Palo Alto Ballet Company, (415) 493-5522.
Peninsula Ballet Theatre, 333 South B St., San Mateo 94401, (415) 343-8485.
Richmond Ballet, Richmond Art Center, Civic Center, Richmond 94804, (415) 237-5065.
San Francisco Ballet Association, 455 Franklin, (415) 861-5600.
San Jose Cleveland Ballet, 99 Almaden Bl, San Jose, (408) 288-2820.

BOOKS

Book Club of California, 312 Sutter St. #510, San Francisco 94108, (415) 781-7532.
Friends of the San Francisco Public Library, Main Library, Civic Center, San Francisco 94102, (415) 558-3770. Sponsors book sales, films, volunteering, parties, exhibits, outings.
Friends of the Santa Cruz Public Library, (408) 429-3495.
Friends of the Sunnyvale Library, (408) 739-2925. 1st Fridays, 10am, Sunnyvale Library.
Mill Valley Literary Society, (415) 381-6671.

BREAKFAST CLUBS

Alameda Breakfast Club, 113 Beverly Dr., Pleasant Hill 94523.
Berkeley Breakfast Club, 3139 Lewiston Ave., Berkeley 94705, (415) 653-0456.
Cosmopolitans, 1499 19th Ave., San Francisco 94122.
Daly City Daybreakers, 2761 Sherwood, San Bruno 94066, (415) 756-2372.
Daly City Sunrisers, 56 Midcrest Way, San Francisco 94131, (415) 826-6550.
Encores, Box 164, Pleasanton 94566, (415) 462-2736.
Esquire Social Club, 201 El Sendero, Vallejo 94590, (707) 642-6104.
Gadabouts, 1552 Jacob, San Jose 95118.
Galavents, 98 La Salle, Piedmont 94610.
Golden Gate Breakfast Club, Press Club, 555 Post, San Francisco 94102, (415) 775-7800.
Lake Merritt Breakfast Club, Skyline Veterinary Hospital, 11183 Skyline, Oakland 94619, (415) 531-8280

BREAKFAST CLUBS (continued)

Lakeview Club, 300 Lakeside Dr. #2800, Oakland 94612, (415) 839-6767.
Leisure League, 278 Cresta Vista, San Francisco 94127.
Los Gatos Social Club, 17774 Navajo Trail, Los Gatos 95030.
Los Robles Social Club, 100 Bel Marin Keys, Novato 94947, (415) 883-8998.
Marinwood Funsters, 775 Miller Creek, San Rafael 94903.
Merry Mixers, 3418 Lynn Oaks Dr., San Jose 95117.
Metropolitan Club, 640 Sutter, San Francisco 94102.
Monday Leisure Club, 70 Dichiera Ct., San Francisco 94112.
Marvelous Marin Breakfast Club, Box 3143, San Rafael 94912.
Networking Breakfasts, San Francisco, Marianna Nunes, (415) 673-6775. Mainly singles.
San Leandro Breakfast Club, Pan American Savings, 510 16th St., San Leandro 94612, (415) 839-6661.
Wednesday Morning Dialogue Club, Box 1201, San Rafael 94913.

BRIDGE

Albany Bridge Club, 7007 Moeser, El Cerrito, (415) 525-6748/232-6689.
Berkeley Live Oak Bridge Club, Live Oak Park, 1301 Shattuck, Berkeley 94709, (415) 845-1718/527-0701.
Bridge Club of San Francisco, 777 Jones, San Francisco 94109, 776-6949.
Campbell Bridge, 175 E. Campbell Ave., Campbell, 378-3711.
Cavendish Bridge Club, 1100 Gough, San Francisco 94109, (415) 776-7080.
Napa Valley Duplicate Bridge Club, 155 Garth St., Napa 94558, (707) 224-1152.
Oakland Bridge Club, Oak Bridge Center, 3026 Broadway, Oakland, (415) 451-4551.
San Francisco Bridge Center, 256 Laguna Honda Blvd., (415) 681-4688.
San Jose Bridge Center, 1190 S. Bascom Ave., San Jose, (408) 279-9573.
UC Bridge Club, UC Student Union, Bancroft & Telegraph, Berkeley 94720, (415) 642-3361/527-4594.

CHAMBER MUSIC

Berkeley Chamber Orchestra, 3071 Kansas, Oakland 94602, (415) 530-8652.
Chamber Music Society of San Mateo County, 829 Vega Cir., Foster City 94404, (415) 345-0879.
Marin Musicfest, 13 Eton Way, Mill Valley 94941, (415) 383-0867.
Mill Valley Chamber Music Society, Box 5121, Mill Valley 94941, (415) 381-4453.
Palo Alto Chamber Orchestra, (415) 856-3848.
San Jose Chamber Music Society, 274 S. 17th St., San Jose, (408) 286-5111.
Trinity Chamber Concerts, 2320 Dana St., Berkeley 94704, 549-3864.

CHARITABLE ORGANIZATIONS

Charitable Organizations frequently sponsor fundraisers and other social events that are good places to meet other singles who are generous and caring.

Aid for Adoption of Special Kids, 3550 Grand Ave., Oakland 94610, (415) 451-1748.
American Cancer Society, 973 Market #550, San Francisco 94103, (415) 974-1592.
American Diabetes Association, 12 Geary #207, San Francisco 94108, (415) 397-3373.
American Foundation for the Blind, 111 Pine St. #725, San Francisco 94111, (415) 392-4845.
American Friends Service Committee, 2160 Lake, San Francisco 94121, (415) 752-7766.
American Heart Association, 120 Montgomery #1650, San Francisco 94104, (415) 433-2273.
American Lung Association, 562 Mission St. #203, San Francisco 94105, (415) 543-4410.
Anti-Defamation League (Jewish), 121 Steuart St #40, San Francisco 94105, (415) 546-0200.
Arthritis Society, 203 Willow #201, San Francisco 94109, (415) 673-6882.
Big Brothers/Big Sisters hold annual joint parties.
   East Bay: 2910 Telegraph Ave., Oakland 94609, (415) 452-1219.
   Fairfield: 1147 Ohio #D, Fairfield 94533, (707) 425-1523.
   Marin - 2175 Francisco #B, San Rafael 94901, (415) 453-3800.
   Napa: 1100 West St., Napa 94559, (707) 255-7634.
   San Francisco: 414 Mason St. #500, San Francisco 94102, (415) 434-4860.
Blind San Franciscans, 2417 Greenwich, San Francisco 94123, (415) 563-4896.
B'nai B'rith (Jewish), 703 Market #550, San Francisco 94102, (415) 541-9293.
City of Hope, 1540 Market #140, San Francisco 94102, (415) 863-7677.
Cystic Fibrosis Society, 116 New Montgomery, San Francisco 94105, (415) 543-9099.
Dawn Society, 846 Bellevue Ave., Daly City 94014, (415) 585-8527.
Easter Seal Society, 6221 Geary, San Francisco 94121, (415) 752-4888.
Epilepsy Society, 1728 Union #211, San Francisco 94123, (415) 474-9075.
Hearing Society, 20 10th St. #200, San Francisco 94103, (415) 863-4710.
Hemophilia Foundation, 7700 Edgewater #710, Oakland 94621.
Leukemia Society, 323 Geary #711, San Francisco 94102, (415) 781-4270.
March of Dimes, 150 N. Hill Dr #14, Brisbane 94005, (415) 468-7400.
Muscular Dystrophy Association, 561 Pilgrim #C, Foster City 94404, (415) 570-6166.
Narcolepsy Association, 335 Quarry Rd., Belmont 94002, (415) 591-7979.

National Association for the Visually Handicapped, 3201 Balboa, San Francisco 94121, (415) 221-3201.
National Multiple Sclerosis Society, 520 3rd St., Oakland 94607, (415) 268-0572.
Northern California Society to Prevent Blindness, 4200 California St., San Francisco 94118, (415) 387-0934.
Operation Concern, 1853 Market, San Francisco 94103, (415) 626-7000.
Pacific Center for Human Growth, Box 908, Berkeley 94701, 548-8283.
Salvation Army, Box 3465, San Francisco 94119, (415) 863-6520.
San Francisco Association for Mental Health, 2393, Pine St., San Francisco 94115, (415) 921-4401.
Sickle Cell Anemia Research Foundation, 1332 Haight, San Francisco 94117, (415) 626-5834.
United Cerebral Palsy Association, 1435 Market St., 2nd Floor, San Francisco 94103, (415) 255-0101.
United Way, 410 Bush, San Francisco 94108, (415) 772-4300.

CHESS

American Tournament Chess Club, 16141 Bertrero Ave., San Lorenzo 94580, (415) 276-0547.
Berkeley Chess Club, Berkeley YMCA, 2001 Allston Way, Berkeley 94704, (415) 652-5324.
Chess Friends of Northern California, 2460 21st Ave., San Francisco 94116, (415) 731-6851.
Fairfield/Suisun Chess Club, (707) 428-7435.
Fremont Chess Club, 4621 Seneca Park Ave., Fremont 94538, (415) 792-0737.
Little House Chess Group, 800 Middle Ave., Menlo Park 94025, (415) 326-2025.
Marin Chess Club, San Rafael Recreation Dept., 50 Canal St., San Rafael 94901, (415) 456-1540/485-3077.
Monterey Chess Center, 430 Alvarado, Monterey 93940, (408) 372-9790.
San Francisco Chess Club, 57 Post St., San Francisco, (415) 421-2258.
Sonoma County Chess Information, (707) 795-9377.
Vallejo Chess Club, 1015 Henry Ct., Vallejo 94590, (707) 642-7270.

COINS

Fairfield Coin Club, Box 944, Fairfield 94533, (707) 427-0482.
Fremont Coin Club, 38991 Farwell Dr., Fremont 94536, (415) 792-1551.
Livermore Valley Coin Club, 1000 S. Livermore Ave., Livermore 94550, (415) 447-8952
Northern California Numismatic Association, Box 5075, San Jose 95150.
Peninsula Coin Club, Box 60484, Palo Alto 94306.
San Francisco Coin Club, Box 27006, San Francisco 94127, (415) 697-2096.

COMPUTERS

The San Francisco Bay Area is the computer capital of the world. There are vast numbers of single men who use computers almost daily. Many of them are computer fanatics who actually think that computers are fun! They are likely to join User Groups, which are listed below. Computer User Groups specializing in business computers and software are excellent places to meet single men, since most women find computers to be boring. Unfortunately, many women think that computer buffs are all nerds. As a person who spends a great deal of time in front of a computer terminal, I disagree with this stereotype. Most of us are fun to be with, as well as intelligent and well-educated. Computer buffs also tend to have good incomes.

In addition to being fertile meeting grounds for singles, Computer User Groups usually have a public domain software library that enables you to get free or almost free software. Assistance and classes are often available to help you use the software.

The clubs are listed below according to the type of computer hardware or software they use. For a current and complete listing of Computer User Groups, meeting times and sites, read MicroTimes, 5951 Canning St., Oakland 94609, (415) 652-3810 or Bay Area Computer Currents, 5720 Hollis St., Emeryville 94608, (415) 547-6800. Both magazines are free.

BEN LOMOND
San Lorenzo Users Group, (408) 338-7348. 2nd Tuesdays, 7pm, Gathering Place, Ben Lomond.
BERKELEY
BMUG, 1442-A Walnut St. #62, Berkeley 94709, (415) 549-BMUG. Huge group. Mainly MacIntosh computers. Main meeting, Thursdays, UC Campus. Special interest groups meet nightly.
Design & Graphics Special Interest Group, 2055 Center St., (415) 849-9114, every other Monday, 8pm.
PC Compatibles User Group, Winners Circle, 2618 Telegraph, (415) 526-4033. 2nd Mondays, 7pm.
PC Desktop Publishers Users Group, 2601 College Ave., (415) 848-8200. 1st Mondays, 7pm.
CAPITOLA
MaCruzer of Santa Cruz, (408) 336-3538. 2nd Wednesdays, 7:30pm, Community Center, 4400 Jade. Desktop Publishing Group, 3rd Thursdays.
Santa Cruz Computer Society, (408) 479-1180/ 3rd Thursdays, 7pm, Santa Cruz County Office of Education, 809 Bay Ave. #H.
CONCORD
Diablo Valley PC User Group, (415) 943-1367. 1st Thursdays, 7:30pm, Carandolet High School, 1133 Winton Dr.
MacIntosh Group, (415) 676-9905. 3rd Tuesdays, Willow Creek Center, 1026 Mohr.

COTATI
North Coast Mac User Group, 3rd Wednesdays, 7:30pm, Sonoma State U., Darwin Hall #108.
CUPERTINO
Mac User Group, (415) 644-9400. 3rd Tuesdays, 7pm, City Center Cafeteria, De Anza at Stevens Creek.
Silicon Valley Computer Society, (408) 286-1271. 4th Wednesdays, 7:30pm, Hewlett-Packard, Bldg 48, Oak Room, Wolfe at Pruneridge.
Silicon Valley Paradox Users Group, (415) 855-1930. 3rd Tuesdays, 6:30pm, 10555 Ridgeview Ct.
Ventura Publisher User Group, (408) 227-5030. 1st Mondays, 6-9pm, Hewlett-Packard, Bldg 48, Oak Room, Wolfe at Pruneridge.
HAYWARD
South County PC Users Group, (415) 642-4442. 2nd Fridays, 8pm, Chabot College Bldg 1560, 2555 Hesperian Bl.
LARKSPUR
Macs of Marin, (415) 459-5707. 2nd Thursdays, 7pm, Redwood High School, 395 Doherty.
MARIN
Marin Autocad Users Group, (415) 491-4722. 1st Thursdays.
PALO ALTO
Mac Users of ComputerWare, (415) 496-1068. 3rd Tuesdays, 7pm, 490 California Ave.
Stanford MacIntosh Users Group, (415) 723-7685.
Stanford/Palo Alto PC Users Group, (415) 329-8252. Last Wednesdays, 7:30pm, Stanford U., Turing Auditorium.
PLEASANTON
Tri-Valley macIntosh User Group, (415) 426-8756 or 830-1283.
SAN CARLOS
Peninsula Computer Club, (415) 593-9981. 2nd Thursdays, 7:30pm, 222 Laurel St., Social Room.
SAN FRANCISCO
Autocad Users Group, American Institute of Architects, 130 Sutter St., 6th Floor, (415) 923-9228. 1st Mondays, 6:30pm.
PC Clone User Group, (415) 861-9321. 2nd Mondays, 7pm, Ft. Mason, Bldg E, Rm 287.
PC Publishers of Northern California, 660 Market St. #215, (415) 635-0159. 3rd Tuesdays, 6pm.
San Francisco Business Computers, (415) 788-5338. 4th Tuesdays, 5:300m, Donatello Hotel, Post at Mason.
San Francisco Computer Society, (415) 929-0252. 1st Mondays, 7pm, Laguna Honda School, 1350 7th Ave.

COMPUTERS (continued)

SAN FRANCISCO (continued)

San Francisco PC User Group, (415) 221-9166. Main Meeting, 3rd Mondays, 7:30pm, UCSF, 3333 California St. Preceding the main meeting at 6:15pm are the following special interest groups meet 6:15pm: Beginners Group, 563-5437; Desktop Video Group, 522-1797; DesqView Group, 841-5628; Lotus Group, 566-9675; New Users Solution Group, 444-4899; PC Jr. Group, 472-7035; WordPerfect Group, 929-1993; Games Group, 255-9516. Other special interest groups include: Professionals Group, 821-1310, 2nd Thursdays, 6:15pm; C Language Group, 355-8352, 2nd Mondays, 6:30pm; Columbia Group, 566-0587.

SAN JOSE

Christian MacIntosh User Group, (408) 980-0338. 1st Thursdays.

P.I.E. IBM Compatibles Special Interest Group, (408) 736-7704. 3rd Wednesdays, 7:30pm, General Disk Corp.

SAN MATEO

Ventura Publisher User Group, (415) 366-5317.

SAN RAFAEL

Golden Gate Computer Society, (415) 927-2909. 4th Mondays, San Rafael Community Center, 618 B St.

SAN RAMON

Mac Diablo User Group, (415) 828-4995 or 829-5501. 4th Wednesdays, 7:30pm, Glendale Savings, 3101 Crow Canyon Rd.

SANTA CRUZ

MUSC Fog Affiliate, (408) 476-0504. 2nd Tuesdays, Green Acres School, 966 Bostwick Ln.

SANTA ROSA

IBM PC User Group of the Redwoods, (707) 527-8737. 2nd Thursdays, 7pm, Veteran Memorial Bldg, E. Dining Rm.

Sonoma County Autocad Users Group, 69 Stony cir., (707) 524-5145. 2nd Thursdays, 5:30pm.

SOUTH BAY

Association of Apple 32 Users, (408) 263-0299. 2nd Saturdays, 10am.

Software Tools & Graphics, (408) 866-7838. 4th Mondays, 7:30pm.

Telecom Group, (408) 243-8781. 1st Mondays, 7:30pm.

MISCELLANEOUS

Bay Talk PC User Group, (415) 486-6411.

FOG International MS-DOS User Group, (415) 755-2000.

CRIBBAGE

Grass Roots Cribbage, Santa Rosa, (707) 585-1577.

Peg-a-Hole Club, (415) 453-4567. Thursdays, 7-9:30pm, Zim's Restaurant, Northgate Shopping Center, Terra Linda.

ESPERANTO

Esperanto League for North America, 5712 Hollis, Emeryville 94608, (415) 653-0998.

San Francisco Esperantists' Regional Organization, 410 Darrell Rd., Hillsborough 94010, (415) 342-1796.

FILMS

Film Arts Foundation, 346 9th St., 2nd Floor, S.F. 94103, (415) 552-8760.

San Francisco International Film Festival, 1560 Fillmore, San Francisco 94115, (415) 567-4641.

FLYING

Aircraft Pilots of the Bay Area, 18136 Reamer Rd, Castro Valley 94546, (415) 376-4104.

Alameda Aero Club, Oakland International Airport, (415) 638-4149.

Alameda Flying Club, (415) 351-2503.

Mt. Diablo Pilots Association, Box 27412, Concord 94527.

Northern California Antique Aircraft Association, Box 434, Campbell 95008, (408) 274-7220.

Palo Alto Flying Club, 1903 Embarcadero Rd., Palo Alto, (415) 494-6946 or 494-7248.

Petaluma Area Pilots Association, 500 Casa Verde, Petaluma 94952, (707) 762-5134.

GEMS & MINERALS

Benicia Rock & Gem Club, 101 Muller, Vallejo 94590, (707) 644-5495.

Berkeley Gem & Mineral Society, Box 755, Berkeley 94701, 387-1376.

California Gem Guild, Josephine Randall Junior Museum, 199 Museum Way, San Francisco 94114, (415) 863-7618 or 589-3388.

California Searchers, Box 3343, San Leandro 94578, (415) 895-1578.

Contra Costa Gem & Mineral Society, Box 4667, Walnut Creek 94596, (415) 689-4676.

Hayward Mineral & Gem Society, Eden YMCA, 951 Palisade, Hayward 94542, (415) 886-4909.

Lapidary Club of Antioch, Box 91, Antioch 94509, (415) 754-5422.

Marin Mineral Society, Box 345, San Rafael 94915, (415) 472-4573.

Mission Peak Gem & Mineral Society, 4515 Ventura Way, Union City 94587, (415) 881-6337, 489-0674, or 656-5688.

Peninsula Gem & Geology Society, Box 952, Los Altos 94022, (415) 325-8898 or 948-8016.

San Francisco Gem & Mineral Society, 4134 Judah, San Francisco 94122, (415) 564-4230.

San Mateo Gem & Mineral Society, 1141 Annapolis, San Mateo 94403, (415) 349-4245.

GENEALOGY

California Genealogical Society, 300 Brannan #409, San Francisco 94107, (415) 777-9936.
Contra Costa County Genealogical Society, Box 910, Concord 94522.
Genealogical & Biographical Society, Box 385, Napa 94559.
Livermore/Amador Valley Genealogical Association, Box 901, Livermore 94550, (415) 447-6861.
Marin County Genealogical Society, Box 1511, Novato 94948.
Napa Valley Genealogical & Biographical Society, 2977 Solano Ave., Napa 94558, (707) 252-9829.
San Ramon Valley Genealogical Society, Box 537, Diablo 94528.
Solano County Genealogical Society, 620 E. Main, Fairfield, (707) 425-6571, 446-6869.

HISTORY

Afro American Historical Society, Ft. Mason, Bldg C, Rm 165, San Francisco 94123, (415) 441-0640.
Alameda County Historical Society, 1066 Ardmore Ave., Oakland 94610, (415) 451-1101.
Alameda Historical Museum, 1327 Oak, Alameda 94501, (415) 521-1233.
Alameda Victorian Preservation Society, Box 1677, Alameda 94501, (415) 523-2877.
Albany Historical Society, 735 Madison St., Albany 94706, (415) 525-2155.
Amador-Livermore Historical Society, Box 573, Pleasanton 94566, (415) 462-2766.
American Indian Historical Society, 1493 Masonic, San Francisco 94117, (415) 626-5235.
Antioch Historical Center, 519 F, Antioch, (415) 757-7351.
Antioch Historical Society, 19 W. 7th, Antioch 94509.
Benicia Historical Society, Box 773, Benicia 94510, (707) 745-5128.
Berkeley Historical Society, 1325 Grant, Berkeley, (415) 524-9880.
Burlingame Historical Society, Box 144, Burlingame 94010, (415) 347-0303.
California Heritage Council, 41 Sutter #307, San Francisco 94104, (415) 981-4860.
California Historical Society, 2090 Jackson, San Francisco 94109, (415) 567-1848.
Chinese Historical Society, 17 Adler Pl, San Francisco 94133, 391-1188.
Clayton Historical Society, Box 94, Concord 94522.
Community Memory Project, 2617 San Pablo, Berkeley 94702.
Concord Historical Society, Box 404, Concord 94522.
Contemporary Historical Vehicle Association, 1316 Rifle Range Rd., El Cerrito 94530.
Contra Costa County Historical Society, 1700 Oak Park Bl, Pleasant Hill, (415) 939-9180.

Dublin Historical Preservation Association, 6600 Donlon Way, Dublin, (415) 828-3377.

East Contra Costa Historical Society, 519 1st St., Brentwood 94513, (415) 634-2691.

El Cerrito Historical Society, 4101 MacDonald, Richmond 94805, (415) 234-4212.

Friends of the Past, Box 11386, Piedmont 94611, (415) 547-0662.

Hayward Area Historical Society & Museum, 22701 Main, Hayward, (415) 581-0223.

Heritage Homes of Petaluma, Box 2152, Petaluma 94953, (707) 763-1100.

History Club of Los Gatos, 123 Los Gatos Blvd., Los Gatos, (408) 354-9825.

Lafayette Historical Society, Box 133, Lafayette 94549.

Livermore Heritage Guild, Box 961, Livermore 94550, (415) 449-9927, 447-5475.

Marin County Historical Society, 1125 B St., San Rafael 94901, (415) 454-8538.

Martinez Historical Society, Box 14, Martinez 94553.

Mill Valley Historical Society, 375 Throckmorton, Mill Valley 94941, (415) 388-2190.

Moraga Historical Society, Box 103, Moraga 94556.

Napa County Historical Society, 1219 1st, Napa 94558, (707) 224-1739.

Napa Landmarks, 1144 Main, Napa 94559, (707) 255-1836.

Novato Historical Guild, 650 McClay Rd., Novato 94948, (415) 897-8669.

Oakland Heritage Alliance, Box 12425, Oakland 94604, (415) 763-9218.

Orinda Historical Society, 56 Meadow View Rd., Orinda 94563.

Petaluma Historical Society, 500 D St., Petaluma 94952, (707) 762-4046.

Petaluma Old Adobe Association, 7766 Beverly Dr., Rohnert Pk 94928, (707) 795-3963.

Pittsburg Historical Society, 40 Civic Ave., Pittsburg, (415) 439-9783.

Pleasant Hill Historical & Cultural Center, 2050 Oak Park Bl., Pleasant Hill, (415) 932-9440.

Redwood City Heritage Association, 627 Hamilton, Redwood City, (415) 365-5564.

Richard III Society (British history), 2161 N. Valley, Berkeley 94702, (415) 848-7097.

San Jose Historical Museum, 635 Phelan Ave., San Jose, (408) 287-2290.

San Leandro Railway Historical Society, 1302 Orchard Ave., San Leandro, (415) 569-2490.

San Mateo County Historical Association, 1700 W. Hillsdale Blvd., San Mateo, (415) 574-6441.

San Ramon Valley Historical Society, Box 521, Danville 94526, (415) 837-4849.

Santa Clara Historical Society, 2635 Homestead Rd., Santa Clara 95051.

Santa Cruz Historical Museum, 118 Cooper, Santa Cruz, (408) 425-2540.

Santa Cruz Mountains Natural History Association, 101 Big Tree Park Rd., Felton, (408) 335-3174.
Society of California Pioneers, 456 McAllister, San Francisco 94102, (415) 861-5278.
Society of Mayflower Descendants
Aptos - 533 Vista del Mar, Aptos 95003.
Oakland - 405 14th St., Terrace Level, Oakland 94612, (415) 451-9599.
Walnut Creek - 19 Oak Knoll Loop, WC 94596, (415) 451-9599.
Solano County Historical Society, 270 Franciscan Dr., Vallejo 94589, (707) 644-3523.
South San Francisco Historical Society, Box 711, S.S.F. 94080, (415) 588-1345.
Sunnyvale Historical Museum, 235 E. California Ave., Sunnyvale, (408) 749-0220.
Sunnyvale Historical Society, (408) 245-5292. 4th Mondays, 7:30pm, Murphy Park, Sunnyvale.
Walnut Creek Historical Society, 2660 Ygnacio Valley Rd., Walnut Creek, (415) 935-7871.
Also see RAILROADS section

INVENTIONS

American Games Association, 308 Spruce St., San Francisco 94118, (415) 567-2747.
Inventors of California, Box 6158, Rheem Valley 94570, (415) 376-7541.

INVESTING

American Association of Individual Investors, 727 Longridge Rd., Oakland 94610, (415) 645-1585.
Investors Community Forum, Box 27695, San Francisco 94127, 661-8966.
Northern California Investors Association, Box 4043, Walnut Creek 94596, (415) 370-9262.

JOB SEEKING

Bay Area Broadcast Skills Bank, 214 Front St. #401, San Francisco 94111, (415) 421-6161.
Bay Area Personnel Association, 109 Minna #531, San Francisco 94105, (415) 788-2150.
Experience Unlimited, 235 12th St. #1008, Oakland 94607, 464-1259.
Forty Plus, 7440 Lockheed, Oakland 94603, (415) 430-2400.
Job Forum, San Francisco Chamber of Commerce, 465 California, 9th Floor, San Francisco 94104, (415) 392-4511.
New Ways to Work, 149 9th St., San Francisco 94103, (415) 552-1000.
San Francisco Job Club, 745 Franklin, San Francisco 94102, 771-1776.

MEDIA

Association for Multi-Image International, 10 Industrial Way, Brisbane 94005, (415) 468-3500.

Bay Area Black Media Coalition, Box 2382, Oakland 94614, (415) 889-8610.

Bay Area Video Coalition, 1111 17th St., San Francisco 94107, (415) 861-3282.

International Television Association, 110 Donoso Plaza, Union City 94587, (415) 786-8820.

Media Alliance, Ft. Mason Ctr, Bldg. D, San Francisco 94123, (415) 441-2557. Classes, forums, parties.

MENSA

Mensa, (415) 369-3252, sponsors parties and other activities throughout the Bay Area. The group is limited to people with high I.Q.s.

Oakland - High IQ Singles (415) 547-4815. Fridays, 6pm, Via Veneto Restaurant, Oakland. Led by Dr. Marilyn Ducati.

San Francisco Regional Mensa, (415) 932-6867.

San Mateo: 1732-A Marina Ct., S.M. 94403.

San Pablo: 2346 Rumrill Rd., S.P. 94806.

Sonoma County: (707) 525-8494.

METAPHYSICAL

Amron Esoteric Center, 2254 Van Ness Ave., San Francisco 94109, (415) 775-0227.

Aquarian Age, Box 919, Cupertino 95015, (408) 253-7644. Discussion group.

Astromatch Dating Service, (800) 64-ASTRO. Matchmaking through astrology.

Avatar Association, San Jose, (408) 249-3953.

Berkeley Psychic Institute, 2436 Haste, Berkeley, (415) 548-8020.

Heart Dance Magazine, Box 5539, Berkeley 94705, (415) 841-1340. Free monthly.

Palo Alto Psychic Institute, 235 Alma, Palo Alto, (415) 325-4124.

Psychic Horizons, 2240 Geary Blvd., San Francisco 94115, (415) 346-7906.

San Francisco Institute of Magical & Healing Arts, Box 410990, San Francisco 94141, (415) 821-7145.

Universal Center for Awareness, 407 Elizabeth St., Vacaville, (707) 448-1455 or 446-1520.

Whole Life Network, Box 2530, Aptos 95001, (408) 462-5810. Publishes magazine filled with information about Metaphysical classes, social events, companies, and organizations.

MINERALS

East Bay Mineral Society, 2506 High, Oakland, (415) 261-4311.
San Francisco Gem & Mineral Society, 4134 Judah, San Francisco 94122, (415) 564-4230.

MUSEUMS

California Academy of Sciences, Golden Gate Park, (415) 752-8268.
Docent Council of the Asian Art Museum, Golden Gate Park, San Francisco 94118, (415) 750-3638.
Ebony Museum of Art, 10343 14th St., Oakland 94607, (415) 763-0141.
Museum Society, De Young Museum, Golden Gate Park, San Francisco, (415) 750-3638.
Napa County Museum Society, Box 2158, Napa 94558, (707)963-7411.
National Maritime Museum Association, Bldg 275, Crissy Field, Presidio of San Francisco 94129, (415) 729-0202.
Oakland Museum Association, 1000 Oak St., Oakland 94607, (415) 893-4257. Quarterly exhibition tours and receptions, catering to singles 21-60s.
Petaluma Museum Association, 20 4th St., Petaluma 94952, (707) 778-4398.
Rock & Roll Museum, Showplace Square, 2 Henry Adams #M-82, San Francisco 94103, (415) 621-4487.
San Francisco Maritime Museum Association, Foot of Polk St., San Francisco 94109.
San Francisco Museum of Modern Art, Van Ness & McAllister, San Francisco 94102, (415) 863-8800.
San Jose Museum of Art Association, 110 S. Market, (408) 294-2787.
Santa Cruz City Museum, 1305 E. Cliff Dr., Santa Cruz, (408) 429-3773.
Vacaville Museum, 213 Buck Ave., Vacaville, 447-4513.
Vallejo Naval & Historical Museum, 734 Marin St., Vallejo 94590, (707) 643-0077.

MUSIC (MISCELLANEOUS)

Albany Community Orchestra, (415) 934-3627.
Aurora Mandolin Orchestra of Little House, 800 Middle Ave., Menlo Pk 94025, (415) 326-2025.
Bach Dancing & Dynamite Society, Box 302, El Granada 94018, (415) 726-4143. Concerts, dinners, socials. Jazz concerts with buffet, Sunday afternoons. Classical Candlelight Dinner Concerts, Friday nights.
Band Foundation, (415) 552-3656.
Berkeley Piano Club, 2724 Haste, Berkeley, (415) 845-8488.
Berkeley Society for the Preservation of Traditional Music, 1111 Addison, Berkeley, (415) 548-1761.
Bread & Roses, 78 Throckmorton, Mill Valley 94941, (415) 381-0320. Provides music for charitable events.

Burlingame Music Club, 3642 Edison St. #C, San Mateo 94403, (415) 341-5281.

Castro Valley Community Band, 19861 Forest Ave., C.V. 94546, (415) 886-1000 or 537-0310.

Community Music Center, 544 Capp, San Francisco 94110, (415) 647-6015.

East Bay Fiddling & Picking Potlucks, 833 San Carlos, Albany 94706, (415) 524-3293.

Etude Music Club, Santa Rosa, (707) 576-1942.

Friends of the Big Band, (415) 332-7340.

Las Gallinas Valley Sanitary District Non-Marching Band, Box 6435, San Rafael 94903, (415) 435-1148.

Livermore Musical Theatre, (415) 449-2113.

New Orleans Jazz Club of Northern California, Box 27232, San Francisco 94127, (415) 398-6652 (taped message).

Oakland Community Concert Association, Box 21035, Oakland 94611, (415) 483-0726.

Oakland Jazz Alliance, (415) 835-1423.

Pacific Musical Society, 170 San Pablo Ave., San Francisco 94127, (415) 661-8555.

Philharmonic Society of Fremont-Newark, Box 104, Fremont 94537, (415) 657-4059.

Pleasanton Community Band, Box 135, Pleasanton 94566, (415) 846-4628/455-4829.

San Francisco Blues Festival, (415) 826-6837.

San Jose Civic Light Opera, 4 N. 2nd St., San Jose, (408) 297-8811.

San Jose Jazz Society, 34 N. 1st St., (408) 288-7557.

San Ramon Valley Community Concerts Association, Box 141, San Ramon 94583, (415) 837-3780.

Serenaders (Big Band), Sunnyvale, (408) 739-4547 (John Nebozuk). Wednesdays, 7:30pm, Braly Park.

Show Folks of America, 827 Hyde, San Francisco 94109, (415) 441-1974.

Sunnyvale Music Association, (408) 736-1480. 1st Wednesdays, 10am-Noon.

Tri-City Concert Association, 625 Virginia, San Mateo 94402, (415) 342-2693/341-4083.

Wagner Society of Northern California, Box 590990, San Francisco 94159.

Also see:
   CHAMBER MUSIC
   OPERA
   SYMPHONY

MYSTERIES

Dashiell Hammett Society, John's Grill, Maltese Falcon Room, 63 Ellis, San Francisco 94102, (415) 986-0069.
Maltese Falcon Society, Box 22544, San Francisco 94122, (415) 665-7644.

NEWCOMERS

Are you new to your area? One of the best ways to get acclimated to a new town is to contact a Newcomers Club or Welcome Wagon. They'll do everything they can to make you feel welcome and help you meet new friends. By the same token, many new people move to your area every day. Often they don't know anyone. That means you get first dibs on all the new singles who move to your area. They'd sure enjoy meeting a friendly person like yourself.

Alameda County Newcomers, (415) 490-8477.
Alamo/Danville Newcomers, 2335 Ostrosky Dr., Alamo 94507.
Belmont Newcomers, Box BG, Belmont 94002, (415) 593-2109.
Burlingame/Hillsborough Newcomers, 1500 Sherman #1B, Burlingame 94010, (415) 344-9747.
Concord Newcomers, Box 21483, Concord 94521, (415) 689-7568.
Concord Welcoming Svc, 1399 Ygnacio Valley, Walnut Creek, 934-7133.
Dublin-San Ramon Newcomers, 12 Lasso Cir., San Ramon 94583 (415) 830-4755/830-8378.
Fairfield/Suisun Newcomers, 4666 Green Valley Ln., Suisun City 94585, (707) 425-6559.
Foster City Newcomers, Box 4102, F.C. 94404, (415) 349-3852.
Fremont Newcomers, 42993 Via Valparaiso, Fremont 94539, 657-8808.
Lafayette Newcomers, 10 El Patio, Vallejo 94590.
Livermore Newcomers, Box 1001, Livermore 94550.
Los Gatos/Monte Sereno/Saratoga Newcomers, 16234 Brooke Acres, Los Gatos 95030, (408) 356-1979.
Marin County Newcomers, 295 Adobestone, San Rafael 94903, 499-0903.
Millbrae Newcomers, 15 Chadwick Ct., Millbrae 94030.
Moraga Newcomers, 11 Merrill Dr., Moraga 94556, (415) 376-1216.
Mountain View Newcomers, 3566 Cambridge Ln, M.V. 94040.
Napa Welcome Wagon, c/o Elks Club, 2840 Soscol, Napa 94558.
New In Town, Box 492, Newark 94560, (415) 471-4485.
Orinda Newcomers, 5 Dale Ct., Orinda 94563.
Palo Alto Newcomers, Box 60824, Palo Alto 94301, (415) 856-7921.
Petaluma Newcomers, 474 Middle Two Rock, Petaluma 94952, 778-8634.
Santa Clara County Newcomers, (408) 998-0313.
Sonoma County Newcomers, 2211 4th St., (707) 545-1995.
Walnut Creek Newcomers, 2532 Quiet Place Dr., Walnut Ck 94598.
Walnut Creek Welcome Wagon, 5604 Alhambra Hills Ct, Martinez 94553.

OPERA

Oakland Opera, 524 18th, Oakland, (415) 832-0559.
Opera San Jose, 12 S. 1st St., (408) 288-8882.
Orfeo Opera Club, 13 Columbus St., San Francisco.
San Francisco Opera Association, War Memorial Opera House, San Francisco 94102, (415) 861-4008.

PHOTOGRAPHY

Advertising Photographers of America, 375 7th St., San Francisco 94103, (415) 621-3915. Fundraising parties & seminars open to public.
American Society of Magazine Photographers, 10 Cleveland St., San Francisco 94103, (415) 863-8395. Social & educational events open to public.
Contra Costa Camera Club, 737 Wiget, Walnut Ck 94598.
Napa Camera Club, 1412 Maxwell, Napa 94559, (707) 225-6104.
Oakland Camera Club, 4424 Howe St., Oakland 94611, (415) 534-5567.
Marin Photography Club, (415) 883-4219.
Petaluma Camera Club, 821 Madison, Petaluma 94952, (707) 762-7861.
Professional Photographers of California, 1873 Market St. #3, San Francisco 94103, (415) 626-2525.
Redwood Empire Camera Club, (707) 539-5135.
Retlaw Camera Club, 2959 Mission St., San Francisco 94110, (415) 647-8737.
Silverado Camera Club, 4149 Linda Vista Ave., Napa 94558, (707) 252-8468. Tuesdays, 7:30pm.
Solano Camera Club meets at the Fairfield Community Center, 1000 Kentucky St., Fairfield, (707) 422-4415.
Sunnyvale Photographic Club, (408) 732-2492. Even Mondays, 7:30-10pm, Sunnyvale Senior Center, Rm 502.

PLANTS

African Violet Society
    East Bay - Lakeside Park Garden Center, 666 Bellevue Ave., Oakland 94612, (415) 273-3186 or 932-6172.
    San Francisco - County Fair Bldg, Golden Gate Park, San Francisco 94122, (415) 558-3602.
    San Mateo County - Garden Center, 605 Parkside Way, San Mateo 94403, (415) 345-7594, 573-6872, or 574-1506.
American Fuschia Society
    Petaluma - 1624 Sarkesian Dr, Petaluma 94952, (707) 778-0828.
    San Rafael - 2227 5th Ave., San Rafael 94901, (415) 457-9210.
    San Bruno - 2600 Leix Way, South San Francisco 94080, (415) 873-1856.
    San Francisco - 651 40th Ave., San Francisco 94121, (415) 752-1623.

PLANTS (continued)

Cactus & Succulent Society
  Marin - 4 Altena, San Rafael 94901, (415) 453-8553.
  Peninsula - 848 Miramar Terrace, Belmont 94002, (415) 592-3366.
  San Francisco - 2659 Post, San Francisco 94115, (415) 346-8552.
California Horticultural Society, Academy of Sciences, Golden Gate Park,
San Francisco 94118, (415) 566-5222.
California Native Plant Society
  Marin County - (415) 883-0157.
  San Francisco Bay Chapter - 105 Sonia St., Oakland 94618, (415) 653-
    0646.
  Santa Clara Valley Chapter - 678 Perth Ct., Milpitas 95035, (408) 946-
    4976.
  Sausalito - 1 Harrison Ave., Sausalito 94965, (415) 332-4048 or 453-
    8243.
Fuji Bonsai Club, 3968 Westbury Rd, Castro Valley 94546.
Garden Club
  Antioch - 3126 S. Francisco, Antioch 94509.
  Belmont - 500 South Rd., Belmont 94002, (415) 593-7523.
  Berkeley - 1056 Ordway, Albany 94706.
  Concord - 3670 Sun View Ct., Concord 94520, (415) 687-2334.
  Danville/Alamo - Box 775, Diablo 94528, (415) 837-3048 or 830-9494.
  Eden Garden Club, Castro Valley Adult School, 19722 Center St.,
    Castro Valley 94546, (415) 538-6884
  El Cerrito - Bay Ridge Chapter, 6847 Glenmawr Ave., E.C. 94530 or
    8045 Terrace Dr., EC 94530, (415) 526-6262 or 524-5116.
  Foster City Garden Club, 968 Marquette, Foster City 94404, (415) 349-
    1782.
  Hillsborough - Box 209, Burlingame 94011, (415) 342-5151.
  Marin - Box 437, Ross 94957, (415) 454-5597.
  Martinez - Muir Chapter, 2112 Swan Lake Ct, Martinez 94553.
  Moraga - 1615 Del Monte Way, Moraga 94556.
  Napa Valley - 2760 Beard Rd., Napa 94558, (707) 252-1263.
  Novato - Box 474, Novato 94948.
  Orinda - Montelindo Chapter, 44 Southwood, Orinda 94563.
  Peacock Gap - 1 Mt. Whitney Dr., San Rafael 94903, (415) 479-1511.
  Sunnyvale - (415) 969-7122. Odd Wednesdays, 10am, Arboretum
    Work Center.
  Walnut Creek - 31 Dellwood Ct, Pleasant Hill 94523, (415) 947-1678
    or 938-7926.
Hayward Community Gardens, 25051 Whitman, Hayward, (415) 537-
8901.
Heather Farm Garden Center Association, 430 las Lomas, Walnut Creek
94598.
Hydroponic Society of America, Box 6067, Concord, (415) 682-4193.
Ikebana International, Hall of Flowers, Golden Gate Park, San Francisco
94118, (415) 566-2976.

PLANTS (continued)

Marin Home & Garden Club, 2385 Las Gallinas, San Rafael 94903.
Pleasant Hill Garden Study Club, 1808 Del Rey, Lafayette 94549.
Rose Society of Vallejo, 35 Muller, Vallejo 94590, (707) 643-5073.
San Leandro Dahlia Society, 1044 Marquette Way, San Leandro 94577.
Sheffield Garden Club, 218 Morlo, Oakland 94605, (415) 653-6127.
Shibui Arrangers, 845 Oakwood, Vallejo 94590, (707) 557-4322.
San Francisco Garden Club, 640 Sutter St., San Francisco 94102, (415) 771-0282.
Strybing Arboretum Society, 9th Ave. & Lincoln Way, San Francisco 94122, (415) 661-1316.
Western Horticultural Society, Box 60507, Los Altos, (415) 851-4492 or 941-1332.

POETRY

Contra Costa Poets Workshop, 79 isabella Ln., Pleasant Hill 94523, (415) 935-3331.
Live Poet's Society, (415) 673-7213. Poetry workshops, Thursdays, 6:30-8pm, State Bldg., San Francisco. Free.
Marin Poetry Center, (415) 454-7644.
San Jose Center for Poetry & Literature, 12 S. 1st St., San Jose, 292-3254.

PROPERTY

Apartment Owners Association of Southern Alameda County, 1260 A St. #110, Hayward 94544, (415) 537-0340.
Belmont Property Owners Association, 400 Davey Glen Rd., Belmont, (415) 593-1492.
Berkeley Property Owners Association, 1940 Virginia, Berkeley, (415) 540-8668.
Building Owners & Managers Association, 465 California #504, San Francisco 94104, (415) 362-8567.
Diablo Valley Property Managers Association, Box 5517, Walnut Creek 94596, (415) 828-5855.
East Bay Building Owners & Managers Association, 80 Grand Ave. #301, Oakland 94612, (415) 893-8780.
Income Property Marketing Group, 444 Market St. #2600, San Francisco 94111, (415) 433-7822.

PUBLIC RELATIONS

International Association of Business Communicators, 870 Market St. #940, San Francisco 94102, (415) 433-3400.
Public Relations Society of America, Ketcham Public Relations, 55 Union St., San Francisco 94111, (415) 984-6282, (415) 984-6282. Speakers, luncheons.

PUBLISHING

Bay Area Publishers Network, (415) 664-5727. Lunch meetings in Berkeley for small publishers.

Bay Area Publishing Forum, 75 Dorado, San Francisco 94112, (415) 331-5576.

International Association of Independent Publishers, Box 703, San Francisco 94110, (415) 922-9490.

PUBLIC SPEAKING

Island City Singles, 1148 Fleet St., Oakland 94610, (415) 865-5024 or 530-4326. Public speaking, Mondays, 7pm, Citicorp Bldg Conference Rm, Haight at Webster, Alameda.

Bay Area Speakers Service, 1408 Via Loma, Walnut Ck 94598, (415) 939-9121.

International Training in Communication Club, 1534 5th Ave. #4, San Rafael 94901 (415) 454-2054. Meets 2nd & 4th Thursdays, 7:30pm.

National Speakers Association, Box 281143, San Francisco 94128, (415) 994-1498.

Toastmasters practice their public speaking skills each week, usually after dinner. Chapters are found throughout the Bay Area. A few are listed below.

Bechtel Toastmasters, 45 Fremont St., 2nd Fl., San Francisco 94105, (415) 768-0445.

Belmont/San Carlos Toastmasters - 669 Edna, San Mateo 94402, (415) 349-7428.

Burlingame, (415) 344-7421.

Cable Car Club, 425 Market St., 2nd Fl., San Francisco 94105.

Capital Speakers, 519 Viewmont, Benicia 94510, (707) 745-0396.

Chinatown, 120 Ripley, San Francisco 94108.

City Hall, San Francisco, (415) 558-3844.

Coffee Beings, (415) 546-4600.

Communications, 73 Sonora, Corte Madera 94925.

Demosthenes, (415) 557-8911.

District Four (South Bay) Toastmasters Membership Hotline, (408) 559-3818.

Downtown, Cal Federal, 2600 Ocean Ave., San Francisco 94132, (415) 334-6706.

East Bay MUD, Box 24055, Oakland 94623.

EPA, (415) 974-8016.

Fightin' 49ers, (415) 397-3078.

First Class, (415) 550-5490.

Forbesmasters, (415) 534-6472.

Fountaingrove Toastmasters, Santa Rosa, (707) 577-3979.

Golden Gate Toastmasters, 363 Golden Gate, San Francisco 94102.

Healdsburg, (707) 431-1933.

Janus Toastmasters, (415) 556-8308.

Land Barons West Portal, (415) 681-1040.
Land End Toastmasters, (415) 221-4810, x3063.
Magic Word, 130 W. Portal Ave., San Francisco 94127.
Mare Island - Box 2171, Mare Island, Vallejo 94592.
Marin - 66 Cascade, Fairfax 94930.
Merritt Toastmasters, 3100 Summit Room C, Oakland 94623.
Motormouths, (415) 565-3935.
Napa Toastmasters, 527 Donwood, Napa 94558.
New Horizons, (415) 994-2956.
North Marin - 54 Birch, Corte Madera 94925.
Oakland - 1221 Broadway, 4th Fl., Oakland 94612.
Oakland City Center, 1221 Broadway, 13th Fl, Oakland 94612.
People Mover Toastmasters, Metro Center, 101 8th St., Oakland 94607.
Petaluma - 700 Sartori, Petaluma 94952, (707) 762-3910, 763-6891 or
    762-6608.
Plaza Speakers, (415) 544-3867.
Positive Thinkers Toastmasters, 341-1707 (Jim Schwandt). Public
    speaking, Mondays, 6:30-7:30am, Denny's Rest., 3190 Campus.
Premium Toastmasters, San Ramon, (415) 842-2432.
Pucksters, (415) 557-0925.
Realtors Toastmasters, (415) 929-7100.
Rohnert Park Friendlies, (707) 584-7193.
San Lorenzo - 17453 Via Carmen, San Lorenzo 94580.
Sierra Speakers, (415) 673-0548.
Singles Toastmasters, Lafayette Orinda Presbyterian Church, 49 Knox,
    Lafayette 94549, (415) 430-2400 (days) or 832-2953 (eve). Mondays,
    7:30-9:30pm.
South Marin - 257 Ricardo, Mill Valley 94941.
Speakeasies, (415) 474-9800.
Sunnyvale Toastmasters, 11916 Los Arboles, Sunnyvale 94087.
Sun Valley - 1789 Woodland Ct, Concord 94521.
Toast of the Town, Santa Rosa, (707) 823-5655.
Vallejo Speakwrights - 65 Garthe, Vallejo 94590 or 266 Woodridge,
    Vallejo 94590, (707) 644-7358.
Vintage Toastmasters, Box 1662, Travis AFB 94535, (707) 447-6810.
West Portal Toastmasters, (415) 369-7328.
Whole Wheat Toastmasters, (415) 556-8277.

RAILROADS

Bay Area Electric Railroad Association, Box 3694, San Francisco 94119.
Black Diamond Lines Model Railroad Club, 425 Fulton Shipyard Rd.,
    Antioch, (415) 779-1964.
California Central Model Railroad Club, 4185 Bassett, Agnew, (408)
    988-4449.

RAILROADS (continued)

Golden Gate Model Railroaders, Inc., Josephine D. Randall Jr. Museum, Museum Dr., near Roosevelt St., San Francisco 94114, (415) 863-1399.
Napa Valley Model Railroaders, Inc., Napa Fairgrounds, Napa 94558, (707) 253-8428/255-9615.
Northwest Pacific Railroad Historical & Technical Society, Box 4413, San Rafael 94913.
Peninsula Model Railroad Association, San Mateo County Fairgrounds, San Mateo 94403, (415) 345-2294.
Railway & Locomotive Historical Society, 978 Emerald Hill Rd., Redwood City 94061.
San Francisco Historical Railway Society, Box 1212, San Leandro 94577, (415) 785-0778.
Vallejo Model Railroad Club, Box 4281, Vallejo 94590, (707) 643-4286.
Walnut Creek Model Railroad Society, 2751 Buena Vista Ave., Walnut Creek, (415) 937-1888.
West Bay Model Railroad Assn., 1090 Merrill, Menlo Park, (415) 322-0685.

RELIGION

Churches are great places to meet single women, since the men who attend are primarily married. Nevertheless, there are tens of thousands of religious single men in the Bay Area that can be found at church. In addition to attending worship services you might consider joining one of the clubs or activities at the church (for example the choir, fundraising committees, or special events committees).

Hundreds of churches in the Bay Area sponsor singles clubs and activities. See the section on singles clubs. Warning: many of the singles clubs that meet at churches are secular. If you want to meet a religious man at a singles club, choose one that sponsors Sunday school classes, Bible readings, or worship services specifically for singles.

SINGING

Barbershop Quartet, 1123 Court St., San Rafael 94901, (415) 456-3064
Mayflower Community Chorus, Mayflower Inn, 1533 4th, San Rafael 94901, (415) 456-1011.
Oakland Symphony Chorus, (415) 652-8834.
Oakland Turnverein Gemischter Chor, (415) 482-1072 or 532-1352. Rehearsals, Wednesdays, 8pm, Bjornson Hall, Oakland. Also social events.
Redwood Chordsmen, Santa Rosa, (707) 528-2661.
San Francisco Civic Chorale, 16 Highland Ave., San Rafael 94901, (415) 453-6501.
San Mateo County Choral Society, 1556 Bernal, Burlingame 94010.
Silver Singers Mixed Chorus, Santa Rosa, (707) 545-8608.

SINGING (continued)

Society for the Preservation & Encouragement of Barbershop Quartet Singing, Box 913, Daly City 94014, (415) 826-1717.
Sunnyvale Singers, (408) 249-3629. Tuesdays, 7:45-9:45pm, Homestead High School.

STAMP COLLECTING

Fremont Stamp Club, Box 1061, Fremont 94536, (415) 797-9568.
Japanese-American Philatelic Society, Box 1049, El Cerrito 94530, (415) 529-1045.
Peninsula Stamp Club, 686 Edna Way, San Mateo 94402, (415) 574-3409.
San Francisco Philatelic Society, 986 Guerrero, S.F. 94110, (415) 647-7637.
San Pablo Pines Stamp Club, 100 Austin Ct., S.P. 94806, (415) 724-6409 or 724-0934.
Stamp Club of Vallejo, Box 4281, Vallejo 94590, (707) 643-4286.
Sunnyvale Stamp Society, (408) 245-6579. Tuesdays, 7-10pm, Raynor Park Building, Sunnyvale.
Tamalpais Stamp Club, Marin County, (415) 454-5524 or 641-5861.

SYMPHONY

Berkeley Symphony Orchestra, 941 The Alameda, Berkeley 94707, (415) 527-3436.
Contra Costa Symphony, 33 Moraga Way, Orinda, (415) 253-1535.
Diablo Symphony Association, Box 2222, Walnut Creek 94595, 935-7764.
East Bay Symphony, 1999 Harrison, Oakland, (415) 446-1992.
Marin Symphony League, Box 32, Ross 94957, (415) 456-2621.
Napa Valley Symphony Association, 2407 California Blvd., Napa 94558, (707) 226-6872.
Nova Vista Symphony, Sunnyvale, (408) 245-1305. Tuesdays, 7:30-10pm, Cumberland School, Sunnyvale.
San Francisco Symphony Association, Louise Davies Hall, San Francisco 94102, (415) 552-8000.
San Jose Symphony Association, 99 Almaden Bl, (408) 287-7383.
Santa Cruz County Symphony, 6500 Soquel, Aptos 95003, (408)462-0553.

TALL CLUBS

Are you hoping to meet new friends or romantic partners that are tall? Join one of the chapters of Tall Clubs International. The height requirement is: Men - 6'2"; Women - 5'10". Most members are single.

Redwood Empire Tall Club, 1055 Montgomery Rd., Sebastopol 95865, (707) 823-9708.
Golden Gate Tip Toppers, 750 Elizabeth, San Francisco 94114, 759-6411.
South Bay Tall Club, (408) 734-1720.

THEATRE

American Conservatory Theatre (A.C.T.), 450 Geary St., San Francisco 94102, (415) 771-3880.
Antioch Performing Arts Guild, (415) 754-8844.
Berkeley Community Theatre, Allston Way & Grove, (415) 845-2308.
Berkeley Repertory Theatre, 2025 Addison, Berkeley, (415) 841-6108.
Black Repertory Group, 1719 Alcatraz, Berkeley 94703.
Chanticleers, Box 2021, Castro Valley 94545, (415) 887-2397.
College Ave. Players, 2125 Essex St., Berkeley 94705, (415) 843-9564.
Duck's Breath Mystery Theater, Box 22513, S.F. 94122, (415) 386-9358.
Fairfield Civic Theatre, Box 887, Suisun, 864-1000.
Hollywood Actors Theatre, Box 5618, Santa Rosa 95402.
Los Altos Conservatory Theatre, Box 151, Los Altos, (415) 941-5228.
The Next Stage, 2336 Market #140, San Francisco 94114, (415) 885-6763 or 253-9602. A theater company, school, and consortium of artists that use theater as a tool to explore and develop human potential.
Oakland Ensemble Theatre, 1428 Alice #289, Oakland 94612.
Oakland Civic Theatre, 666 Bellevue Ave., Oakland, (415) 452-2909.
Oakland Ensemble Theatre, 1428 Alice, Oakland, (415) 763-7774.
Orinda Starlight Village Players, Box 204, Orinda 94563, (415) 253-1191/254-5530.
Palo Alto Players, 1305 Middlefield Rd., Palo Alto, (415) 329-2623.
Pittsburg Community Theatre, (415) 439-7529.
Pleasanton Playhouse, Box 1445, Pleasanton, (415) 462-2121.
Ross Valley Players, Box 437, Ross 94957, (415) 456-9555.
San Francisco Conservatory of Ballet & Theater Arts, 347 Dolores, San Francisco, (415) 626-1001.
Santa Clara Players, 1509 Warburton AVe., Santa Clara, (408) 248-7993.
Santa Cruz County Actor's Theatre, 1001 Center, S.C., (408) 425-7529.
Santa Cruz Performing Arts Alliance-Theatre Hotline, Box 1058, Santa Cruz, (408) 476-2166.
Sunnyvale Community Players, Sunnyvale Community Ctr, 736-0520.
Theatre Bay Area, 2940 16th St., #102, San Francisco 94103, 621-0427.

TRAVEL

Have you ever noticed how different people are when they're on vacation? The new locale liberates many people so that they're friendlier and more open to new friends and romantic relationships. It's not unusual for people to fall madly in love on a cruise or at a vacation resort with someone they wouldn't even notice if they lived next door!

The problem with romance away from home is that frequently you have a problem sustaining the relationship over a long distance. With that warning out of the way, you may consider looking for love on your next trip. With luck your new friend might live reasonably close to you. Call up your travel agent and ask which cruises or vacations have the most single people in the age range that interests you. Some cater predominantly to middle-aged and older; some to couples; some to singles in their 20s and 30s.

Club Med is probably the most popular vacation package for singles (although couples also attend). Your travel agent can give you the details. Incidentally, in case you've never called a travel agent, they usually work on a commission basis, which means their services are free to you, the customer. Listed below are services and organizations that specialize in meeting the needs of the single traveler.

NATIONWIDE TRAVEL SERVICES FOR SINGLES

New Horizon Adventures Singles Travel Club, Box 1228, Yreka, CA 96097, (916) 842-4181 or 842-2112. Myra Benson.

Partners-in-Travel, Box 491145, Los Angeles, CA 90049, (213) 476-4869.

Singles International Travel, 668 Main St., Hyannis, MA 02601, (508) 790-0050.

Singleworld Tours, (800) 223-6490 or (212) 758-2433.

Solo Flights, 127 S. Compo Rd., Westport, CT 06880. Quarterly newsletter. Travel networking. Free.

Travel Companion Exchange, Box 833, Amityville, NY 11701, (516) 454-0880.

Travelers Exchange, Box 14567, Las Vegas, NV 89114.

Travel Match, Box 6991, Orange 92613, (714) 997-5273. Computerized matching service for single travelers. Members are matched on the basis of a 4 part questionnaire & as geographically convenient as possible. Same sex or opposite sex matches as the members prefer. $60 per year includes up to 12 matches per year and a monthly newsletter. The newsletter includes articles about travel.

Travelmate, (619) 258-0220. Computer dating service that matches singles nationwide who like to travel.

Travel Partners Club, Box 2368, Crystal River, FL 32629, (904) 796-1117.

Umbrella Singles, Box 157, Woodbourne, NY 12788, (914) 434-6871. Giant singles weekends at fine hotels in the U.S. & abroad. Tennis, volleyball, swimming, ice skating, calisthenics, dance lessons, parties, rap sessions, lectures, educational programs.

World Travel Club, Colpitt's Travel Center, Westgate Mall, Brockton, MA 02401, (800) GO-TOURS or (617) 588-5660.

LOCAL TRAVEL SERVICES (specializing in Singles)

Blue Marble Travel, 530 Alameda del Prado, Novato 94949, 883-2424.

Club Voyage Marin, Greenbrae Travel, 332 Bon Air Center, Greenbrae 94904, (415) 461-4815. Singles Travel Club.

Gateway Travel, 1762 Technology Dr., San Jose, (408) 295-5600 or (800) 248-3273.

Just for Single Travelers Club, 1601 El Camino, Belmont 94002, (415) 591-8747.

SeaFit Fitness & Singles Cruises, 370 Turk St. #113, San Francisco 94102, (415) 626-0212 or (800) 626-0211.

LOCAL TRAVEL SERVICES specializing in Singles (continued)
    Shields World Travel, 5321-J Hopyard Rd., Pleasanton 94566, (415)
        460-0555.
    Single Travelers, 421 W. MacArthur Blvd., Oakland 94609, (415) 420-
        1381 (Dave). Socials, 4th Tuesdays, in San Francisco.
    Travelin' Singles, Box 386, Aptos 95001, (408) 724-6246 or 761-9977.
        Gloria Dodson is Northern California representative for this group
        based in Southern California. Primarily international travel.
    Travel Time, 2307 Van Ness, San Francisco 94109, (415) 775-8725.
    Vagabond Travel, 2290 W. El Camino Real, Mt. View 94040, (415)
        962-0990.

VEGETARIANISM

Vegetarian Potlucks for Singles, San Rafael, (415) 456-3341. 2nd & 4th
    Fridays.
Vegetarian Society of San Francisco, 1450 Broadway, San Francisco
    94109.

VOLUNTEER CENTERS

10% of all romantic relationships start on the job. But what do you
do if you have the kind of job situation where no one is appropriate for
you? Or what if you're unemployed? One alternative is to take on a
volunteer job. There are thousands of non-profit organizations
throughout the Bay Area that need help. You'll be donating your time
in a good cause, meeting new friends, and possibly find a romantic
partner.

Some of the volunteer jobs involve working with the public. Others
allow you to serve on a board of directors. In each case you'll be
meeting new friends. In addition, non-profit organizations often throw
staff parties, particularly during the holiday season. As an example, Big
Brothers/Big Sisters pair up adults with boys and girls who need a
father/mother figure. Big Brothers/Big Sisters frequently throw joint
parties, so you'll be able to meet men.

Another good way to new friends is to volunteer to be a docent for
one of the museums. You'll be able to meet your fellow docents as well
as the general public. In choosing from so many volunteer
opportunities, it makes sense to choose a job where you are likely to
meet the kind of person you seek.

Call up your local Volunteer Center listed below. They'll be glad to
meet with you personally and match you up with a job suitable to your
talents and that you will enjoy. Don't be afraid to be honest and say that
you're hoping to meet new friends. They'll be glad to suggest a
volunteer position where you'll be likely to find the kind of person you
seek.

VOLUNTEER CENTERS (continued)

ANTIOCH - 213 G St., (415) 778-3308.
BEN LOMOND - 8500 Hwy. 9, Ben Lomond 95005, (408) 336-2257.
HAYWARD - 21455 Birch St., (415) 538-0554.
MONTEREY - 444 Pearl, Monterey 93940, (408) 373-6177.
NAPA - 1700 2nd, (707) 252-6222.
OAKLAND - 477 15th St., (415) 893-6239.
PETALUMA - 7 4th Ave., Petaluma 94952, (707) 762-0111.
PLEASANTON - 333 Division, (415) 462-3570
REDWOOD CITY - 940 Douglas Ave., (415) 364-7770.
RICHMOND - 3905 MacDonald Ave., (415) 233-5558.
SALINAS - 971 N. Main, (408) 758-8488.
SAN FRANCISCO - 1090 Sansome, (415) 982-8999.
SAN JOSE - 110 E. Gish Rd., (408) 288-6868.
SAN MATEO - 450 Peninsula Ave., 415) 342-0801.
SAN RAFAEL - 70 Skyview Terrace, San Rafael 94903, (415) 479-5660.
SANTA CRUZ - 1100 Emeline Ave., Santa Cruz, (408) 423-0554.
WATSONVILLE - 15 Madison, Watsonville 95076, (408) 722-6708.

WINE

Cityscape, San Francisco, (415) 776-0215. Monthly wine tastings.
Friends of the Vineyards, Box 1191, Livermore 94550.
Napa Valley Wine Train, 1275 McKinstry, Napa 94559, (707) 253-2111.
Vintners Club, Box 3298, San Rafael 94901, (415) 485-1166.
Wine Institute, 165 Post St., San Francisco 94108, (415) 986-0878.

WRITING & JOURNALISM

American Society of Journalists & Authors, 881 Haight, San Francisco 94117, (415) 864-6369.
Asian-American Journalists Association, 1765 Sutter #1000, San Francisco 94115, (415) 346-2051.
Bay Area Black Journalist Association, (415) 893-8366/834-7897.
Bay Area Writers Workshop, Box 620327, Woodside 94062, (415) 430-3127.
California Lawyers for the Arts, Ft. Mason, San Francisco 94123, (415) 775-7200. Workshops on copyrights, video contracts, and literary agreements for artists, writers, attorneys
California Writers Club, (415) 841-1217.
Comedy Writers Association, Box 211, San Francisco 94101, (415) 626-3292.
International Black Writers & Artists, 5312 Normandie, Oakland 94619, (415) 839-4116. 3rd Saturdays, Diamond Branch Library, 3565 Fruitvale. Speakers, discussions, poetry workshops.
Mill Valley Literary Society, (415) 381-6671.

MISCELLANEOUS SOCIAL CLUBS

Active 20-30 Club
Napa - Box 12, Napa 94559, (707) 253-2030.
Santa Rosa - Box 692, Santa Rosa 95404.
Alta Mira Club, 15090 Beatty St., San Leandro 94577.
Athenian Nile Club, 410 14th St., Oakland 94612.
Campidoglio Social Club, 535 Broadway, San Francisco, (415) 392-8390.
Chatterbox Club, 282 Daffodil Dr., Fairfield 94533, (707) 425-7030.
Community Hospitality Club, 1105 4th Ave., Napa 94558.
Comstock Club, 1409 Sutter St., San Francisco 94109.
Concord Social Activities Center, 2290 Willow Pass Rd., (415) 680-9861.
Concord Summer Festival Association, 2888 Willow Pass Rd., 682-6770.
East Side Social Club, 2377 University Ave., E. Palo Alto, (415) 323-7232.
Far East Social Club, 885 4th St., San Rafael 94901, (415) 459-9022.
Golden Gate Breakfast Club, c/o Press Club, 555 Post St., San Francisco 94103, (415) 775-7800.
Lovers of the Stinking Rose (Garlic), 1621 5th Ave., Berkeley 94710, (415) 527-5171.
North Bay Nite Caps, Box 4212, Vallejo 94590.
North Star Social Club, 45 Jackson, San Jose, (408) 293-3529.
Old-Timers Club, 1821 Steiner, San Francisco, (415) 929-9603.
Over 40 Club, 560 Helen Dr., Millbrae 94030.
Peninsula Social Club, 100 N. B, San Mateo, (415) 343-7981.
Senior Friendship Club, (707) 255-1800. Tuesdays, 1-4 pm, at the Senior Center, 1500 Jefferson St., Napa.
Skylions, Box L, Daly City 94015.
University Club of Palo Alto, 327 Miranda Ave., Palo Alto 94304.
We & Our Neighbors Club, 15480 Union Ave., San Jose, (408) 559-9868.
Wednesday Club of Suisun, 225 Sacramento, Suisun 94595, 425-2745.

MISCELLANEOUS SPECIAL INTERESTS

Alcoholics Anonymous, 1046 Irving St., San Francisco 94122, (415) 661-1828.
American Chemical Society, 2140 Shattuck #1101, Berkeley 94704, (415) 848-0512. Monthly lectures open to the public.
Association of Space Explorers, 3263 Sacramento #B, San Francisco 94115, (415) 931-0585.
Bay Area Skeptics, 4030 Moraga St., San Francisco 94122. Critically examines paranormal claims. Free public meetings; monthly newsletter. $11,000 reward for proven psychic ability.
Berkeley Piano Club, 2724 Haste, Berkeley, 845-8488.
Brain Exchange, 826-8248.
California Handicapables, INC., 2326 Jones St., San Francisco 94133, (415) 273-5447. Discussion groups, lectures on new legislation affecting the handicapped. Free transportation is provided for anyone who calls a few days before a scheduled meeting. All ages.

East Bay Go Association, 2547 8th St. #41, Berkeley, (415) 843-1973.
Elvis Now Fan Club, Box 6581, San Jose 95159.
Homebrew Club (Beer), Hopland, (707) 463-1551.
Napa Valley Dining Club, 1303 Jefferson #200B, Napa 94559.
National Association to Advance Fat Acceptance (NAAFA), 477 15th St., #200, Oakland 94612, (415) 834-7897, 793-3908, or 886-3550. Dinners, dances.
Near Escapes, Box 193005, San Francisco 94119, 386-8687. Kay Grant, Director. Visits to museums, aquariums, baseball games, amusement parks. 60% single.
North Bay Connection, Jerry Lipkin, 55 Valle Vista #912, Vallejo 94590, (707) 747-6407. Singles & couples.
Oakland Switchboard, 1909 73rd Ave., Oakland, (415) 569-6369.
The Olympic Club, 524 Post St., San Francisco 94102, (415) 775-4400.
Pacific Union Club, 1000 California, San Francisco 94108, (415) 775-1234.
Peninsula Treasure Hunters, 812 Bower Rd., Pacifica 94044, (415) 355-0379 or 876-6555.
Press Club of San Francisco, 555 Post, San Francisco 94103, (415) 775-7800.
Radio-Controlled Glider Club, Pleasanton, (415) 462-9141.
Romantasy, 199 Moulton, S.F. 94123, (415) 673-3137. Parties & classes. Mainly singles. Also an erotic boutique.
San Francisco Bay Area Puppeteers Guild, (415) 552-1009. Mainly women.
San Francisco Model Yacht Club, 36 Kennedy Dr., Golden Gate Park, San Francisco 94118, (415) 386-9762.
San Francisco Bay Area Postcard Club, 104 Harbor Dr., Novato 94947, (415) 897-9137.
San Francisco Sex Information Hotline, Box 640054, SF 94164, (415) 621-7300. Volunteers answer sexual questions over the phone. Occasional parties.
Santa Rosa Mah Jong Club, (707) 579-1310.
Star Trekkers of the Bay Area, 1255 Detroit #20, Concord 94520, (415) 671-9341.
Variety Club, 585 Market, Preview Rm 101, San Francisco 94104, (415) 781-3894.

SERVICE CLUBS

There are many service clubs, such as Rotary, Kiwanis, Lions, and Elks, that are ideal for meeting new friends and making business connections. Members usually are from a broad range of businesses and professions. As a member you would also be supporting many charitable activities. Until recently these clubs were limited to men, but recent court decisions require them to open up membership to women. Most of the members are married, but a reasonable percentage will be single.

ELKS CLUBS

ALAMEDA - 2255 Santa Clara Ave., Alameda, (415) 522-1015.

HAYWARD - 24962 Mission Blvd., Hayward, (415) 537-1867.

NAPA - 2840 Soscol Ave., Napa 94558, (707) 255-4522.

REDWOOD CITY - Wilmington Way & Jefferson Ave., (415) 365-1991.

KIWANIS CLUBS

ALAMEDA - 1119 College Ave., Alameda 94501, (415) 523-1905.

ALBANY/EL CERRITO - 1009 Solano, Albany 94706, (415) 527-4927.

ANTIOCH - 341 Woodcrest, Oakley 94561, (415) 675-2473.

BELMONT - Box AB, Belmont 94002.

BENICIA - 1554 E. 2nd St., Benicia 94510, (707) 745-0205.

BERKELEY - Box 323, Berkeley 94701, (415) 526-8439 or 808 Park Central, Richmond 94803, (415) 222-3416.

BURLINGAME - Box 174, Burlingame 94011, (415) 340-0421.

CONCORD - 40 Oakbrook, Pittsburg 94565.

CUPERTINO - Box 98, Cupertino 95015, 252-6078, 255-2654, 253-0751.

EAST COUNTY - 1244 Putnam or 3900 Kite, Antioch 94509, 946-3153.

EL CERRITO/ALBANY - Plaza Professional Bldg #211, El Cerrito 94530, (415) 526-4186.

FAIRFIELD - Box 156, Fairfield 94533, (707) 426-0545 or 425-4625.

FOSTER CITY - Smith-Habel, 2031 Pioneer Ct. #2, San Mateo 94403, (415) 345-9292, 889-8000 or 582-8277.

GREATER HAYWARD - Bodycraft Co., 16348 E. 14th St., San Leandro 94578, (415) 276-1600.

LAFAYETTE - 1212 Pleasant Hill Rd., Lafayette 94549.

LOS ALTOS - 18611 Decatur Rd., Monte Sereno 95030, (408) 948-4441.

MENLO PARK - Sequoia - 1030 Curtis St. #200, M.P. 94025, 327-1313.

MILLBRAE/SAN BRUNO - 715 Cypress Ave., S.B. 94066, 589-2595.

MORAGA - 400 Donald Dr., Moraga 94556, (415) 376-7516.

MORAGA VALLEY - Box 503, Moraga 94556.

MT. VIEW - 578 Division, Campbell 95008, (415)969-5637, (408)739-1947.

NAPA
   Greater Napa Chapter, 2330 Lake Park Dr., Napa 94558, 252-0587.
   Napa Chapter, KVON, 1124 Foster, Napa 94558, (707) 252-1440.

NEWARK - Pacific Creditors, 400 Bristol Blvd., San Leandro 94577, (408) 985-0294.

NOVATO - Box 450, Novato 94948.

OAKLAND
Grand Lake Chapter, 17074 Broadway Terr., Oakland 94611, 547-0236.
Oakland Chapter, 1301 30th Ave., Oakland 94601, 534-6666, 444-3188.
Oakland Coliseum Chapter, Intl Bancorp, 7452 Limerick Ave., Dublin 94528, (415) 829-1218.

PALO ALTO
Palo Alto Chapter, Box 149, P.A. 94302, (415) 858-3940.
Peninsula Chapter, Box 1025, P.A. 94302.

PETALUMA - Box 2071, Petaluma 94953, (707) 762-6721.

PITTSBURG - Box 1110, Pittsburg 94565.

PLEASANTON - IFS, 157 Main St., Pleasanton 94566, (415) 462-1040.

REDWOOD CITY
Redwood City Chapter, Box 624, R.C. 94064.
Woodside Terrace Chapter, 711 Woodside Dr., R.C. 94061.

RICHMOND - West Coast Fabrication, 700 S. 32nd St., Richmond 94804, (415) 529-0177.

SAN CARLOS - 2606 Ponce, Belmont 94070, (415) 592-1251.

SAN FRANCISCO
Mission Chapter, 3060 16th St., SF 94103, (415) 826-3627.
San Francisco Chapter, California Parlor Cars, 1101 Van Ness, SF 94109, (415) 771-8474.
Golden Gate Chapter, 1880 Jackson St. #503, SF 94109, (415) 441-5375.

SAN LEANDRO - Box 758, San Leandro 94578, (415) 351-7460.

SAN LEANDRO, SOUTH - Allstate Insurance, 14895 E. 14th, S.L. 94578.

SAN MATEO - 345 N. Delaware, San Mateo 94401.

SAN RAFAEL - Box 353, San Rafael 94915.

SANTA CLARA - Box 2358, Santa Clara 95051, (408) 723-0775.

SOUTH SAN FRANCISCO - 3130 La Selva #206, San Mateo 94403, (415) 873-6116/579-0615.

ST. HELENA - 1390 Adams St., St. Helena 94574, (707) 963-2777.

SUNNYVALE - Silicon Valley Chapter - 1075 Rockefeller Dr., Sunnyvale 94087, (408) 245-8335.

TRI VALLEY - 3720 Thistle, Pleasanton 94566.

VALLEJO
Vallejo Chapter, 101 Corporate Place, Vallejo 94590, (707) 544-4611.
Suburban Chapter, 3626 Georgia, Vallejo 94590, (707) 557-5571.

WALNUT CREEK
Rossmoor Chapter, Box 2037, W.C. 94595, (415) 934-9086.
Walnut Creek Chapter, W.C. Florist, 1668 Locust, W.C. 94598, (415) 934-2396.
Ygnacio Valley Chapter, 849 Stonehaven Dr., Walnut Ck 94596.

For an updated listing of Bay Area Kiwanis Chapters contact Kiwanis International - 8000 Capwell Dr., Oakland 94621, (415) 832-6464.

LIONS CLUBS

ALAMEDA - 2052 San Antonio St., Alameda 94501.
ALBANY - 1331 Liberty #7, El Cerrito 94530.
AMADOR VALLEY - 1555 Trimingham Dr., Pleasanton 94566.
AMERICAN CANYON - 260 American Canyon Rd #176, Vallejo 94590.
APTOS - 170 Bowen Ave., Aptos 95003.
ATHERTON - 450 Oakgrove Ave. #107, Menlo Pk 94025.
BELMONT - 1469 El Camino Real, Belmont 94002, (415) 593-5376.
BENICIA
    Benicia Chapter, 4592 E. 2nd St., Benicia 94510, (707) 745-8855.
    Benicia Capitol Chapter, 464 Mills Dr., Benicia 94510, (707) 745-3356.
BERKELEY
    Host Chapter, Box 560, Berkeley 94701, (415) 848-5420.
    Berkeley West Chapter, Box 2188, Berkeley 94702.
BETHEL ISLAND - Box C1, Bethel Island 94511.
BRENTWOOD - 122 Broderick, Brentwood 94513.
BOLINAS - Briones Chapter, Box 516, Bolinas 94924.
BURLINGAME - Box 206, Burlingame 94011, (415) 344-5741 or 344-5466.
CALISTOGA - Box 855, Calistoga 94515.
CASTRO VALLEY
    Castro Valley Chapter, 21168 Redwood Rd #130, Castro Valley 94546.
    Host Chapter, 5581 Trailside Ct, Castro Valley 94522, (415) 537-3174.
CLAYTON VALLEY - Armand's Draperies, 3391 Mt. Diablo Blvd.,
    Lafayette 94549, (415) 283-8717.
CONCORD - Box 430, Concord 94522.
CORTE MADERA - Box 606, Corte Madera 94925.
CROCKETT - 716 2nd Ave, Crockett 94525, (415) 787-1471.
CUPERTINO
    De Anza Chapter, 830 Stendahl, Cupertino 95014, (408) 257-3833.
    Host Chapter, Box 642, Cupertino 95015.
DALY CITY Host - 7525 Mission St., Daly City 94015, (415) 991-8025.
DANVILLE - 541 Ferncroft Ct, Danville 94526.
DISCOVERY BAY - Box 665, Bethel Island 94511.
DUBLIN - 11742 Solana Dr., Dublin 94568.
EL CERRITO - 314 Rugby Ave., Kensington 94708.
MILLBRAE - 850 Taylor Blvd., Millbrae, (415) 692-0251.
OAKLAND
    Chinatown Chapter, 66 Jack London Sq., Oakland 94607.
    Coliseum Chapter, Box 2084, Oakland 94607, (415) 834-7897.
    Elmhurst Chapter, 1608 78th Ave., Oakland 94621, (415) 638-5407.
    Lake Merritt Chapter, 4617 Camden, Oakland 94619.
    Montclair Chapter, New World Travel, 1955 Mountain Blvd., Oakland
        94611, (415) 339-1335.
    Oakland Chapter, 5521 Columbia, Richmond 94804 (415) 525-7829.
FAIRFAX - 189 Deer Hollow Rd., San Anselmo 94960.

FAIRFIELD
  Fairfield Chapter, Box 126, Fairfield 94533, 422-5411/425-0198.
  FAST Chapter, Box 308, Fairfield 94533.
FREMONT
  Centerville Chapter, 4785 Hansen Ave., Fremont 94536.
  Central Chapter, 1165 Sand Beach Pl., Alameda 94501, (415) 522-3485.
  Industrial Chapter, 4957 Mansbury Ct., Fremont 94538.
  Vista Chapter, 2009 Oro Dr., Fremont 94536.
HAYWARD
  Hayward Chapter, 1065 A St., Hayward 94541.
  Hayward South Chapter, 38353 Cubberly, Hayward 94545.
LAFAYETTE - 3581 Mt. Diablo Blvd., Lafayette 94549, (415) 283-8502.
LARKSPUR - Box 21, Larkspur 94939.
LIVERMORE - (415) 455-1506.
LOS GATOS - Box 522, Los Gatos 95031, (408) 356-1266.
MENLO PARK Host - 2150 Harkins, Menlo Pk 94025, (415) 324-9272.
MILL VALLEY - Box 374, Mill Valley 94942.
MILLBRAE - 703 Clearfield Dr., Millbrae 94030.
MT. EDEN - Box 76, Mt. Eden 94557, (415) 743-0231.
NAPA - Box 3015, Napa 94558.
NEWARK - 159 Blaisdell, Fremont 94536.
NOVATO - Box 346, Novato 94947 or Box 1458, Novato 94948.
OAKLEY - 1766 Ashwood Dr., Oakley 94561.
ORINDA - 3840 Quail Ridge Rd., Lafayette 94549.
PALO ALTO
  Host Chapter, 935 Middlefield Rd., Palo Alto 94306, (415) 321-7992.
  Palo Alto South Chapter, 2290 Birch, Palo Alto 94306, (415) 326-7610.
PETALUMA
  Adobe Chapter, 1290 St. Anthony Ln., Petaluma 94952, (707) 763-6947.
  Petaluma Chapter, Box 447, Petaluma 94953, (707) 763-4104.
  Seven-Eleven Chapter, 709 Petaluma Blvd. N., Petaluma 94952, (707)
    763-0564.
PINOLE/HERCULES - 1124 Parkridge, Richmond 94803.
PITTSBURG - Ambrose Chapter - 3105 Willow Pass Rd., Pittsburg 94565,
  (415) 458-1601.
PLEASANT HILL - 2937 Salvio, Concord 94519, (415) 689-1680.
PLEASANTON - Box 266, Pleasanton 94566.
REDWOOD CITY
  Downtown Chapter, 401 Marshall, Redwood City 94063.
  Sunrise Chapter, Box 573, Redwood City 94064, (415) 327-7551.
RICHMOND - Box 2508, Berkeley 94702, (415) 652-6602.
SAN RAFAEL - Box 458, San Rafael 94912.
SAN RAMON - 7365 Sedgefield Ave., San Ramon 94583.
SANTA CLARA - 2679 Toledo, Santa Clara 95050, (408) 246-4490.

SANTA ROSA
  Coddingtown Chapter, Box 6765, Santa Rosa 95404.
  Santa Rosa Chapter, Box 1074, Santa Rosa 95409.
SAUSALITO - Box 1049, Sausalito 94966.
SOUTH SAN FRANCISCO - Bank of America, 955 El Camino, S. San
  Francisco 94080, (415) 273-5305.
SUISUN VALLEY- Box 153, Fairfield 94533.
SUNNYVALE - 137 Cumulus Ave., Sunnyvale 94087.
UNION CITY - 3161 Orwell, Fremont 94536.
VALLEJO
  Executive Chapter, Box 4427, Vallejo 94590, (707) 554-6080.
  Greater Vallejo Chapter, 357 Skyline, Vallejo 94590.
  Host Chapter, 128 Maher Ct., Vallejo 94590, (707) 552-2863.
  Marina Chapter, 1553 Redwood, Vallejo 94590, (707) 643-7508.
  Vallejo-Reveille Chapter, 115 Clark Dr., Vallejo 94590, (707) 643-3062.
WALNUT CREEK - Ygnacio Valley Commuters - 173 Maxine, Pleasant
  Hill 94523.
WEST MARIN - Box 65, Pt. Reyes Station 94596.

OPTIMISTS CLUBS

CAMPBELL - Box 2273, Saratoga 95070, (408) 446-3230.
CUPERTINO
  Cupertino Chapter, Box 92, Cupertino 95014.
  DeAnza Chapter, 3535 Ross Ave. #203, San Jose 95124, (408) 269-0946.
MILL VALLEY - Box 2668, San Rafael 94912.
NAPA - 2265 Big Ranch Rd., Napa 94558 or 2163 Euclid, Napa 94558.
OAKLAND
  Oakland Chapter, Dodge Pre-Fab, 717 Kevin Ct., Oakland 94621, (415)
    436-6545.
  Oakland North Chapter, 18 Oval, Oakland 94611, (415) 547-2502.
PALO ALTO
  Downtown Chapter, Box 1224, Palo Alto 94302, (408) 727-4050.
  Palo Alto Chapter, Box 505, Palo Alto 94302, (415) 854-3300.
  Palo Alto-Menlo Park Chapter, 1123 Blue Lake Sq., Mt. View 94040,
    (415) 968-4287.
  Palo Alto South Chapter, 844 E. Meadow, P.A. 94303, (415) 493-9024.
PETALUMA - Breakfast Chapter, 346 Keokuk, Petaluma 94952, (707)
  763-6375.
REDWOOD CITY - Box 1138, Redwood City 94064, (415) 366-1392.
SAN CARLOS - Paramount Awards, 940 Washington, San Carlos 94070,
  (415) 593-9339.
SAN FRANCISCO - 500 Montgomery, S.F. 94111, (415) 788-4700 x5.
SAN LEANDRO - 13730 E. 14th St., San Leandro 94577, (415) 489-8565.
SAN RAFAEL - 1104 4th St., San Rafael 94901.
SANTA ROSA - High Noon Chapter, 2729 Yulupa Ave., S.R. 95404

ROTARY CLUBS

ALAMEDA - 3104 Gibbons, Alameda 94501, (415) 521-4500.
ALAMO - Grubb & Ellis, 1646 N. California #540, W.C. 94596, 932-6760.
ALBANY - 603 Key Route Blvd., Albany 94706, (415) 525-1130.
ANTIOCH - Box 692, Antioch 94509.
BELMONT - Box 448, Belmont 94002.
BENICIA - Box 421, Benicia 94510.
BERKELEY - 1836 University Ave., Berkeley 94703, (415) 841-2319.
BRENTWOOD - 402 Sherwood Dr., Brentwood 94513, (415) 634-2509.
BURLINGAME - Box 1297, El Granada 94018, (415) 726-6038 or 574-7000 or 696-2300.
CALISTOGA - Box 754, Calistoga 94515, (707) 942-6973.
CAMPBELL - 1527 Monteval, San Jose 95120, (408) 260-0800.
CASTRO VALLEY - Sunrise Chapter, 322 Davis St., San Leandro 94577, (415) 886-8765.
CONCORD - 2080 Diamond Blvd., Concord 94520, (415) 798-2270.
CUPERTINO - Box 637, Cupertino 95015, (408) 253-1806/248-2772.
DALY CITY - Box 3026, Daly City 94017, (415) 744-0490.
DUBLIN - Family Service of East Bay, 7080 Donlon, Dublin 94568, (415) 828-3538.
FAIRFIELD - Box 477, Fairfield 94533, (707) 422-3200.
FOSTER CITY - Box 8111, Foster City 94404, (415) 341-1290.
FREMONT
    Fremont Chapter, Tri-City Office Machines, 43466 Ellsworth, Fremont 94539, (415) 657-1535.
    Mission San Jose Chapter, Box 538, Fremont 94537.
    Niles Chapter, 38355 B Logan Dr., Fremont 94536, (415) 796-4410.
GILROY - 1534 Calabrese, Gilroy 95020, (408) 842-5112.
HAYWARD - 22205 Prospect, Hayward 94541, (415) 784-2640.
HOLLISTER - 1070 San Benito, Hollister 95023, (408) 637-7423.
IGNACIO - 283 Robin Ave., Cotati 94928.
LAFAYETTE - Box 103, Lafayette 94549, (415) 284-4862.
LIVERMORE
    Livermore Chapter, 1740 Perry Way, Livermore 94550, (415) 373-5325.
    Livermore Valley Chapter, 1617 Warsaw Ave., Livermore 94550, (415) 449-4661.
LOS ALTOS - Box 39, Mt. View 94042, (415) 964-8000.
LOS GATOS - 19600 Redberry Dr., Los Gatos 95030, (408) 354-2950.
MARIN COUNTY
    Central Chapter, Box 438, Corte Madera 94925, (415) 459-0303.
    Evening Chapter, 25 Suffield Ave., San Anselmo 94960.
MARTINEZ - ESI, 10 Douglas #100, Martinez 94553, (415) 372-8600.
MENLO PARK - 1148 Crane St., Menlo Pk 94025, (415) 323-5169.
MILL VALLEY - Box 374, Mill Valley 94941, (415) 388-1818.
MILLBRAE - 50 Bel Aire Ct., Hillsborough 94010, (415) 956-6555 x300.
MILPITAS - 1 N. Main St., Milpitas 95035.

ROTARY CLUBS (continued)

MORAGA
Moraga Chapter, Box 122, Moraga 94553, (415) 376-4411 x385.
St. Mary's College Chapter, 3621 Walnut #1, Lafayette 94549.
MOUNTAIN VIEW - Box 39, Mt. View 94042, (415) 964-8000.
NAPA
Napa North Chapter, Box 493, Napa 94559, (707) 224-3121.
NOVATO - 1450 Grant Ave., Novato 94947.
OAKLAND
East Oakland Chapter, 11 Dover Ct., Orinda 94563, (415) 893-7233.
International Fellowship of Flying Rotarians, Box 449, Oakland 94604, (415) 834-2430.
North Oakland/Emeryville Chapter, 107 Mandala, Walnut Ck 94596.
Oakland Chapter, 1736 Franklin St. #200, Oakland 94612, 451-2120.
Piedmont/Montclair Chapter, Office of Charles Triay, 2030 Franklin, Oakland 94612, (415) 452-1360.
Sunrise Chapter, 1425 Leimert, (415) 428-0300 or 398-3534.
ORINDA - Box 44, Orinda 94563.
PALO ALTO
Palo Alto Chapter, Transition Capital, 5 Palo Alto Sq., #1022, Palo Alto 94306, (415) 493-1051.
Palo Alto Bayshore Chapter, 408 Cambridge Ave., Palo Alto 94306, (415) 326-6384.
Stanford Area Chpater, Box 465, Los Altos 94023, (415) 961-1473.
PETALUMA
Petaluma Chapter, Box 5655, Petaluma 94953, (707) 763-5224.
Petaluma Valley Chapter, 14 West St., Petaluma 94952, (707) 762-7319.
Pittsburg - Cypress Corp., 1200 Concord Ave. #130, Concord 94520, (415) 674-0401.
PLEASANTON
Pleasanton Chapter, Box 1185, Pleasanton 94566.
Pleasanton North Chapter, 206 Blue Mound Ct., San Rafael 94583.
REDWOOD CITY
Redwood City Chapter, 1107 Shasta, Redwood City 94063, (415) 368-7879 or 364-6440.
Redwood Shores Chapter, 750 Middlefield Rd., Redwood City 94063, (415) 363-4516.
RICHMOND - 3220 Blume Dr., Richmond 94806, (415) 222-6000.
ROSS VALLEY - Deer Park Villa, Bolinas Rd., Fairfax 94930, 472-7470.
SAN CARLOS - Box 513, San Carlos 94070, (415) 592-1251.
SAN FRANCISCO
San Francisco Chapter, 55 New Montgomery #5010, San Francisco 94105, (415) 546-0644.
Stonestown Chapter, Box 31420, San Francisco 94131.

SAN JOSE
 Almaden Chapter, 6573 Crystal Springs Dr., San Jose 95120, 227-9697.
 Cambrian Park Chapter, 5730 San Lorenzo Dr., San Jose 95123, (408)
  295-2900.
 San Jose Chapter, 998 Park Ave., San Jose 95126, (408) 297-6100.
 San Jose East Chapter, 3414 Woody End Ct., San Jose 95121.
 San Jose International Airport Chapter, 1725 Seville, San Jose 95131.
 San Jose North Chapter, 830 Jury Ct. #1, San Jose 95112.
 San Jose South Chapter, 5524 Deep Purple, San Jose 95123.
 San Jose West Chapter, 18950 Graystone Ln, San Jose 95120.
SAN LORENZO - 185 C Norris Canyon, San Ramon 94583, 886-1500.
SAN MATEO - New York Life, 520 S. El Camino #916, San Mateo 94402,
 (415) 342-0856.
SAN PABLO - Box 222, San Pablo 94806, (415) 231-0202.
SAN RAFAEL
 Mission San Rafael Chapter, Box 1378, San Rafael 94915.
 San Rafael Chapter, 138 El Condor Ct., San Rafael 94903.
 Terra Linda Chapter, 585 Kernberry, San Rafael 94903.
SANTA CLARA
 Santa Clara Chapter, American Components, 1871 Main St., Santa
  Clara 95050, (408) 224-6344.
 Santa Clara North Chapter, 5088 Lone Hill Rd., Los Gatos 95030.
 Santa Clara West Chapter, 3276 Ravenswood Way, San Jose 95148.
SANTA CRUZ COUNTY
 Mid-County Chapter, 7120 Viewpoint Rd., Aptos 95003, 724-4725.
 San Lorenzo Valley Chapter, 163 Taylor, Santa Cruz 95062, 335-5117.
 Santa Cruz Chapter, 135 Rulofson, Santa Cruz 95060.
 Santa Cruz Sunrise Chapter, 148 Spreading Oak, Scotts Valley 95066.
 Scotts Valley Chapter, 160 Lunar Dr., Scotts Valley 95066.
SANTA ROSA
 Santa Rosa Chapter, Box 2785, Santa Rosa 95404.
 Santa Rosa East Chapter, Box 2785, Santa Rosa 95404.
SARATOGA
 Saratoga Chapter, Box 96, Saratoga 95071, (408) 867-2252.
 West Valley, 13851 River Ranch Cir., Saratoga 95070.
SAUSALITO - Box 897, Sausalito 94966.
SOUTH SAN FRANCISCO - 1486 Huntington Ave. #200, S.S.F. 94080.
ST. HELENA - Box 211, St. Helena 94574.
SUNNYVALE - 4666 Capay Dr #3, San Jose 95118, (408) 942-8744.
TIBURON - 98 Main St., Tiburon 94920.
VALLEJO - Box 3188, Vallejo 94590, (707) 644-1141.
WALNUT CREEK
 Rossmoor Chapter, Box 2177, Walnut Ck 94595.
 Walnut Creek Chapter, Box 4191, Walnut Ck 94596.
WATSONVILLE - 34 La Casa Ct., Freedom 95019.

CIVIC ORGANIZATIONS

ECOLOGY ORGANIZATIONS

Abalone Alliance
  East Bay - (415) 655-1715.
  Marin - 1024 Sir Francis Drake Blvd., San Anselmo 94960, 456-4377.
  San Francisco - 2940 16th St. #310, SF 94103, (415) 861-0592.
American Shore & Beach Preservation Association, University of California, 512 O'Brien Hall, Berkeley 94720.
Audubon Society
  Golden Gate Chapter - 1550 Shattuck #204, Berkeley 94705, (415) 843-2222.
  Marin Chapter - Box 599, Mill Valley 94942, (415) 388-7888, 331-0730, or 383-1770.
  Mt. Diablo Chapter, Box 53, Walnut Creek 94597.
  Oakland Chapter - Box 11176, Oakland 94611, (415) 834-6666.
  Napa/Solano Chapter, 1015 Borrette, Napa 94558, (707) 252-3439.
  National Chapter, 376 Greenwood Beach Rd., Tiburon 94920, (415) 388-2524.
  Santa Clara Valley, 2253 Park Blvd., Palo Alto 94306, (415) 329-1881.
  Sequoia Chapter, 720 El Camino #403, Belmont 94002, (415) 493-7368.
Bay Area Community Council, Emeryville, (415) 652-5373, 843-2479, or 526-4362.
Bay Area Environmental Protection, 1125 Hensley St., Richmond 94801, (415) 233-8001.
Bay Area Greenbelt Congress, 512 2nd St., 4th Fl., San Francisco 94107, (415) 543-4291, 423-8987, or 846-1906.
Berkeley Bayfront Council, Box 181, Berkeley 94701, (415) 845-6135 or 548-2393.
Berkeley Design Advocates, (415) 893-6834, 548-5700, or 845-6475.
Big Sur Land Trust, Box 221864, Carmel 93922, (408) 625-5523. Helps preserve open space in Big Sur, Carmel Valley, & Monterey Peninsula.
Carlmont Whole Earth Program, 2811 San Carlos Ave., San Carlos 94070, (415) 591-9623.
Citizens for an Appropriate Urban Shoreland Environment, 1334 Peralta, Berkeley 94702, (415) 525-1486.
Citizens for a Better Environment, 2131 University Ave., #421, Berkeley 94704.
Clean Bay, 2070 Commerce Ave., Concord 94520, (415) 685-2800.
Committee for Green Foothills, 2253 Park Blvd., Palo Alto 94306, (415) 327-5906.
Contra Costa Hills Club, 4000 Broadway, Oakland 94609, (415) 232-7475.
Earth Regeneration Society, 470 Vassar, Berkeley 94708, (415) 525-4877.
East Bay League of Conservation Voters, Box 3191, Oakland 94609, (415) 652-8063.

Ecology Center
  Berkeley - 1403 Addison St., Berkeley 94702.
  San Francisco - 13 Columbus, San Francisco 94111, (415) 391-6307.
Electric Vehicle Association, 1460 Summit Rd., Berkeley 94708, (415) 848-1468.
The Elmwood Institute, Box 5765, Berkeley 94705, (415) 845-4595. Energy Conservation Program, 7101 Edgewater Dr., Oakland 94621, (415) 642-4911.
Environmental Defense Fund, 2606 Dwight Way, Berkeley 94704, (415) 548-8906.
Environmental Federation of California, Kalman Stein, 116 New Montgomery #231, San Francisco 94105, (415) 882-9330.
Environmental Volunteers, 2253 Park Blvd., Palo Alto 94306, (415) 327-8107.
Friends of Aquatic Park, 1210 Shattuck, Berkeley 94709, (415) 843-1743.
Friends of Claremont Canyon, Box 5108, Berkeley 94705, (415) 841-0339.
Friends of the Earth, 1045 Sansome, San Francisco 94111, (415) 433-7373.
Friends of the River, Fort Mason, Bldg C, San Francisco 94123, (415) 771-0400.
Friends of Trees, 2021 Waverly St., Napa 94558, (707) 224-4224.
Friends of the Yard, Berkeley, (415) 849-4993.
Green Belt Alliance, 116 New Montgomery #640, San Francisco 94105, (415) 543-4291.
Greenpeace Pacific Southwest, Ft. Mason, Bldg. E, San Francisco 94123, (415) 474-6767.
Hayward Area Planning Association, 2787 Hillcrest Ave., Hayward 94542, (415) 538-3692.
Marin Agricultural Land Trust, 520 Mesa Rd., Pt. Reyes 94956, (415) 663-1158.
Marin Conservation League, 35 Mitchell Blvd. #11, San Rafael 94903, (415) 456-1912.
Marin Conservation League, North Marin, 110 San Mateo Way, Novato 94947.
Mono Lake Committee, 1045 Sansome #404, S.F. 94111, (415) 956-7532.
Nature Conservancy, 785 Market, 3rd Fl., S.F. 94103, (415) 777-0487.
Nature Explorations, 2253 Park Blvd., Palo Alto 94306, (408) 325-8737.
Neighbors for Clean Air, 1610 Curtis St., Berkeley, (415) 524-2724.
Northern California Solar Energy Association, Box 3008, Berkeley 94703.
Oakland Neighborhood Tree Program, (415) 834-7897.
People for Open Space, 116 New Montgomery #640, San Francisco 94105, (415) 543-4291.
Peninsula Conservation Center Foundation, 2253 Park Blvd., Palo Alto 94306, (415) 328-5313.
Planet Drum Foundation, Box 31251, San Francisco 94131, 285-6556.
Preserve Area Ridgelands Committee, 1st Presbyterian Church, 2490 Grove, Castro Valley 94546, (415) 538-3692.

Rain Forest Action Network, 301 Broadway #A, San Francisco 94133, (415) 398-4404.

Safe Water Coalition, 41 Sutter #709, San Francisco 94104, (415) 421-2608.

San Francisco Beautiful, 41 Sutter #709, San Francisco 94104, (415) 421-2608 or 986-1010.

Santa Cruz Greens, (408) 335-3216.

Save the Bay Association, Box 925, Berkeley 94701, (415) 849-3053.

Save the Hills Association, 7065 Marlborough Terr., Berkeley 94705.

Save Mt. Diablo, Box 25, Concord 94522, (415) 685-5315.

Save the Redwoods League, 114 Sansome #605, SF 94104, (415) 362-2352.

Save San Francisco Bay Association, 2140 Shattuck, Berkeley 94701, (415) 849-3053.

Save Wetlands in Mayhews, 36493 Bridgepointe, Newark 94560, (415) 792-8291.

Sierra Club

Contra Costa Chapter - 85 Monte Cresta, Pleasant Hill 94523.

Loma Prieta Chapter, 2253 Park Blvd., Palo Alto 94306, (415) 966-3655.

Marin Chapter, 7 Crest Rd., Fairfax 94930, (415) 456-6944.

San Francisco Bay Chapter, 6014 College Ave., Oakland 94618, (415) 653-6127.

San Francisco Chapter - 530 Bush, SF 94108, (415) 981-8634.

Silicon Valley Toxics Coalition, 760 N. 1st, San Jose, 287-6707.

Tamalpais Conservation Club, 870 Market St. #562, San Francisco 94102, (415) 391-8021 or 861-5636.

Trees for the City, 740 Francisco, San Francisco 94133, (415) 775-1695.

Tri-City Ecology Center, Box 674, Fremont 94537, (415) 793-6222.

Trust for Public Land, 116 New Montgomery, 4th Floor, San Francisco 94105, (415) 495-4014.

Underwater Society of America, Box 628, Daly City 94017.

University New Conservationists, Box 362, Campbell 95009, (408) 241-5769.

Urban Care, Box 181, Berkeley 94708, (415) 845-6135.

Urban Creeks Council, 2634 Grant, Berkeley 94703, (415) 540-5118.

Urban Ecology, 1939 Cedar, Berkeley 94709, (415) 548-7801.

Walnut Creek Action for Beauty Council, 1820 Stratton Cir., Walnut Ck 94598.

INTERNATIONAL AFFAIRS ORGANIZATIONS

American Global Association, 180 Grand Ave., Oakland 94612, (415) 655-4700.

Amnesty International, 655 Sutter #402, San Francisco 94102, (415) 563-3733 or 441-3733.

Asia Foundation, 550 Kearny, San Francisco 94108, (415) 982-4640.

Bay Area Free South Africa Movement, 5425 E. 14th St., Oakland 94601, (415) 752-7766, 261-3094, or 653-0329

Burlingame/Cuernavaca Sister Cities Association, Box 1154, Burlingame 94011, (415) 343-4768.

Campaign Against Apartheid, UC, 613 Eshleman Hall, Berkeley 94720, (415) 642-7783.

East/West Exchange, Box 4028, San Rafael 94915, (415) 472-3493.

Food First: Institute for Food & Development Policy, 145 9th St., San Francisco 94103, (415) 864-8555. Fights world hunger.

Global Cooperation for a Better World, 401 Baker St., San Francisco 94117, (415) 563-4459.

Marin Chinese Culture Group, Box 6051, San Rafael 94913, 457-0313.

Oakland Africa Sister City Cultural Center, 59 Garland, Oakland 94611, (415) 893-2293.

Oakland/Dalian Friendship City Society, Ms. Lelia White, Main Library, 125 14th St., Oakland 94610.

Oakland/Fukuoka Sister City Society, 681 Santa Ray, Oakland 94610.

Pan American Society, 3040 22nd St., San Francisco 94103, 550-9252.

UNESCO Association, 5815 Lawton, Oakland 94618, (415) 654-4135.

UNICEF, 3419 Sacramento, San Francisco 94118, (415) 567-9755.

United Nations Association
  Oakland - 477 15th St. #200, Oakland 94612, (415) 849-1752.
  San Francisco - 312 Sutter St. #602, SF 94108, (415) 982-6677.

U.S.-China Peoples Friendship Association, 50 Oak St., #502, San Francisco 94102, (415) 863-0537.

World Affairs Council, 312 Sutter St. #200, San Francisco 94108, (415) 982-2541.

World Forum of the Silicon Valley, 110 E. San Carlos, San Jose 95112, (408) 298-8342.

World Trade Association, 465 California, 9th Fl., San Francisco 94104, (415) 392-2705.

WORLD PEACE ORGANIZATIONS

Alameda County Nuclear Weapons Freeze, 4042 Broadway, Oakland 94611.

American-Soviet Friendship Society, 1819 10th St., Berkeley 94710, (415) 232-6249.

Beyond War
  Fremont Chapter - 4216 Mattos Dr., Fremont 94536, (415) 792-4927.
  Marin Chapter - 12 Ninestone Ct., San Rafael 94903, (415) 479-5100.
  Oakland Chapter - Box 523, 5251 Broadway, Oakland 94618, (415) 444-1750 or 524-6324.
  Palo Alto Chapter - 222 High St., P.A. 94301, (415) 328-7756.
  Sonoma County Chapter - 6113 Bridgewood Dr., Santa Rosa 95405, (707) 539-1944.

WORLD PEACE ORGANIZATIONS (continued)

Center for Peacemaking, 5701 Thornhill Dr., Oakland 94611, (415) 339-1131.

Circle of Concern, Berkeley Area Interfaith Council, 2340 Durant Ave., Berkeley 94704, (415) 841-0881 or 848-8055.

Disarmament Resource Center, 942 Market #708, San Francisco 94102, (415) 495-0526.

Foundation for the Arts of Peace, 1918 Bonita, 3rd Fl., Berkeley 94704, (415) 486-0264.

Hayward Area Peace Fellowship, Box 3493, Hayward 94540, (415) 782-5795.

Livermore Action Group, 3126 Shattuck Ave., Berkeley 94705, (415) 644-3031 or 644-2028.

Institute for the Practice of Nonviolence/Veterans Peace Action Teams, (415) 753-2882.

Marin Center for Peace & Justice, 1024 Sir Francis Drake Blvd., San Anselmo 94960, (415) 459-5676. Network of Marin County organizations committed to stopping the nuclear weapons and creating a safe environment.

Mid-Peninsula Peace Center, 555 Waverly, Palo Alto 94301, (415) 326-8837.

Northern California War Tax Resistance, (415) 843-9877.

Nowhere to Run/Turnaround Race for Peace, Box 20249, Oakland 94620, (415) 658-7805, 658-6503, or 452-0872.

Nuclear Weapons Freeze, Napa, (707) 944-2235.

Organization for a Workable Peace, 1442 A Walnut #182, Berkeley 94709, (415) 836-4294.

Peace A Community Task, 75 Hill Rd., Berkeley 94708, (415) 841-9189.

Peace Center of Marin, 1024 Sir Francis Drake Blvd., San Anselmo 94960, (415) 459-5676.

Peace Navy, (415) 398-1201. Nonviolent water-based theater. Supports peace social justice, and ecology.

Peace Ribbon Action, Santa Cruz, (408) 688-7021.

Peace the 21st, (707) 762-8916, visualizes and meditates for world peace.

Physicians for Social Responsibility, 2288 Fulton #307, Berkeley 94704.

SANE/FREEZE Campaign for Global Security supports ending the arms race and building an economy based on peace.
Regional Office, (415) 621-7770.
San Francisco, (415) 621-0858.
Alameda County, (415) 655-6872.
Contra Costa County, (415) 372-7161.
Marin County - 72 Kensington, San Anselmo 94960 (415) 459-1530.
San Mateo County - Box 425, San Mateo 94401, (415) 342-3404.
Napa County, 1556 Jefferson, Napa 94559, (707) 253-2125.
Santa Clara County, (408) 866-5582.
Santa Cruz County, (408) 458-9975.

WORLD PEACE ORGANIZATIONS (continued)

San Francisco Bay Area Peace Council, 347 Dolores, (415) 621-5210.
Swords to Plowshares, 400 Valencia, San Francisco 94103, 552-8804.
Voting Power Action Committee, 5825 Telegraph Ave. #53, Oakland 94609, (415) 268-0282.
Walnut Creek Peace Center, 65 Eckley Ln., W.C., (415) 933-7850.
War Resisters League, 924 Market #705, San Francisco 94102, 433-6676.
Witness for Peace, 2124 Kittredge St. #92, Berkeley 94704, (415) 763-5344 or (408) 425-3749.
World Citizens Assembly, 312 Sutter #506, San Francisco 94108, (415) 421-0836 or 525-5057.
World Without War Council, 1730 Martin Luther King Jr., Berkeley 94709, (415) 845-1992.

PEACE IN CENTRAL AMERICA ORGANIZATIONS

Bay Area Central America Peace Campaign, c/o Cispes, 760 Valencia, San Francisco 94110, (415) 648-8222
Central American Hotline, (415) 845-3123.
Central American Refugees Organization Project, (415) 864-7400.
Committee in Solidarity with the People of El Salvador, Box 3326, Berkeley 94703, (415) 648-8222.
CRECE, (415) 824-5928.
Earth Island Environmental Project in Central America, (415) 788-3666.
East Bay Sanctuary Covenant, (415) 540-5296.
Emergency Response Network, (415) 655-1177.
Guatemala News & Information Bureau, (415) 835-0810.
Marin Interfaith Task Force on Central America, (415) 454-0818.
Neighbor to Neighbor, (415) 824-3355.
New El Salvador Today, (415) 864-7755.
Nicaraguan Information Center, (415) 549-1387.
Nicaraguan Interfaith Committee for Action, (415) 433-6057.
Pledge of Resistance, (415) 771-1276.
Pueblo to People, (415) 648-8068.
San Francisco Jewish Sanctuary Coalition, (415) 282-2636.
San Francisco Sanctuary Covenant, (415) 824-6274.
SHARE, (415) 644-2642.
Tecnica, (415) 848-0292.

POLITICAL PARTIES

Democrats
    Alameda County Democratic Central Committee, 1122 B St #211, Hayward 94541.
    Berkeley Democratic Club, 2519 Hawthorne Terr., Berkeley 94708, (415) 845-0608.

Democrats (continued)
Napa County Democratic Central Committee, 1415 Jefferson, Napa 94559, (707) 252-3067.
Orinda-Moraga Democratic Club, Box 31, Orinda 94563.
Petaluma Democratic Club, Box 2850, Petaluma 94953, 762-2706.
Union City Democratic Club, 31249 San Andreas Dr., Union City 94587, (415) 887-7355.
San Francisco Democratic Party, (415) 626-1161.
San Ramon Valley Democrats, 1135 San Ramon Valley Blvd., Danville 94526.
Sonoma County Democratic Headquarters, 607 4th St., Santa Rosa 95404, (707) 575-3029.
Libertarians
Peninsula Libertarians, Box 3331, Redwood City 94064, 368-8148.
Republicans
Napa County Republican Party, (707) 226-9151.
San Francisco Republican Party, 540 Van Ness, San Francisco, (415) 255-7668.
Sonoma County Republican Headquarters, 50 Santa Rosa Ave. #203, Santa Rosa 95404, (707) 542-7066.

TAXPAYERS ORGANIZATIONS

Alameda County Taxpayers Assoc., 1305 Franklin, Oakland, 893-3341.
Berkeley Taxpayers Association, (415) 524-8083.
Contra Costa Taxpayers Association, 820 Main, Martinez, (415) 228-5610.
Marin United Taxpayers Association, 819 A St., San Rafael 94901, (415) 456-7910.
San Francisco Taxpayers Association, 446 Corbett Ave., San Francisco, (415) 864-2344.
Solano County Taxpayers Association, 740 Texas, Fairfield, 425-8145.
Sonoma County Taxpayers Association, (707) 542-0442.
Union City Homeowners & Taxpayers Committee, 103 Decoto Rd., Union City, (415) 429-9767.
Mental Health Association, 2398 Pine St., San Francisco 94115, 921-4401.

MISCELLANEOUS CIVIC ORGANIZATIONS

A Dream for Berkeley, 828 Spruce St., Berkeley 94707, (415) 527-8242
Alameda County War on Drugs, 2450 Washington Ave., San Leandro, (415) 352-5006
All Berkeley Coalition, 1400 Shattuck #7-36, Berkeley 94709, (415) 548-7290 or 524-5232
American Civil Liberties Union, 1663 Mission #460, San Francisco 94103.
Americans for Non-Smokers Rights, 2054 University Ave. #500, Berkeley 94704.

MISCELLANEOUS CIVIC ORGANIZATIONS (continued)

American Society on Aging, 833 Market, San Francisco 94103, (415) 543-2617.
American Civil Liberties Union, 814 Mission St., San Francisco 94103, (415) 621-2488.
Association for California Education, 2929 Castro, San Pablo 94806, (415) 236-4962.
The Bay Area Council, 847 Sansome, San Francisco 94111, (415) 981-6600.
Bay Area Educational Television Association, 500 8th St., San Francisco 94103, (415) 864-2000.
Bay Area Physicians for Human Rights, Box 14564, San Francisco 94114.
Bay Area Urban League, 344 20th St., Oakland 94612, (415) 922-5050.
Bay Planning Coalition, 666 Howard St. #301, San Francisco 94105, (415) 543-3830.
Berkeleyans for Fair Traffic Management, Box 5108, Berkeley 94703, (415) 549-3093.
Berkeley Architectural Heritage Association, 2105 Bancroft Way, Berkeley, (415) 841-2242.
Berkeley Citizens Action, 3122 Shattuck Ave., Berkeley, (415) 549-0816.
Berkeley Citizens United, Box 44, Berkeley 94701, 525-0783 or 524-1331.
Berkeley City Club, 2315 Durant, Berkeley 94704, (415) 848-7800.
Berkeley Roundtable on the International Economy, (415) 642-3067.
Berkeley Tenants Union, 2022 Blake, Berkeley, (415) 843-6601.
Berkeley Victory Civic Club, 1305 66th St., Berkeley 94702.
Black Cultural & Political League, 4287 Oakdale Pl., Pittsburg 94565.
Black Political Association, Box 1851, Pittsburg 94565, (415) 439-2061.
Cabrillo Civic Club, 300 East M St. #58, Benicia 94510.
California Club, 1750 Clay St., San Francisco 94108, (415) 474-3516.
California Council for Environmental & Economic Balance, 215 Market #1311, San Francisco 94105, (415) 495-5666.
California Educators for Social Responsibility, 477 15th St. #200, Oakland 94612, (415) 268-9898.
California Institute for Effective Action, 959 12th St., Oakland 94606, (415) 839-1569.
Century Club, Box 1055, Concord 94522, (415) 682-8521.
Chinese-American Citizens Alliance, 1044 Stockton, San Francisco 94108.
Churchill Club, Palo Alto, (415) 494-6678.
Citizens Action League
  Box 3702, Oakland 94609.
  1113 MacDonald, Richmond 94801, (415) 236-8232.
  2988 Mission, San Francisco 94110, (415) 647-8450.
Citizens Council for Napa Tomorrow, 905 Caymus, Napa 94559.
Citizens for Law & Order, Box 13308, Oakland 94661, (415) 531-4664.
Citizens League of Marin, Box 9351, San Rafael 94915, (415) 457-0650.
Coalition for Better Housing, 1801 Van Ness #350, San Francisco 94109, (415) 474-6987.

Coalition for the Right to Know (anti-censorship), 464 19th St., Oakland 94612, (415) 835-4692.
Coalition of Concerned Medical Professionals, 2205 14th Ave., Oakland 94606, (415) 436-8020.
Committee to Save the Cable Cars, 201 3rd St. #900, San Francisco 94103, (415) 956-3777.
Common Cause of Marin, (415) 388-4423.
Commonwealth Club of California, 681 Market, San Francisco 94105, (415) 543-3353 or 362-4903.
Community Action Committee, 85 Marina Center, Suisun City 94585, (707) 422-1221.
Concerned Citizens Committee, 369 Orange, Oakland 94610.
Consumers Coop of Berkeley, Box 4030, 4805 Central Ave., Richmond 94804, (415) 526-0440.
Contra Costa Crisis & Suicide Intervention, Box 4852, Walnut Creek, (415) 939-1916.
Contra Costa Law League, 24 Cragmont Ct., Walnut Creek 94598, (415) 943-1524.
Council for Civic Unity, 870 Market, San Francisco 94105, (415) 781-2033.
Council of Neighborhood Associations, Box 1217, Berkeley 94701, (415) 849-2103.
Downtown Association, 582 Market, San Francisco 94104, (415) 362-7842.
Federation of Oakland Residents, 4569 Merrill Ave., Oakland 94619.
Foster City Association of Black Residents, 470 Bodega, Foster City 94404.
Group Against Smoking Pollution (GASP), Box 4400, San Francisco 94101.
Hayward Neighborhood Alert, 24864 Kay Ave., Hayward 94545.
Hunger Project, 1388 Sutter, 4th Floor, San Francisco 94109, (415) 928-8700.
League of United Latin American Citizens, 3004 16th St. #211, San Francisco 94103.
Livermore Education Association, 1874 Catalina Ct., Livermore, (415) 447-1199.
Livermore Main Street Project, 2222 2nd, Livermore, 373-1795.
Marin Coalition, Box 709, San Rafael 94915.
Market Street Development, 870 Market, San Francisco 94102, (415) 362-2500.
Martinez Citizens Advisory Committee, 525 Henrietta St., Martinez 94553, (415) 372-3520.
Mexican-American Political Association, 3810 Crestview Dr., Pittsburg 94565.
Monterey Civic Club, 540 Calle Principal, Monterey 93940, (408) 372-9489.
Napa County Alliance, (707) 224-4340.
Napa County Right to Life, Box 3293, Napa 94558, (707) 226-8874.

National Association for the Advancement of Colored People (NAACP).
El Cerrito - Box 844, EC 94530, (415) 234-9296.
Hayward - 3580 Skyline Dr., Hayward 94542.
Fairfield - 15 El Cerrito Ct. #14, Fairfield 94533, (707) 426-1123.
Oakland - 663 35th St., Oakland 94609, (415) 652-8493.
Pittsburg - Box 1026, Pittsburg 94566.
Vallejo - Box 4451, Vallejo 94590, (707) 554-4993.
National Coalition to Stop Food Irradiation, Box 59-0488, San Francisco 94159, (415) 566-CSFI, 848-4424.
New Oakland Committee, 505 14th St. #300, Oakland 94612, (415) 464-8005.
Northern California Association for Non-Profit Housing, 82 2nd St. #204, San Francisco 94105, (415) 495-2273.
Northern California Committee Against Repressive Legislation, Box 640354, San Francisco 94164, (415) 346-7350, (408) 624-7562.
Northern California Interfaith Committee on Corporate Responsibility, 3410 19th St., San Francisco 94110, (415) 863-8060.
Oakland Community Organizations, 3914 E. 14th St., Oakland 94601.
Oakland Development Council, 500 E. 8th St., Oakland, (415) 839-6961.
Oakland Education Association, 270 E. 12th, Oakland, (415) 763-4020.
Oakland Homeless Project, 1530 Martin Luther King Jr. Way, Oakland, (415) 465-0881.
Oakland Housing Coalition, (415) 652-2118.
Oakland Service Club, 4786 Geranium Pl., Oakland 94619
Orinda Association, Box 97, Orinda 94563, (415) 254-0800.
Pittsburg Community Organizing Project, 455 W. 4th, Pittsburg, (415) 439-1004.
Pleasant Hill Civic Action Committee, 3300 N. Main St., Pleasant Hill 94523.
Pride in Pinole Committee, 2620 Shady Draw, Pinole 94564, (415) 758-5460.
Redwood City Heritage Association, 627 Hamilton, 365-5564.
Safety Awareness for Everyone (SAFE), Bateman Eichler, 850 Bryant #553, San Francisco 94103.
San Franciscans for Good Government, (415) 564-5904.
San Franciscans for Neighborhood Enterprise, 3700 Sacramento, (415) 668-7363.
San Franciscans for Reasonable Growth, 241 Bartlett, (415) 285-5065.
San Francisco Area Pro-Choice Coalition, 3543 18th, (415) 255-1989.
San Francisco Bay Conservation & Development, 30 Van Ness #2011, San Francisco 94102, (415) 557-3686.
San Francisco Coalition of Business & Labor, (415) 982-5139.
San Francisco Forward, 690 Market #800, San Francisco 94104, (415) 434-4466.
San Francisco Planning & Urban Research Association (SPUR), 312 Sutter, San Francisco 94108, (415) 781-8726.

MISCELLANEOUS CIVIC ORGANIZATIONS (continued)

San Francisco 2000 Committee, 1 Montgomery, (415) 394-2654.
San Mateo County Service League, 879 Main, Redwood City, (415) 364-4664.
Society for the Preservation of English Language & Literature, 365 1st St., Los Altos, (415) 948-8202 or 349-2915.
Suicide Prevention, 3940 Geary, San Francisco 94118, (415) 752-4866.
TURN (Toward Utility Rate Normalization), 639 Mission, San Francisco 94103.
Urban Care, Box 181, Berkeley 94708.
Vacaville Community Action Council, 819 Davis, Vacaville, 446-4888.
Vacaville Fiesta Committee, 400 E. Monte Vista Ave, Vacaville, 448-4613.
Vallejo Beautification Advisory Committee, Box 3068, Vallejo 94590, (707) 648-4527.
Zero Population Growth, Box 9393, San Jose 95157, (408) 379-1213.

BUSINESS ORGANIZATIONS

Why not mix business with pleasure? Most cities in the Bay Area have Chambers of Commerce that sponsor mixers, networking parties, and educational events that are ideal for meeting new friends as well as potential customers. Most of the members are married, but there still are plenty of single men to meet. The Junior Chamber of Commerces (Jaycees) have younger men. This chapter also includes a many other types of business organizations.

CHAMBERS OF COMMERCE

ALAMEDA COUNTY

Alameda Chamber of Commerce, City Hall, Alameda 94501, 522-0414.
Albany Chamber of Commerce, 1108 Solano Ave., (415) 525-1771.
Berkeley Chamber of Commerce, 1834 University Ave., (415) 845-1212.
California Hispanic Chambers of Commerce, 4580 Central Ave., Fremont, (415) 797-0844.
Castro Valley Chamber of Commerce, 21096 Redwood, (415) 537-5300.
Emeryville Chamber of Commerce, 2000 Powell, Emeryville 94608, (415) 658-8327.
Fremont Chamber of Commerce, 39650 Liberty, Fremont, 657-1355.
Hayward Chamber of Commerce, 22300 Foothill Blvd., (415) 351-8292.
Korean-American Chamber of Commerce, 160 Indian Rd., Piedmont 94610, (415) 397-9170.
Mission San Jose Chamber of Commerce, Box 3396, Mission San Jose 94539, (415) 656-1249/657-5982.
Northern California Black Chamber of Commerce, 654 13th St., Oakland 94612, (415) 451-9231.
Oakland Chamber of Commerce, 1939 Harrison, (415) 451-7800.
Oakland Chinatown Chamber of Commerce, 701 Franklin St., Oakland 94607, (415) 893-8979.
Pacific-Indonesian Chamber of Commerce, 1946 Embarcadero, Oakland 94606, (415) 536-1967.
Pleasanton Chamber of Commerce, 450 Main #202, Pleasanton 94566, (415) 846-5858.
Union City Chamber of Commerce, 33484 Alvarado-Niles Rd., (415) 471-3115.
San Leandro Chamber of Commerce, 262 Davis, (415) 351-1482.

CONTRA COSTA COUNTY

Antioch Chamber of Commerce, 212 H St., (415) 757-1800.
Bethel Island Chamber of Commerce, Box 263, B.I. 94511, (415) 684-0254.
Brentwood Chamber of Commerce, Box 773, Brentwood 94513, (415) 634-3344.

CONTRA COSTA COUNTY (continued)

California Hispanic Chambers of Commerce, Box 8668, Pittsburg 94565, (415) 427-4664.
Concord Chamber of Commerce, 1982 Concord Ave., (415) 685-1181.
Contra Costa Black Chamber of Commerce, 3101 MacDonald Ave., Richmond 94804, (415) 235-3738.
Crockett Chamber of Commerce, Box 191, Crockett 94525, (415) 787-1155.
Danish-American Chamber of Commerce, 230 Orinda Way, Orinda 94563, (415) 254-8433.
Dublin Chamber of Commerce, 7986 Amador Valley, (415) 828-6200.
El Cerrito Chamber of Commerce, 10506 San Pablo, (415) 527-5333.
El Sobrante Chamber of Commerce, Box 1924, E.S. 94803, (415) 223-0757.
Hispanic Chamber of Commerce, Box 5396, Concord 94524, (415) 674-0496.
Lafayette Chamber of Commerce, 1003 Oak Hill Rd., (415) 284-7404.
Martinez Chamber of Commerce, 620 Las Juntas, (415) 228-2345.
Moraga Chamber of Commerce, 1450 Moraga Rd., (415) 376-0150.
Oakley Chamber of Commerce, Hwy. 4, (415) 625-1035.
Orinda Chamber of Commerce, 70 Moraga Way, (415) 254-3909.
Pinole Chamber of Commerce, Box 1, Pinole 94563, (415) 724-4484.
Pittsburg Chamber of Commerce, 2010 Railroad, (415) 432-7301.
Pleasant Hill Chamber of Commerce, 1881 Contra Costa, (415) 671-0700.
Richmond Chamber of Commerce, 117 Park Pl., Richmond 94801, (415) 234-3512.
Rodeo Chamber of Commerce, Box 548, Rodeo 94572, (415) 299-7351.
San Pablo Chamber of Commerce, 1 Alvarado Sq., S.P. 94806, (415) 234-2067.
San Ramon Chamber of Commerce, 2333 San Ramon Valley, 831-9500.
Valley Chamber of Commerce, 274 S. Hartz, Danville, (415) 837-4400.
Walnut Creek Chamber of Commerce, 1501 N. Broadway, 934-2007.
Walnut Creek Jaycees, Box 280, Pleasanton 94566.

MARIN COUNTY

Corte Madera Chamber of Commerce, 498 Tamalpais, (415) 924-4888.
Larkspur Chamber of Commerce, (415) 924-3330.
Marin County C. of C., 30 N. San Pedro, San Rafael 94903, 472-7470.
Mill Valley Chamber of Commerce, 38 Miller Ave., (415) 388-9700.
Novato Chamber of Commerce, 807 DeLong, (415) 897-1164.
San Anselmo Chamber of Commerce, 1000 Sir Francis Drake, 454-2510.
San Rafael Chamber of Commerce, 1030 B St., (415) 454-4163.
Sausalito Chamber of Commerce, 333 Caledonia, (415) 332-0505.
Tiburon Chamber of Commerce, 96 Main St., (415) 435-5633.
West Marin Chamber of Commerce, Box 94, 8165 Hwy 1, Olema 94950, (415) 663-9232.

MONTEREY COUNTY

Carmel Business Association, San Carlos & 7th, Carmel, 625-2212.
Marina Chamber of Commerce, 3200 Del Monte, (408) 384-9155.
Monterey Peninsula Chamber of Commerce, 380 Alvarado, Monterey 93940, (408) 649-1770.
Pacific Grove Chamber of Commerce, Forest & Central Ave., 373-3304.
Salinas Chamber of Commerce, 119 E. Alisal, (408) 424-7611.
Seaside Chamber of Commerce, 505 Broadway Ave., (408) 394-6501.

NAPA COUNTY

Angwin Chamber of Commerce, Box 111, Angwin 94508.
Calistoga Chamber of Commerce, 1458 Lincoln Ave., (707) 942-6333.
Lake Berryessa Chamber of Commerce, Box 9164, L.B. 94558.
Napa Chamber of Commerce, 1900 Jefferson, Napa 94558, (707) 226-7455.
St. Helena Chamber of Commerce, Box 124, S.H. 94574, (707) 963-6000.
Yountville Chamber of Commerce, Box 2064, (707) 944-0334.

SAN FRANCISCO

Australian Chamber of Commerce, 2939 Broderick, San Francisco 94123, (415) 921-5613.
British-American Chamber of Commerce, 3150 California, San Francisco 94104, (415) 567-6128.
Canadian-American Chamber of Commerce, Box 2931, San Francisco 94126, (415) 495-6021.
Chinese Chamber of Commerce, 730 Sacramento St., San Francisco 94108, (415) 982-3000.
Chinese-American Chamber of Commerce, 737 Grant Ave. #B, San Francisco 94108, (415) 362-4306.
Filipino-American Chamber of Commerce, 447 Sutter, San Francisco 94108, (415) 221-7366.
French-American Chamber of Commerce, 425 Bush St. #401, San Francisco 94108, (415) 398-2449.
German-American Chamber of Commerce, 465 California, San Francisco 94104, (415) 392-2262.
Japanese Chamber of Commerce, 685 Market #820, San Francisco 94105, (415) 543-8522.
San Francisco Black Chamber of Commerce, 111 New Montgomery, (415) 777-0944.
San Francisco Chamber of Commerce, 465 California, 9th Floor, San Francisco 94104, (415) 392-4511.
San Francisco Junior Chamber of Commerce, 5 3rd St. #225, San Francisco 94103, (415) 495-5333.
Southeast Asian-American Chamber of Commerce, 775 Commercial, (415) 781-6160.

SAN FRANCISCO (continued)

Soviet-American Chamber of Commerce, 317 12th Ave., 752-4093.
Swedish American Chamber of Commerce, World Trade Center #268,
San Francisco 94111, (415) 781-4188.
U.S.-Arab Chamber of Commerce, 1231 Market, (415) 552-8202.

SAN MATEO COUNTY

Belmont Chamber of Commerce, 1365 5th Ave., (415) 595-8696.
Brisbane Chamber of Commerce, 42 Visitacion Ave., (415) 467-7283.
Burlingame Chamber of Commerce, 306 Lorton, (415) 344-1735.
Burlingame Jaycees, Box 504, Burlingame 94011, (415) 348-8909.
Daly City Chamber of Commerce, 244 92nd St., (415) 755-8526.
Foster City Chamber of Commerce, 1125 E. Hillside Blvd., (415) 573-7600.
Half Moon Bay Chamber of Commerce, 225 S. Cabrillo Hwy., 726-5202.
Menlo Park Chamber of Commerce, 1100 Merrill, (415) 325-2818.
Millbrae Chamber of Commerce, 316 Broadway, (415) 697-7324.
Redwood City Chamber of Commerce, Jefferson & Middlefield, (415)
364-1722.
San Bruno Chamber of Commerce, 668 San Mateo Ave., (415) 588-0180.
San Carlos Chamber of Commerce, 1250 San Carlos Ave., (415) 593-1068.
San Mateo Chamber of Commerce, 2031 Pioneer Ct., (415) 341-5679.
San Mateo Jaycees, Box 602, San Mateo 94401.
South San Francisco Chamber of Commerce, 226 Miller, (415) 588-1911.
U.S. Chamber of Commerce, 500 Airport Bl #240, Burlingame 94010,
(415) 348-4011.

SANTA CLARA COUNTY

California Jaycees, 375, McKendrie, San Jose 95110, (415) 292-8211.
Campbell Chamber of Commerce, 328 E. Campbell Ave., (408) 378-6252.
Cupertino Chamber of Commerce, 20455 Silverado, (408) 252-7054.
East Palo Alto Chamber of Commerce, 1475 E. Bayshore, (415) 328-5769.
Gilroy Chamber of Commerce, 7780 Monterey, Gilroy, (408) 842-6437.
Gilroy Hispanic Chamber of Commerce, 7365 Monterey, Gilroy, (408)
848-5780.
Los Gatos Chamber of Commerce, 5 Montebello Way, Los Gatos, (408)
354-9300.
Los Gatos Jaycees, Box BB, Los Gatos 95030, (408) 248-3612.
Milpitas Chamber of Commerce, 75 S. Milpitas Blvd., Milpitas, (408)
262-2613.
Morgan Hill Chamber of Commerce, 18320 Monterey, M.H. 95037, (408)
779-9444.
Palo Alto Jaycees, Box 1321, Palo Alto, (415) 323-7252/941-5100.
San Jose Chamber of Commerce, 180 S. Market, (408) 998-7000.
San Jose Jaycees, 410 Shadow Graph, San Jose 95110, (408) 987-1060.
Sunnyvale Jaycees, Box 64047, Sunnyvale 94087, (408) 248-2169.

SANTA CLARA COUNTY (continued)

Santa Clara Chamber of Commerce, 4699 Old Ironsides Dr., Santa Clara, (408) 296-6863.
Saratoga Chamber of Commerce, 20460 Saratoga-Los Gatos Rd., Saratoga, (408) 867-0753.

SANTA CRUZ COUNTY

San Lorenzo Valley Chamber of Commerce, (408) 338-3563 or 354-0177.
Santa Cruz Chamber of Commerce, 105 Cooper, Santa Cruz, (408) 423-1111.
Santa Cruz Jaycees, (408) 425-5645.

SOLANO COUNTY

Benicia Chamber of Commerce, 831 1st St., Benicia 94519, (707) 745-2120.
Benicia Jaycees, Box 722, Benicia 94510, (707) 745-9657.
Dixon Chamber of Commerce, 201 S. 1st St., Dixon 95620, (707) 678-2650.
Fairfield-Suisun Chamber of Commerce, 1111 Webster, Fairfield 94533, (707) 425-4625.
Vacaville Chamber of Commerce, 400 E. Monte Vista Ave., Vacaville 95688, (707) 448-6424.
Vallejo Chamber of Commerce, 2 Florida, Vallejo 94590, (707) 644-5551.
Vallejo Jaycees, 843 Annette Ave., Vallejo 94591, (707) 237-5252.

SONOMA COUNTY

Cotati Chamber of Commerce, 8000 Old Redwood Hwy, (707) 795-5508.
Cloverdale Chamber of Commerce, Box 476, (707) 894-2862.
Healdsburg Chamber of Commerce, 217 Healdsburg Ave., (707) 433-6935.
Petaluma Chamber of Commerce, 314 Western Ave., (707) 762-2785.
Petaluma Jaycees, 139 Lakeville St., Petaluma 94952, (707) 763-0915.
Rohnert Park Chamber of Commerce, 6050 Commerce Blvd., (707) 584-1415.
Russian River Chamber of Commerce, Box 331, (707) 869-9009.
Santa Rosa Chamber of Commerce, 637 1st St., (707) 545-1414.
Santa Rosa Christian Businessmen's Committee, (707) 887-1448.
Sonoma Chamber of Commerce, 453 1st St. E., Sonoma 95476, 996-1033.

ENTREPRENEURS ORGANIZATIONS

Community Entrepreneurs Organization (CEO), Box 2781, San Rafael 94912, (415) 435-4461. Brainstorming, lectures, and networking for current and aspiring entrepreneurs. Typical donation is $5 per meeting. 1st Tuesdays, 7:30-9:30pm, Zim's Restaurant, Northgate, Terra Linda.

ENTREPRENEURS ORGANIZATIONS (continued)

Entrepreneurs Association of Diablo Valley, Box 23482, Pleasant Hill 94523, (415) 934-8550.

High Technology Entrepreneurial Council, 6200 Antioch St., Oakland 94611, (415) 339-3895.

International Entrepreneurs of America, 465 Cal;ifornia St., San Francisco 94104, (415) 398-6871.

National Association for the Self-Employed, (415) 933-2934. Free seminars.

MISCELLANEOUS BUSINESS ORGANIZATIONS

Burlingame Leads Club, (415) 348-7546.

Business Alliance, 495 California St, 9th Floor, San Francisco 94104, (415) 392-4520.

Business Executives Association of Marin, 24 Marsh, Mill Valley 94941, (415) 381-3816. Weekly breakfast in San Rafael. Networking.

Connections, 479-4509 (Margaret). Lunch & networking, Tuesdays, La Toscana Restaurant, San Rafael.

Clayton Business & Professional Association, Box 436, Clayton 94517, (415) 671-1646.

Contra Costa Council, 1 Annabel Ln. #214, San Ramon 94583, (415) 934-2009.

East Bay Briar Patch, 2524 Benvenue #35, Berkeley 94704, (415) 548-6659.

Executives Association

Alameda County - 1611 Telegraph Ave. #1001, Oakland 94612.

Contra Costa - Box 21304, Concord 94521, (415) 825-1379.

San Francisco - 914 Hearst Bldg #3, SF 94103, (415) 781-6461.

Family Firm Network, 2169 Union St., San Francisco 94123, (415) 922-1323.

Federated Employers of the Bay Area, 582 Market St. #412, San Francisco 94104.

Fremont Leads Club, 40792 Fremont Blvd., Fremont 94538.

Golden Gate Business Association, 1550 California St. #21, San Francisco, CA 94109, (415) 441-3651.

Golden State Business League, 333 Hegenberger Rd. #315, Oakland 94621, (415) 635-5900.

Greater Alameda Business Association, 1903 Encinal Ave., Alameda 94501, (415) 522-2628.

Institute of Business Designers, 600 Townsend St. #50E, San Francisco 94103, (415) 621-4713.

Last Monday Club, 3871 Piedmont, Oakland 94611, (415) 428-0909.

Marin Leads Club, (415) 435-3919 or 388-7179.

Marin Professional Women's Network, Diana Good, Western Federal Savings, (415) 383-6110. Breakfast & networking, Tuesdays, 7:30am.

Men & Women's Professional Networking Organization, 1746 Leavenworth, San Francisco 94133, (415) 673-6775.

National Alliance of Business, 350 Sansome St. #1040, San Francisco 94104, (415) 391-4061.

North Bay Ad Club, (415) 492-9226.

OZ, St. Francis Hotel, San Francisco, (415) 774-0235, sponsors elegant business networking parties.

Napa Valley Private Industry Council, 2447 Old Sonoma Rd., Napa 94558, (707) 253-4291.

San Carlos Business Association, Box 156, San Carlos, (415) 592-9463.

San Franciscans for Neighborhood Enterprise, 3700 Saramento St., San Francisco 94118, 668-7363.

San Francisco Commercial Club, 465 California St., San Francisco 94104, (415) 982-2929.

San Francisco Leads Club, 562 Mission St. #405, San Francisco 94105, (415) 543-8666.

San Leandro Manufacturer's Association, 262 Davis, San Leandro, (415) 357-5600.

Santa Clara Valley Business Association, 1830 Hamilton, San Jose, (408) 378-2457.

South Bay Community Business Association, Box 23525, San Jose 95153, (408) 578-8550.

Work Alone Professionals, Santa Cruz, (408) 427-1968. For solo workers.

ETHNIC ORGANIZATIONS

AUSTRALIAN
Australian-American Association, 400 California, 13th Floor, San Francisco 94104, (415) 772-9229.
Australian Chamber of Commerce, 360 Post, San Francisco 94104, (415) 362-6168.

BLACK
Bay Area Black Media Coalition, Box 2382, Oakland 94614, 889-8610.
Black Business Exchange, Box 2635, Oakland 94612, (415) 352-2970.
Contra Costa Black Chamber of Commerce, 3101 MacDonald Ave., Richmond 94804, (415) 235-3738.
Ebony Social Set, 142 Versailles, Pittsburg 94565.
Northern California Black Chamber of Commerce, 654 13th St., Oakland 94612, (415) 451-9231.

BRITISH
British-American Club of Northern California, 4255 Williams Rd., San Jose 95129, (408) 257-2221 or 948-9784.
British American Club of Northern California, 3 W. 37th Ave. #14, San Mateo, (415) 573-6440.

CANADIAN
Canadian-American Society, Box 2931, San Francisco 94126.

CHINESE
Chinese-American Chamber of Commerce, 737 Grant Ave. #B, San Francisco 94108, (415) 362-4306.
Chinese-American Citizens Alliance 1044, Stockton St., San Francisco 94108, (415) 982-4618.
Chinese Calligraphy Society, 633 Post St. #734, San Francisco 94109, (415) 626-4664.
Chinese Chamber of Commerce, 730 Sacramento St., San Francisco 94108, (415) 982-3000.
Chinese Club of Foster City, 844 Polaris, F.C. 94404.
Chinese Club of Vallejo, 1416 Florida, Vallejo 94590, (707) 642-2776
Chinese Culture Center, 750 Kearny St., S.F. 94108, (415) 986-1822.
Marin Chinese Culture Group, Box 6051, San Rafael 94913.
National Association of Chinese-Americans, 737 Grant Ave., San Francisco 94133, (415) 391-2069.
Organization of Chinese-Americans, 1251 W. Tennyson, Hayward 94544, (415) 787-6888 or 794-6956.
South Bay Chinese Club, Box 12, Fremont 94537, (415) 791-1400.

CROATIAN
Croatian-American Social Club, 415 Grand Ave., South San Francisco, (415) 952-3830.

FILIPINO
Filipino-American Chamber of Commerce, 353 Sacramento #740, San Francisco 94111, (415) 421-5400.
Filipino-American Club, Box 4042, Foster City 94404.

FILIPINO (continued)
Filipino-American Club of Livermore/Amador Valley, Box 767, Livermore 94550, (415) 443-2153.
Filipino-American Federation, 111 Rhea Ct., Vallejo 94590, (707) 552-2456.
Filipino-American Senior Citizen Center, 3483 Mission, San Francisco, (415) 285-2076.
Filipino Club, Our Lady of Perpetual Help, 1019 Nimitz, Daly City 94014.
Filipino Community Center, 3361 Fulton Rd., Fulton, (707) 546-2795.
Filipino Community of San Francisco, 2970 California, San Francisco 94115, (415) 346-7252.
Filipino Community of Solano County, 820 Sonoma Blvd., Vallejo 94590, (707) 644-4716.
Filipino Senior Citizens Club, 83 6th St., San Francisco, (415) 974-5871.
Sons of Philippines, 44 Carol Dr., Pittsburg, 94565.
FRENCH
Alliance Francaise, 1345 Bush, San Francisco 94109, (415) 775-7755.
Alliance Francaise of the East Bay, (415) 548-1520.
Cercle de L'Union, 414 Mason St., San Francisco 94102, (415) 362-5956.
GERMAN
German-American Club, Santa Cruz, (408) 427-0557.
German-American Society of Marin, Box 1276, Novato 94948, (415) 897-7985. Activities include dances and parties.
Goethe Institute, 530 Bush, San Francisco, (415) 391-0370, promotes German culture through films, concerts, art exhibits, classes, books, and parties.
HISPANIC
Alianza Argentina, 464 Reynolds Circle, San Jose, (408) 436-0748.
Amigos de las Americas, 125 Feliz Ct., Danville 94526.
Argentina Circulo de San Jose, 824 N. 12th, San Jose, (408) 998-3123.
Arriba/Juntos, 2017 Mission, 2nd Floor, San Francisco 94110, (415) 863-9307.
Association Guadalupana, 755 Laguna Ct., Fairfield 94533, (707) 422-8771.
California Hispanic Chambers of Commerce, Box 8668, Pittsburg 94565, (415) 427-4664.
Hispanic Chamber of Commerce, 2601 Mission St., San Francisco 94110, (415) 647-0224.
Hispanic Chamber of Commerce, Box 5396, Concord 94524, 674-0496.
Mexican-American Cultural Association, Box 614, Concord 94522, (415) 687-6222.
Mission Cultural Center, (Hispanic Culture) 2451 Harrison, San Francisco, (415) 821-1155.
Pittsburg Spanish Speaking Cultural Center, 411 E. 10th, Pittsburg, (415) 439-7515.
Puerto Rican Club, 3249A Mission St., San Francisco, (415) 550-9323.
Spanish Club, 1805 Emeleth Ave., San Leandro 94577.

INDONESIAN
Pacific Indonesian Chamber of Commerce, 1946 Embarcadero, Oakland 94606, (415) 536-1967.

IRANIAN
Society of Iranian Professionals, Box 3753, Santa Clara 95055.

IRISH
Irish Center, Inc., 2123 Market, San Francisco 94114, (415) 621-2200.

Irish Social Club, (408) 265-7512.

United Irish Culture Center, 2700 45th Ave., San Francisco, (415) 661-2700. Weekend dances, Irish bands, concerts, and lectures.

ITALIAN
Italian-American Citizens Club, 143 School St., Daly City 94014.

Italian-American Club, 151 El Camino Dr., Pittsburg 94565, (415) 432-2568/439-9977.

Italian-American Social Club, 958 Oak Ln., Menlo Pk, (415) 322-8933.

Italian-American Social Club, 1727 Indiana, Vallejo 94590, 552-1727.

Italia Oggi, (415) 673-2200. For young professionals interested in Italy. You need not be Italian to join.

Club Italia of Marin, 11 Ayala Ct., San Rafael 94903.

Museo Italo Americano, Ft. Mason, Bldg C, S.F. 94123, (415) 673-2200.

Sons & Daughters of Italy, 3367 Petaluma Hill Rd., Santa Rosa 95404.

Sons of Italy

Petaluma - 4990 D St. Extension, Petaluma 94952, (707) 763-0091.

Pittsburg - 23 Barrie Ct., Pittsburg 94565, (415) 432-3463.

San Francisco - 5051 Mission, SF 94112.

Vallejo - 267 Valle Vista, Vallejo 94590.

JAPANESE
American-Japanese Social Club, 1721 Gershwin Cir., Fairfield 94533, (707) 422-8930.

Japanese American Club

Concord - 3165 Treat, Concord, (415) 680-9768.

Walnut Creek - 3356 Chamberlain Ct., Walnut Ck 94598

Japanese-American Association of San Francisco, 1759 Sutter St., San Francisco 94115, (415) 921-1782.

Japanese-American Citizens League

Diablo Valley - (415) 838-9148.

Pleasanton - 11 Carpenter Ct., Pleasant Hill 94523.

San Francisco - 1765 Sutter, S.F. 94115, (415) 921-5205.

Sebastopol - 7986 Washington Ave., Sebastopol 95472.

Japanese-American Philatelic Society, Box 1049, El Cerrito 94530, (415) 529-1045.

Japan Society of San Francisco, 312 Sutter, San Francisco 94108, (415) 986-4383.

Japan Society of Northern California, 350 Sansome St. #630, San Francisco 94104, (415) 986-4383.

Tri-Valley Japanese American Citizens League, (415) 833-2561.

Watsonville Japanese American Citizens League, 150 Blackburn, Watsonville, (408) 724-4028.

KOREAN
Korean-American Chamber of Commerce, 160 Indian Rd., Piedmont 94610, (415) 397-9170.
NEW ZEALAND
New Zealand-American Association, 291 Geary St. #510, San Francisco 94102, (415) 986-3566.
POLISH
Polish Arts & Culture Foundation, 1290 sutter, San Francisco 94109, (415) 474-7070.

Polish Club, 3040 22nd St., San Francisco, (415) 550-9252.
RUSSIAN
Russian-American Community Services, 300 Anza, San Francisco 94118.

Russian Center of San Francisco, 2450 Sutter, San Francisco, (415) 921-7631.
SCANDINAVIAN
Danish-American Chamber of Commerce, 1640 Stanley Dollar Dr. #1A, Walnut Creek 94595, (415) 945-8937.

Danish Society, Box 41, Petaluma 94953, (707) 454-4837

Sons of Norway
Hayward - 1241 McBridge Ln., Hayward 94544
Pleasant Hill - 2095 Morella, Pleasant Hill 94523
Santa Rosa - 617 W. 9th St., Santa Rosa 95404
Vallejo - 201 Grapewood, Vallejo 94590

Swedish American Chamber of Commerce, World Trade Center #268, San Francisco 94111, (415) 781-4188.

Young Scandinavians Club, 6A Cazneau Ave., Sausalito 94965, (415) 331-6463.
SCOTTISH
Caledonian Club, 1310 Mercer St., Richmond 94804.

Caledonian Club of San Francisco, (415) 897-4442.
SWISS
Swiss Club Tell, 551 Edgewood Ave., Mill Valley 94941, (415) 388-9993.
UKRAINIAN
Ukrainian National Association, 215 Silliman St., San Francisco 94134, (415) 468-2601.

FOR MORE INFORMATION

NATIONAL PERIODICALS

Christian Single, 127 9th Ave. N., Nashville, TN 37234, (615) 251-2289.
Concerned Singles Newsletter, Box 555, Stockbridge, MA 01262. Monthly
newsletter for peace-oriented singles.
Jewish Singles Magazine, Box 247, Newton, MA 02159, (617) 244-5677.
Miss Mom, Box 547, Moab, UT 84532, (801) 259-5090. Monthly. Free.
News & Views, Single Life Institute, 810 Milford, Abilene, TX 79601,
(915) 673-8687. Monthly newsletter for singles ministries.
Single Adult Ministry Information, Box 11394, Kansas City, MO 64112.
Monthly newsletter for coordinators of Christian singles clubs.
Single Adult Ministries Journal, Colorado Springs, (303) 579-6471.
Monthly newsletter for coordinators of Christian singles clubs.
Single Impact, 7245 College, Lima, NY 14485. Christian Quarterly.
The Single Parent, Parents Without Partners (P.W.P.). 8807 Colesville Rd.,
Silver Spring, MD 20910, (301) 588-9354. Monthly.
Singles Scene, Box 454, Crossville, TN 38557, (615) 456-0021. Christian.
Today's Single, 1933 Wisconsin, Milwaukee WI 53233, (414) 344-7300.

LOCAL PERIODICALS

Coast Singles Magazine, Box 3097, Salinas 93912, (408) 449-8243. For
Santa Cruz & Monterey County. Articles, personals.
Enjoy Life Singles Magazine, Box 2593, Santa Rosa 95405, (707) 575-1006.
Bimonthly. Violet Young, Editor. Publishes singles calendar for the
North Bay, articles, and personal ads.
In the Know, 1042 Sanchez, San Francisco 94114, (415) 647-5567. Juliette
Smith, Editor. Monthly singles calendar.
The Intimacy Advocate, 414 41st St., Oakland 94609. Susan Page, Editor.
Includes articles and personal ads for singles.
Lifestyle, 421 W. MacArthur Blvd., Oakland 94609, (415) 420-1381. Bi-
monthly. Dave Sawle, Publisher. Includes singles calendar, articles,
and personal ads.
Single Again, Box 384, Union City 94587, (415) 793-6315. Monthly
magazine for divorced, separated, and widowed. Len Harris,
Publisher. Includes articles and personal ads for singles.
Trellis Singles Magazine, 1260 Persian Dr., Sunnyvale 94089, (415) 941-
2900 or (408) 747-1455. Bi-monthly singles calendar throughout Bay
Area. Singles events listings over the phone, (900) 844-4445. 89 cents
per minute. Also personal ads.

BOOKS

Brief Encounters, E. Coleman & B. Edwards. Garden City, NY: Anchor Books, 1979.

The Challenge of Being Single, M. Edwards & E. Hoover, NY: New American Library, Inc., 1975.

Classy Classifieds, Toni Bowes & David Kindopp. Send $9.50 to Hedon Enterprises, Box 280, San Anselmo CA 94979, (415) 257-5259.

Cohabitation Agreement & Guide, designed to protect both individuals who are living together. Singular Approaches, Box 1045, Tres Pinos, CA 95075.

Coming Apart: Why Relationships End and How to Live Through the Ending of Yours, Kingma, Daphne Rose, Berkeley: Conari Press, 1987. To order a copy send $8.43 per copy to Conari Press, 713 Euclid Ave., Berkeley, CA 94708.

Catholic Singles Book Club, Box 1920, Evanston, IL 60204.

Clubs, Organizations, & Associations: A Guide to Getting Involved, San Francisco Chamber of Commerce, 465 California, 9th Floor, San Francisco 94104, (415) 392-4511.

The Dance-Away Lover, Daniel Goldstine. NY: William Morrow & Co., 1977.

The Divorce Book, Gosse, Richard, et al, New Harbinger Publications, 1984. Send $11.66 to Singles, 4 Highland Ave., San Rafael, CA 94901.

Finding Love, Dr. Margaret O'Connor & Dr. Jane Silverman. NY: Crown Publishers, 1989.

First Person Singular: Living the Good Life Alone, S.M. Johnson. NY: New American Library, Inc., 1978.

Game Free: The Meaning of Intimacy, Thomas Oden. NY: Harper & Row, 1974.

The Great American Man Shortage, William Novak. NY: Rawson Associates, 1983.

How to Find a Lasting Relationship, 3rd Edition, Richard Gosse, Marin Publications, 1991. Send $11.66 to 4 Highland Ave., San Rafael, CA 94901. (415) 459-3817.

How to Pick Up a Man, Dian Hanson. NY: G.P. Putnam's Sons, 1982.

How to Pick Up Girls, Eric Weber. NY: Symphony Press, 1970.

If I'm So Wonderful Why Am I Still Single?, Susan Page. Grafton Books, 1988.

Launching & Sustaining Successful Singles Ministry, Dick Dunn. $37.75 to Singles Ministry Resources, Box 1472, Roswell,GA 30077, 587-1691.

Letting Go: A 12 Week Personal Action Program to Overcome a Broken Heart. Zev Wanderer & Tracy Cabot. NY: Warner Books, 1981.

The Little Black Party Book, Juliette Smith. Singles clubs and other social organizations. $7 to In the Know, 634 Broderick, San Francisco 94117.

Looking for Love Through the Personals, Judy Knoll. $9.95 to Personal Connections, Box 880004, San Diego, CA 92108.

BOOKS (continued)

Lover Shopping: How to Be Married One Year from Today, Dr. Martin V. Gallatin. Send $14.95 to Shapolsky Publishers, 56 E. 11th St., New York, NY 10003 or call (212) 505-2505.

Making Contact, A. Wassmer. NY: The Dial Press, 1978.

National Single Adult Ministries Resource Directory, Box 730, Redmond, OR 97756, (800) 452-1104, x76. $11.95. Jerry Jones, Editor.

National Square Dance Directory, Box 54055, Jackson, MS 39208, (601) 825-6831. Gordon Goss. $9. Includes many singles square dance clubs.

101 Creative & Effective Ways to Meet Worthwhile Men, Betsy Reifman. Singles Calendar, Box 3044, Laguna Hills 92654, (714) 855-2347.

Pairing, G.R. Bach & R.M. Deutzch, NY: Avon Books, 1970.

Passive Men; Wild Women, Pierre Mornell. NY: Ballantine Books, 1979.

Personal ADventures, Jay Wiseman. Send $7 to Jay Wiseman, Box 1261, Berkeley 94701.

Professional Singles Manual, Renee Namaste, Ph.D. Also known as Solo Power. ARC Publications, 3142 Cork Ln, Costa Mesa 92626.

The Psychology of Romantic Love, Nathaniel Branden. NY: Bantam Books, 1981.

Single File: How to Live Happily Forever After With or Without Prince Charming, Susan Deitz. NY: St. Martin's Press, 1989.

Singles Ministry Handbook, Douglas L. Fagerstrom, National Assoc. of Christian Singles, 1933 W. Wisconsin Ave., Milwaukee, WI 53233. The

Single Mother's Survival Manual, Barbara Duncan. Send $14.45 to R & E Publishers, Box 2008, Saratoga, CA 95070.

Single, Straight Men: 106 Guaranteed Places to Find Them, Dr. Diana Sommerfield. St. Martin's Press, $9.95.

Singles: The New Americans, Simenauer, J. & Caroll, D. NY: Simon and Schuster, 1982.

Starting a Singles Ministry Kit. $34.95 to Mobilized to Serve, Elim Fellowship, 7245 College, Lima, NY 14485, (716) 582-2790.

Too Close, Too Soon, Jim Talley & Bobbie Reed. Nashville: Thomas Nelson Publishers, 1982.

The Whole Single Person's Catalog, E. Collins. NY: Peebles Press, 1979.

Twenty Tips to More Dates in the 90's, Marie France. San Francisco: Paris Press, 1990.

SINGLES RESOURCES
with Rich Gosse

Rich Gosse is Chairman of American Singles, a nationwide, non-profit organization. He teaches classes for singles at more than 55 American colleges. Now you can experience the wit and wisdom of Rich Gosse in the privacy of your home or car with audio cassette tapes of his most popular college classes. These tapes, together with his informative and entertaining books, will give you all the resources you need to enjoy your single lifestyle.

ORDER FORM

Please mail me the following items:

___ Looking for Love in All the Right Places (tape)
___ How to Be Happily Single (tape)
___ Romantic Charisma (tape)
___ Initiating Contact & the Art of Flirting (tape)
___ How to Select the Right Partner/Eliminating the
      Competition (tape)
___ Self-Esteem for Singles (tape)
___ How to Find a Lasting Relationship (book)
___ Singles Guide to the San Francisco Bay Area (book)
___ Singles Guide to the L.A. Area (book)
___ The Divorce Book

$9.95 + $1.71 shipping & handling = **$11.66 per book or tape.**

Enclosed is my check for $_____.
Please charge my VISA or MC # _____
Name _____
Address _____
City, State, Zip, Phone _____

Mail to: Richard Gosse & Associates, 4 Highland Ave., San Rafael, CA 94901 or order over the phone, (415) 459-3817.

FREE DATING SERVICE

Sponsored by California Singles

Attractive single people like yourself are waiting to meet you. As a member of California Singles Dating Service you will receive their profiles in the mail. You can contact them directly or can allow them to contact you after they have read your profile.

Directions: Fill in all or as many of the blanks below as you wish. If you give your telephone number you will greatly increase the number of members who contact you. If you don't give a number, all letters will be mailed to us, then forwarded to you.

YOUR PROFILE
(to be sent to other members)

First Name _____
Phone (optional) (___)_____
Race _____Age _____
Sex: Male _____   Female _____
Occupation _____
Education _____
Ages of Children Living With You:

_____
Height _____   Weight _____
Color of Hair _____   Eyes _____
3 adjectives that describe you best:

_____
Leisure Activities _____

_____
Smoke: Y N   Alcohol: Y N   Drugs: Y N
Purpose: Dating Only _____
Open to a committed relationship _____
Open to marriage _____

PERSON YOU SEEK

Race(s): _____
Age range _____
Education _____
Smoke: Y N   Alcohol: Y N   Drugs: Y N
Location: How many miles can the person live from you: _____
Describe the person you want to meet:

_____

APPLICATION (confidential)

Name _____
Address _____
City, State, Zip _____
Phone (___)_____

I apply for membership in a non-profit dating service operated by California Singles, hereinafter refered to as CAS. I certify that I am single and not currently in a commited relationship.

I give permission to CAS to release all information provided by me on the profile form. I understand that CAS does not screen members.I agree to hold harmless CAS from any liability regarding the dating of individuals met through CAS.

I understand that my membership in this dating service is free and that the service is made possible by voluntary donations from members.

Enclosed is my donation of:
____ $100 ____$25 ____$10 ____ Other
____ I do not choose to donate.

_____
(signature)   (date)

Please forward this application and any donation you may wish to make to:
California Singles, 4 Highland Ave., San Rafael, CA 94901